# Bloom's Modern Critical Views

# Bloom's Modern Critical Views

*Modern Critical Views*

# LANGSTON HUGHES

*Edited and with an introduction by*

## Harold Bloom
Sterling Professor of the Humanities
Yale University

CHELSEA HOUSE PUBLISHERS
New York ◇ Philadelphia

© 1989 by Chelsea House Publishers,
a subsidiary of Haights Cross Communications.

Introduction © 1988 by Harold Bloom

Printed and bound in the United States of America

10

Library of Congress Cataloging-in-Publication Data
Langston Hughes/edited and with an introduction by Harold
Bloom.
     p.    cm.—(Modern critical views)
     Bibliography: p.
     Includes index.
     Summary: A collection of twelve critical essays on Hughes
and his work, arranged in chronological order of their original
publication.
     ISBN 1–55546–376–2   0-7910-7810-8 (paperback)
     1. Hughes, Langston, 1902–1967—Criticism and
interpretation. 2. Afro-Americans in literature. [1. Hughes,
Langston, 1902–1967—Criticism and interpretation.
2. American literature—History and criticism.] I. Bloom,
Harold. II. Series.
PS3515.U274Z668   1988
818'.5209—dc19
                                                  87-22186
                                                    CIP
                                                     AC

# Contents

# Editor's Note

This book brings together a representative selection of the best criticism devoted to the writings of Langston Hughes, poet and chronicler of the Harlem Renaissance. The critical essays are reprinted here in the order of their original publication. I am grateful to Daniel Duffy for his aid in editing this volume.

My introduction follows Arnold Rampersad's *Life of Langston Hughes* in considering the relation between Hughes's human and poetic origins. Darwin T. Turner begins the chronological sequence with a consideration of Hughes's career as a dramatist, after which George E. Kent sets Hughes in the context of black American folk and cultural traditions.

Hughes's novel, *Not without Laughter,* is analyzed by Roger Rosenblatt, while Raymond Smith studies the total shape of Hughes's poetic stance. Onwuchekwa Jemie, a fierce defender of Hughes's poetry, attempts to work out the effect of jazz upon those poems, after which R. Baxter Miller considers Hughes's representation of women. An overview of Hughes by Martha Cobb is followed by Susan L. Blake's account of Hughes's "urban folktales."

Another overview, by Richard K. Barksdale, commends Hughes as a humanist wholly appropriate to his own era, a judgment which is consonant with Chidi Ikonne's argument that Hughes centered upon affirming the black self.

*The Ways of White Folk* is studied in its narrative procedures by David Michael Nifong, after which Arnold Rampersad strongly concludes this volume with his sensitive meditation upon the poetic will in Langston Hughes.

# Introduction

Twentieth-century black American literature is so varied that adequate critical generalization is scarcely possible, at least at this time. A literary culture that includes the fiction of Ellison and Hurston, the moral essays of Baldwin, and the extraordinary recent poetry of Jay Wright is clearly of international stature. Langston Hughes may be the most poignant and representative figure of that culture, more so even than Richard Wright. Clearly an authentic poet, Hughes nevertheless seems to lack any definitive volume to which we can turn for rereading. His best book of poems is certainly *Fine Clothes to the Jew* (1927), which retains some freshness and yet has palpable limitations. Ideological defenses of Hughes's poetry are now common and necessarily are represented in this volume. Folk traditions ranging from blues to spirituals to jazz songs to work chants to many other modes do get into Hughes's poetry, but his poems on the whole do not compare adequately to the best instances of those cultural models. Other critics find Hughes Whitmanian, but the subtle, evasive, and hermetic Whitman—still the most weakly misread even as he is the greatest of our poets—had little real effect upon Hughes's poetry. The authentic precursor was Carl Sandburg, and Hughes, alas, rarely surpassed Sandburg.

Social and political considerations, which doubtless will achieve some historical continuity, will provide something of an audience for Hughes's poetry. His first autobiography, *The Big Sea,* may be his most lasting single book, though its aesthetic values are very mixed. Rereading it, plus his second autobiography, *I Wonder as I Wander,* his *Selected Poems,* and *The Langston Hughes Reader,* I come to the sad conclusion that Hughes's principal work was his life, which is to say his literary career. This conclusion is partly founded upon the contrast between Hughes's own writings and the admirable biography by Arnold Rampersad, *The Life of Langston Hughes, Volume I: 1902–1941* (1986). Reading Rampersad's *Life* is simply a more vivid and valuable aesthetic and human experience than reading the

1

rather faded verse and prose of Hughes himself. Hughes's courage and his persistence made the man more crucial as a representative figure than his intrinsic strength as a writer by itself might have allowed him to have become.

Rampersad, a biographer of uncommon distinction, memorably condenses the essence of Hughes's personal vision in the fifth paragraph of his *Life:*

> As successful as his life seemed to be by its end, with honors and awards inspired by more than forty books, and the adulation of thousands of readers, Hughes's favorite phonograph record over the years, spun in his bachelor suite late into the Harlem night, remained Billie Holiday's chilly moaning of "God Bless the Child That's Got His Own." Eventually he had gotten his own, but at a stiff price. He had paid in years of nomadic loneliness and a furtive sexuality; he would die without ever having married, and without a known lover or a child. If by the end he was also famous and even beloved, Hughes knew that he had been cheated early of a richer emotional life. Parents could be so cruel! "My theory is," he wrote not long before he died, "children should be born without parents—if born they must be."

Most of Hughes's writing, like his overt stances in life, is a reaction-formation away from that origin. Rampersad's skilled devotion uncovers the trace of sorrow that moves remorselessly from a grim family romance (or lack of it) through a refusal to abide or end in alienation. The refusal may be ascribed to Hughes's profound, almost selfless love for his own people, and makes him an authentic and heroic exemplar for many subsequent black American writers. Whatever the inadequacies of Hughes's various styles, his place in literary history is an assured one.

Rampersad, in his essay on Hughes's poetic origins reprinted in this volume, shrewdly notes the mixture of will and passivity that combines in Hughes's art, and relates the passivity to Hughes's apparent asexuality. I wish only that the poetic will in Hughes had been stronger, as it was in Whitman and is now in John Ashbery and Jay Wright, among other contemporaries. What Hughes lacked, perhaps, was a sufficient sense of what Nietzsche called the will's revenge against time, and time's "It was." Absorbing his own plangencies, Hughes chose not to take revenge upon his familial past. His pride in his family and in his race was too great for that, but what made him a hero of a pioneering black literary life may also have weakened his actual achievement as a poet. Rampersad defends Hughes by comparing him to Whitman, who also had the sense that his life was a larger poem than any he could write. But the poet of "Crossing Brooklyn Ferry" and "As I Ebb'd with the Ocean of Life" could afford that sense better than could the poet of "The Weary Blues" and "Reverie on the Harlem River."

Yet there are moments in Hughes that are unique and testify to a mode of irony almost his own. In *The Big Sea*, Hughes recalls an exchange with his friend of Harlem Renaissance days, the black writer Wallace Thurman. The brief sketch of Thurman, followed by the wise passivity of Hughes's self-revelation, is like a fragment of an art, humorous and wise, that cultural and personal circumstances did not permit Hughes to perfect. Still, it remains a strong testament:

> Wallace Thurman laughed a long bitter laugh. He was a strange kind of fellow, who liked to drink gin, but *didn't* like to drink gin; who liked being a Negro, but felt it a great handicap; who adored bohemianism, but thought it wrong to be a bohemian. He liked to waste a lot of time, but he always felt guilty wasting time. He loathed crowds, yet he hated to be alone. He almost always felt bad, yet he didn't write poetry.
>
> Once I told him if I could feel as bad as he did *all* the time, I would surely produce wonderful books. But he said you had to know how to *write*, as well as how to feel bad. I said I didn't have to know how to feel bad, because, every so often, the blues just naturally overtook me, like a blind beggar with an old guitar:
>
> > *You don't know,*
> > *You don't know my mind—*
> > *When you see me laughin',*
> > *I'm laughin' to keep from cryin'.*

DARWIN T. TURNER

# Hughes as Playwright

Throughout his professional writing career of forty-six years, Langston Hughes maintained keen interest in theater. He published his first play, "The Gold Piece," in 1921. In 1935, he had his first Broadway show—*Mulatto,* which established a record by remaining in production on Broadway longer than any other play which had been written by a Negro. During the thirties and early forties, he founded three Negro dramatic groups—The Suitcase Theater in Harlem, the Negro Art Theater in Los Angeles, and the Skyloft Players in Chicago. As late as 1963, Hughes was still polishing *Emperor of Haiti,* which had been produced as *Drums of Haiti* twenty-seven years earlier.

Langston Hughes took pride in his achievements in the theater. Truly, for a Negro writer, they were remarkable. In addition to the record-setting *Mulatto* and *Simply Heavenly,* which appeared on Broadway in 1957, he wrote seven other plays which were produced professionally. He also wrote musicals, a movie script, radio drama, a passion play, and the lyrics for the musical version of Elmer Rice's *Street Scene.* Nevertheless, despite his extensive efforts, Hughes never became outstanding as a dramatist. The reasons for his failure are evident in a close examination of his works.

Produced in 1935, but written in 1930, *Mulatto* is an emotionally engaging drama, marred by melodrama, propaganda, and crudities common to inexperienced playwrights. Developed from a short story, "Father and Son," *Mulatto* dramatizes the conflict between Colonel Norwood, a wealthy white man, and Robert, his "yard child." Since he was seven years old,

From *CLA Journal* 11, no. 4 (June 1968). © 1968 by the College Language Association.

Robert has hated his father for refusing to recognize their relationship, of which he himself had been proud. During his summer's vacation from college, Robert has strained tension to a breaking point by defying the morés of his father and of the Georgia town in which they live. Finally, on the scheduled day of Bert's return to college, the tension snaps. Incensed to learn that Bert has defied a white woman, has sped past a white man, and has entered the front door of the house regularly, Norwood threatens to kill Bert. Bert kills his father and flees; but, chased by a posse, he returns to the house, where he kills himself.

Much of the power of the play derives from the subject itself. A traditional subject in drama, father-son conflict inevitably generates excitement and frequently produces memorable characters and confrontations: Oedipus and Laertes, Hamlet and Claudius, Theseus and Hippolytus are only a few. In this instance, the excitement was intensified for American audiences by the first professional dramatization of a conflict between a mulatto and his father.

The play gains strength also from Hughes's characterizations of Bert and Cora. Although he is obviously modeled on the proud and noble slaves of Negro literary tradition, Bert is an interesting character. His contempt for other Negroes, his stubborn insistence that he be recognized as a man, and his arrogant defiance of custom symptomize a fatal *hubris*. In his deliberate provocation of trouble, a manifestation of what seems almost a suicidal complex, he anticipates James Baldwin's protagonist in *Blues for Mr. Charlie,* written a generation later.

Cora too seems a familiar figure from American stories about the antebellum days. At first, she is merely the docile servant who, for many years, has lived with the master, nurtured him, and borne his children without concern for herself and without complaint. After Norwood's death, however, Cora assumes more significant dimensions. Revealing that love had caused her to excuse Norwood's faults and cling to him, she now repudiates him because his death threatens her son, who is even more precious to her. Unfortunately, as Hughes has written the scene, a reader is uncertain whether Cora is insane or is, for the first time, rationally aware of the manner in which she has been abused by Norwood. Regardless of the reason for her transformation, Cora, like all of Hughes's other heroines, appears more carefully delineated and more admirable than the male figures who dominate her life.

Even Colonel Norwood is interesting as a character. Although Hughes, writing protest drama, stereotyped him from racial bigots of his own day and slave masters of the previous century, Norwood gains reality in his final confrontation with Bert. Transcending racial identity, he becomes, like Hughes's own father, a man in conflict with his son. When Norwood cannot pull the trigger of his gun to kill Bert, Bert strangles him. Although Bert could only wonder why Norwood did not fire, a reader suspects, romantically perhaps, that, at the critical moment, Norwood realized that Bert was actually his flesh and blood, not merely a "yard child" whom he could ignore.

Despite the subject and the interesting characterizations of Bert and Cora, the play is weak artistically in plot structure, language, and thought. From the moment of Norwood's death, the action moves with the rapidity and inexorability of Greek tragedy. Prior to the death, however, it too frequently seems painfully slow and digressive. For example, Bert's sister Sally appears in act 1, talks, and then leaves for college. Rather than contributing to the plot or background, she merely distracts the reader, who puzzles about the reason for her existence. One can almost argue artistic justification for the play's producer, who revised the play to cause Sally to miss her train in the first act and be raped in the third. Even though the producer was motivated by the commercial possibilities of sensationalism, he at least provided dramatic reason for Sally's presence and carried to their logical conclusion hints which Hughes planted casually and forgot.

Hughes forgot some other matters in the drama. From the opening scene onward, he reiterated the fact that Norwood does not permit Negroes to use the front door. Negro servants who haul a huge trunk down the front hall steps are required to carry it out the back door. When Norwood learns that Bert frequently enters through the front door, he threatens to break Bert's neck. Nevertheless, only a few moments after Norwood has voiced his threat, a Negro servant helps his master enter through the front door and leave through the same portal. Nothing in the stage directions indicates that Norwood pays any attention to this dark transgression of his hallowed sill.

Because Hughes was a talented poet, it is difficult to understand his apparent insensitivity to language and to effective usage in *Mulatto*. His faults are various. "Kid" and "old man" seem inappropriate slang for rural Georgia of the early 1930's. Even more incongruous is the use of "papa." Norwood slapped seven-year-old Bert for calling him "papa." One wonders how the word came into Bert's vocabulary since no one else in the play uses it. Cora uses "daddy" and "pappy." Bert's brother says, "Pa." Norwood says, "Pappy." Even Bert himself fails to use the counterpart when addressing his mother. He calls her, "Ma."

Other words are questionable. It is doubtful that a Southerner would use "lynching" to describe an activity in which he participated. It is improbable that Norwood would emphasize his own immorality by calling his son a bastard. It is unnecessary for the overseer to inform the audience that he will form a posse from *white* men.

Quibbling about words may seem petty criticism of a writer. Nevertheless, one assumes that a poet, more than other writers perhaps, would exercise care in selecting words. Occasionally but too infrequently, Hughes demonstrated ability to use language effectively when he chose to. The most appealing scene in the play is that in which Cora, in a monologue, recalls her early relationship with Norwood. The speech rings true in every respect. It is colloquial, faithfully representative of the dialect of Southern Negroes, and poetic. Hughes also demonstrated incisive use of language in the ironic moment at which a Negro servant, disregarding Norwood's five Negro children, agrees with a white undertaker's assertion that Norwood had no relatives.

Part of Hughes's difficulty with language resulted from his desire to be certain that spectators understood the full implications of the characters' statements. In order to assure himself that no one would miss the point, Hughes sometimes overstated it. For example, Norwood, explaining his financial security, says that he has "a few thousand put away." A wealthy man who is not boasting would probably say merely that he has a few *dollars* put away. But Hughes wanted the spectator to realize Norwood's wealth. Similarly, Higgins, a white man, says, "All this postwar propaganda on the radio about freedom and democracy—why the niggers think it's meant for them." Psychologically, the statement is false. A bigot would not verbalize his awareness of a difference between the condition of the Negro and America's promise to its citizens. In fact, he probably would not be aware of any difference. But Hughes, using a white man as mouthpiece, wanted to emphasize the discrepancy in the minds of his audience.

Finally, in *Mulatto*, Hughes slipped into improbable contradictions which sometimes are amusing. For instance, to emphasize the sacredness of the Colonel's library, Cora says that even she has never been permitted to enter it in thirty years. Surely someone, however, cleaned the room at least once during that time. Certainly, Colonel Norwood was not a man to clean and dust a room; certainly also, the individual who most probably would be assigned the task would be Cora, the most trusted servant.

Not amusing, but even more improbable, is the picture of life in the Norwood house. Except for allusions to contemporary personalities and inventions, one might assume that the story was set in the antebellum South. For instance, there is never any mention of paying the servants. Surely, however, most working Negroes in Georgia in 1930 at least touched the money they earned even if they immediately handed it on to a creditor.

*Little Ham,* written during the thirties, is set in the Harlem Renaissance of the twenties. Webster Smalley has described it as a folk comedy. To a Negro reader, however, it is a slow-moving, frequently dull, artificial attempt to present within a single play all of the exotic elements which distinguish life in Harlem from life in the rest of America. Here, jumbled together like the animals in a box of animal crackers, are shoe shiners, beauticians, numbers runners, homosexuals, West Indians, followers of Father Divine, gangsters, middle-class Negroes. They cut, shoot, drink, make love, gossip, play numbers, flirt, but rarely utter a significant thought.

The slight and confused story, better suited for musical comedy where it might be obscured by attractive songs and dances, recounts the adventures of Hamlet Hitchcock Jones, a "sporty" ladies' man. When Little Ham, who flirts with all women, meets fat Tiny Lee, a beauty parlor owner, his conversation ends in a promise to escort her to a Charleston contest the following evening. Soon afterwards, he purchases a stolen coat for his new girlfriend, wins $645 playing the numbers and is given a job as a numbers runner. When he visits Tiny at her shop, he is surprised to find Mattie Bea, his married girlfriend, who, expecting to accompany him, bought the contest tickets which Ham has given to Tiny and who believes that Ham will give her the stolen coat which he has already given to Tiny. When she discovers the true situation, she attacks Tiny; but Ham is arrested by the police, who assume that he is beating her. Later, Gilbert, Tiny's former boyfriend, visits her apartment to take her to the Charleston contest. His efforts are interrupted by the arrival of Ham, who has secured his release from jail by charming a female judge. To forestall trouble, Tiny hides Gilbert in a closet and locks him in. Still later, at the dance, Mattie Bea and Gilbert, both arriving late, threaten to continue their quarrels with Tiny and Ham. Coincidentally, however, it is revealed that Mattie Bea and Gilbert are husband and wife. Finding themselves together for a change, they become reconciled, and all the couples participate in a frenzied Charleston contest, which is won by Ham and Tiny.

A play with such insignificant action needs to be redeemed by characterization, language, humor, or thought. *Little Ham,* unfortunately, is weak in each of these.

The language probably is the most effective element of the play. In the Harlem dialect and slang, with which he was familiar, Hughes wrote more freely and more accurately than in *Mulatto.* The language constitutes a significant source for the humor of the play. Hughes wrote effective quips:

"She is just a used blade, and I got a new razor"; "I don't duel, I duke"; "love is taking 'til you can't give no mo." Hughes also drew comedy from the strangeness of the Harlem dialect—"she-self," "perzactly"—and from such malapropisms as "reverted" (instead of "converted") and "prostitution" (instead of "prostration").

Like Zora Neale Hurston he assumed that non-Negro audiences would be amused by the colorful language of Negroes, especially the language of invective. This is effectively illustrated by Tiny's tirade directed towards Mattie Bea:

> TINY: I'm a real good mama that can shake your peaches
> down. . . . I hear you cluckin', hen, but your nest must be
> far away. Don't try to lay no eggs in here.

Unfortunately, however, some of the expressions already had been overworked by the time Hughes wrote the play. Now they seem hackneyed: "I'm from Alabam, but I don't give a damn"; "God don't love ugly."

Hughes based his comedy almost as much on slapstick actions and situations, such as that in which Gilbert, locked inside a closet, quarrels with and shoots at Ham, who is outside. Hughes found humor in low comedy, such as the ridicule of the effeminate movements and cowardice of a homosexual and Tiny's accidental burning the head of a middle-class woman who is her client. In general, the comedy is heavy rather than subtle.

The characterization too is heavy and stereotypic. Ham is a wise-cracking, fast-talking ladies' man. Tiny is fat, pleasant, and undistinguished. The other characters are such obvious types that Hughes frequently did not even name them. They are listed merely as "West Indian," "Staid Lady," "Youth," "Shabby Man," etc.

The action is heavily foreshadowed and overly dependent upon chance and coincidence. For example, the complicated love triangles of Tiny and Ham are eased by the improbable coincidence that their former lovers are married to each other. Motivation is puzzling. For example, although love is reputed to work marvels, a critical reader might wonder what attracts Ham to Tiny. Is he enchanted by her money, or is he conquered by her dominance? Without the necessary explanation, the incongruous pairing seems comic rather than sentimental.

Although serious ideas do not intrude upon the apparently continuous gaiety of the Harlemites, shadows of a troubled world appear at the edge of the gay and the comic. Such a shadow is the pathetic joy of the Shabby Man, who has secured a job for the first time in two years. Such a shadow appears in the wish-fantasies and self-delusions of the numbers players who, praying for the one wonderful windfall, overlook the vast sums which they are dribbling away by daily dimes and quarters. Shadowy too are social protests: a janitor's complaint about long hours, the silence of Madam Lucille and Ham when police, without a warrant, search the shoe shine parlor for evidence of gambling.

*Don't You Want to Be Free?*, also written in the thirties, is a poetic drama—or, more appropriately, a pageant—which traces the history of the American Negro from the original enslavement to the Depression. The scenes are predictable—a slave auction, a slave rebellion which ends in massacre. Nevertheless, effective narration provides pride for Negro spectators by recounting Negroes who struggled for freedom—Nat Turner, Denmark Vesey, Harriet Tubman, Sojourner Truth. Furthermore, Hughes effectively underscored the emotion by using lyrics and melodies of spirituals and the blues. A product of the thirties, however, the pageant overemphasizes a call for a uniting of the workers of the world. In language and in thought, the play was the most artistic which Hughes had written, but its obvious aiming at a Negro audience made it unsuitable for commercial production on Broadway.

*The Sun Do Move* (1942) echoes, expands, individualizes, and dramatizes the thought which was narrated in *Don't You Want to Be Free?* After two Negro porters strip to reassume their identity as Africans, the play begins with the auction of two young Africans, Rock and Mary. After a period of time Rock is sold before he has time to see the birth of his child. On the new plantation, he becomes friends with Frog and resists the advances of Bellinda, who has been chosen as his new mate. When they attempt to escape, Frog is killed and Rock is recaptured. Meanwhile, on the other plantation, Mary, Rock's wife, has reared their son. When Little Rock attempts to protect his mother from her mistress's brutality, he is sent to another plantation, where he dies. Escaping again, Rock this time reaches Mary and, with her, flees to the North, where, assisted by Quakers, they become free.

Despite structural weaknesses caused by cinematic flashes from scenes of Rock to those of Mary or Little Rock and despite Hughes's characteristic interpolations of irrelevant low comedy, the play is much more forceful and dramatically interesting than the earlier one. The dispassionate historicity of the pageant is emotionalized by Hughes's focus upon Mary and Rock, struggling to live as human beings rather than chattel.

*Simply Heavenly* (1957), designed for the commercial theater, reached Broadway in a state weaker than *Simple Takes a Wife*, the book upon which the play was based. The major sufferer in the adaptation is Jesse B. Semple himself. In the tales and dialogues of the Simple books, Jess assumes the dimensions of a folk hero. Even though he drinks, cavorts with women, has difficulty paying rent, talks ungrammatically and excessively, his foibles never detract from his dignity; for, like the Greek gods and the heroes of various myths, he is larger than life. It may be appropriate even to say that he, like Joseph Conrad's Kurtz, is remembered primarily as a voice, in this instance a voice which utters common sense even when the speaker seems emotional and illogical. Reduced to actable dimensions, however, Simple, losing his grandeur, shrinks into a more sincere, more conservative, and more thoughtful Ham. In the play, he peeks beneath his legs to watch Joyce, his fiancée, change clothes; he turns somersaults; he is thrown from a car to land on his "sit-downer"; he is propped comically in a hospital bed with his legs in traction; sentimentally and pathetically, he tries to reform and to win Joyce. In short, Simple's reality as the embodied spirit of the Negro working class is reduced to the Harlem barfly; the Chaplinesque Comic Hero shrinks to a farcical fall guy of the pattern of Stan Laurel and Lou Costello.

The second major injury resulting from the transformation from the book to the play is suffered by the material itself. Even though incidents occur in the book, they generally serve merely as acceptable devices to generate Simple's philosophizing. Consequently, what matters is not what happens but what reaction it stimulates from Simple. For a Broadway musical, however, it was necessary to emphasize action and to minimize Simple's reflections. As a result, undue attention is given to Simple's un-successful efforts to seduce Joyce, to the Watermelon Man's pursuit of Mamie, and to the domestic difficulties of Bodidilly and Arcie.

Judged merely in its own terms, however, without reference to the Simple material which it distorts and cheapens, *Simply Heavenly* is vastly superior to *Little Ham*. Simple is more likable than Ham. Joyce and Zarita are less grotesque than Tiny, whose type reappears in Mamie, a secondary lead.

Similarly, the ideas of *Simply Heavenly* have significance missing from *Little Ham*, where Harlemites seemed to concern themselves only with numbers, gossip, parties, sex, and killing. In fact, the differences in *Simply Heavenly* underscore the fact that *Little Ham* was intended as a commercial exploitation of Harlem's exoticism rather than as a presentation of its actuality. In *Simply Heavenly*, the people occupy the same socio-economic level as those in *Little Ham;* they take interest in numbers, gossip, parties, and sex; but they also think and talk about racial problems, economic problems, and domestic problems.

Hughes reacted sensitively to the allegation that he had stereotyped the characters of his earlier books and plays. When a middle-class man says that the denizens of Paddy's bar are stereotypes, Mamie, defender of the race, answers furiously:

> Why, it's getting so colored folks can't do nothing no more without some other Negro calling you a stereotype. Stereotype, hah! If you like a little gin, you're a stereotype. You got to drink Scotch. If you wear a red dress, you're a stereotype. You got to wear beige or chartreuse. Lord have mercy, honey, do-don't like no blackeyed peas and rice! Then you're a down-home Negro for true—which I is—and proud of it! I didn't come here to Harlem to get away from my people. I come here because there's more of 'em. I loves my race. I loves my people. Stereotype!

Nevertheless, it is true that Hughes generally created stereotypes. Ham, Tiny, Robert Norwood, Cora Norwood—all are stereotypes. Even in *Simply Heavenly,* Hughes clung to gross, time-honored models. Joyce is a loving but prim heroine, who probably will become a shrew. A good-hearted, fun-loving girl, who wears her morals loosely, Zarita is from a tradition as old as literature itself.

Both comedy and language seem improved in *Simply Heavenly.* In addition to writing better quips, Hughes, writing lyrics for songs, was able to display his poetic talent more persuasively than in earlier plays. Using the contemporary idiom of Harlem, he created a free and natural dialogue, sometimes rising to colloquial eloquence, as in Simple's recollection of his aunt's efforts to reform him.

Despite the improvement, Hughes continued to relish sentimentality and farce which too frequently detracts from the reality of the characters. For example, it is difficult to believe Boyd's honesty when he describes Simple's crying at night.

During the sixties, Hughes worked on his two best plays—*Emperor of Haiti* and *Tambourines to Glory. Emperor of Haiti* was a generation old. Hughes first presented it as *Drums of Haiti* (1936), rewrote it as *Troubled Island,* an opera, revised it further, and completed his final revisions in 1963, shortly before he presented a script to the Schomburg Collection in Harlem.

*Emperor of Haiti* is the story of Jean-Jacques Dessalines's progress from slave to emperor to corpse. Beginning during the Haitian blacks' rebellion against their French masters and treating historical fact freely, the play focuses on the economic and personal problems of Dessalines's rule as emperor. Economically, the kingdom suffers because Dessalines refuses to require labor from the liberated blacks. When he finally realizes the need, they turn against him. Personally, Dessalines fails in Hughes's play because, after becoming emperor, he rejects his uneducated wife Azelea, who loves him. In her place, he takes Claire Heureuse, a pawn of the mulattoes who seeks to overthrow him. The play climaxes and ends when, riding to crush a rebellion, Dessalines is killed in the trap set by mulattoes. Melodramatically, Azelea, now a penniless street seller, discovers his body and mourns his death while Claire flees with her mulatto lover and two passing Haitians fail to recognize their emperor.

The play has artistic and historical flaws. As in much of Hughes's drama, low comic relief is overworked while the plot lags. For instance, prior to the climactic arrival of Dessalines at the trap, street sellers talk and joke interminably. Furthermore, history is distorted. Although Toussaint is mentioned, the play suggests that Dessalines is the only leader of the slaves' rebellion. Moreover, Dessalines's character is given a moral bath. The libertinism which characterized Dessalines after his becoming emperor is reduced to his affair with Claire Heureuse.

Nevertheless, the historical events provided Hughes with plot, thought, and character superior to those which generally emerged from his imagination. Although Azelea is perhaps idealized as a devoted, self-sacrificing wife, Dessalines is well-drawn, even in outline.

Hughes's final play, *Tambourines to Glory,* was adapted from his novel of the same name. It is a modernized morality play and, as such, is surprisingly good. To make money, Laura Reed, a gay girl like Zarita, persuades staid, religious Essie Johnson to join her in establishing a church. They are assisted and protected by Big-Eyed Buddy Lomax, who actually is the Devil. Gradually Laura slips further and further into sin as Buddy's mistress. She swells membership by giving tips on numbers; she sells tap water as holy water. Vainly, she tries to thwart Buddy's pursuit of Gloria, a singer, and Marietta, Essie's teen-aged niece. Finally, fearing him, Laura stabs Buddy. Essie is arrested but released when Laura confesses. Laura is charged with self-defense.

There is more development in this plot than in any Hughes had written previously; and, although the action is tinged with melodrama, it is free from the irrelevant comedy and improbable coincidence which characterize most of Hughes's work. The characters are not new, but they are smoothly delineated—perhaps because Hughes's frequent recreation of the same types enabled him to know them fully. As has been explained, Laura is modeled after Zarita, and Essie is a quieter, more mature, less attractive Joyce.

More than in any work since *Don't You Want to Be Free?* Hughes used poetry to develop thought. Instead of being entertaining diversions, as in *Simply Heavenly,* the lyrics of the songs explain the motivation and personalities of the characters. For example, Laura sings her love for Buddy; Buddy sings the blues characterizing life in Harlem; Marietta sings her purity.

Perhaps the chief reason for Hughes's success is that the musical morality play permitted him to display his major talents without straining the credulity of the audience. Stereotyped characters and heavy underlining of ideas are accepted in morality plays, and colloquial poetry and broad comedy have a place in musicals.

As Webster Smalley has pointed out, Langston Hughes must be credited with establishing several all-Negro professional dramatic groups. In doing so, he contributed significantly to the development of drama among Negroes. In his own work, however, even though he continued to write and to be produced through two generations, he never developed the artistry of a Louis Peterson or Lorraine Hansberry. Least successful when he catered to the predictable taste of Broadway audiences, he was most artistic when he wrote simply and lyrically of the history and aspirations of Negroes.

GEORGE E. KENT

# Hughes and the Afro-American Folk and Cultural Tradition

Langston Hughes's literary career began with a commitment to black folk and cultural sources as one important basis for his art. The folk forms and cultural responses were themselves definitions of black life created by blacks on the bloody and pine-scented Southern soil and upon the blackboard jungle of urban streets, tenement buildings, store-front churches, and dim-lit bars. Thus the current generation of black writers, who are trying to develop artistic forms that reflect a grip upon realities as they exist from day to day in black communities discover that Langston Hughes is an important pioneer, in his non-ideological way, who has already "been there and gone."

From the animal tales to the hipsterish urban myth-making, folk tradition has *is-ness*. Things are. Things are funny, sad, tragic, tragicomic, bitter, sweet, tender, harsh, awe-inspiring, cynical, other-worldly, worldly—sometimes, alternately expressing the conflicting and contradictory qualities; sometimes, expressing conflicting qualities simultaneously. Thus a Brer Rabbit story is full of the contradictions of experience—an expression of the existing order of the world and Brer Rabbit's unspecific sense of something "other." And there are times in Brer Rabbit stories during which the existing order and Brer Rabbit's "other" have almost equal validity.

The black preacher can be a revered personage, but also a figure of comedy, and the oppressed can be sad as victim but comic as a person. As creative artist, Langston Hughes had more of an instinctive, than intellectual, sense of the folk acceptance of the contradictory as something to be

From *Blackness and the Adventure of Western Civilization*. © 1972 by George E. Kent. The Third World Press, 1972.

borne, climbed on top of, confronted by the shrewd smile, the cynical witticism, the tragicomic scratch of the head, the tense and sucked-in bottom lip, the grim but determined look beyond this life, and, more familiarly, the howl of laughter that blacks have not yet learned to separate from the inanities of minstrel tradition.

Thus, upon entering the universe of Langston Hughes, one leaves at its outer darkness that *type* of *rationality* whose herculean exertions are for absolute resolution of contradictions and external imposition of symmetry. For at many points, though not at all points, Hughes is full of the folk.

And in the face of the stubborn contradictions of life, the folk could frequently call upon their spirits and selves to mount on up a little higher, and simply acknowledge: "It be's that way."

Failure to understand the instance in which the folk do more to move their spirit than to move "objective" reality can lead the critic of the folk and Hughes into a fantasia of misinterpretation. Thus blues critic Samuel Charters in *The Poetry of the Blues* complains because blues singer Bessie Smith's "Long Old Road" expresses great determination to stand up to the terrors of life's journey and to shake hands at journey's end with a friend, but ends in a futility that eliminates the value of the journey: "Found my long lost friend, and I might as well stayed at home." However, Bessie's resolution is in the face-up-to-it-spirit, a tone of pathos, outrage, and defiance mingled, not in the rhetoric of formal rationality.

And thus Robert Bone in his work of criticism, *The Negro Novel in America* (1958), makes neat, clever remarks about ideological confusion in Hughes's novel, *Not without Laughter,* upon discovering that the story advocates both "compensatory" laughter in the face of life's pain and achievement based upon "the protestant ethic." But expressions such as "the success drive," and "the protestant ethic" simply flatten out into lifeless categories the rich density of the folk hope, which is better expressed by its own terms: "being somebody" and "getting up off your knees." The folk tend to be community oriented; thus in *Not without Laughter* Aunt Hager and Aunt Harriett (representative of the religious and blues traditions, respectively) tend to see the central character's achievement possibilities in the form of community uplift. It is Aunt Tempy who more nearly represents something that could be called "protestant ethic," and she is rejected. As will be seen later in the essay, the novel does have problems, but it is unlikely that they would be resolved under the neat dichotomies with which Bone deals.

A third major quality that folk tradition reflects in its less self-conscious form is an *as ifness.* Whereas one feels behind self-conscious black literature the unarticulated knowledge that America for Blacks is neither a land of soul nor of bread, a good deal of folklore suggests a complete penetration of its universe, a possession of the land and self in a more thoroughgoing way than that expressed by white American literature. Spirituals, for example, suggest a complete mining of their universe. Many of the animal tales and general folk stories also suggest that a universe has been possessed and defined. The *blues,* however, as a more self-conscious folk form, achieves this confident embracement only in specific songs, since so many of them feature a wanderer and throw such terrible weight upon the individual self. What Langston Hughes and Claude McKay (and possibly Jean Toomer in *Cane*) were able to retain, though sometimes insecurely, were a bounce and warm vitality whose fragile supports are everywhere apparent even when the entire work seems to be devoted to their celebration. The sudden appearance of aggressive symbols of the white world would bring many of the celebrations to a halt or reveal, at least, the high cost of soul. As a result, some black novels end in an otherwise inexplicable romanticism.

Despite the difficulties, Langston Hughes chose to build his vision on the basis of the folk experience as it had occurred in the South and as it appeared modified in the modern industrial city. Judging from his autobiography, *The Big Sea*, his choice proceeded from the center of his being. He liked black folks. He liked their naturalness, their sense of style, their bitter facing up, their individual courage, and the variety of qualities that formed part of his own family background. He was also in recoil from the results of his father's hard choices of exile, hatred of blacks, self-hatred, and resulting dehumanization. His manifesto of 1926, "The Negro Artist and the Racial Mountain" revealed that choosing the life of the black folk was also a way of choosing himself, a way of possessing himself through the rhythms and traditions of black people. His choice enabled him to allow for prevailing ideologies without being smothered by them, since folk vision could suddenly shift from tenderness to biting cynicism and since within its womb a pragmatic embracement of ideological impulses that promised survival was a secure tradition. Thus, whereas pre-1920s black writers, devoid of a land of soul and a land of bread, found themselves completely at the mercy of that complex of ideas in the social arena known as the American Dream, Hughes brings in aspects of the Dream at will, but so many bitter notes accompany it that he can hardly be said to put much confidence in it. I speak, of course, in the light of the large number of poems that are devoted to other matters. The individual poems, such as "I, Too," which speak of an America that will come to its senses are scattered here and there among poems that discharge the sudden drop of acid. Hughes prized decency in the individual person and could look with compassion upon those corrupted by delusions and systematized prejudice, but in several poems he responded with outrage, bitterness, anger and threat.

It is easily forgotten that one part of "I, Too," speaks of eating well and growing strong, so that no one would *dare* say to the Black, "Eat in the kitchen." In *Selected Poems,* bitterness and desperation are especially apparent in the sections entitled "Magnolia Flowers" and "Name in Uphill Letters," but also directly and indirectly in individual poems among the other sections. In the two sections mentioned, the poems "Roland Hayes Beaten" and "Puzzled" convey the sense of a coming explosion. But one needs merely to range over the body of published poems, in order to sense within Hughes a very powerful ambivalence. Nevertheless, he adopted a psychological approach for his readings to black audiences, described in his second autobiographical book, *I Wonder as I Wander,* an approach which allowed for laughter, then serious and grim situations, and finally the hopeful and stoical stance. Such poems as "I, Too," and "The Negro Mother" gave the positive note without shoving aside the ogres that threatened.

In Langston Hughes's vision, both in regard to the folk and to himself, the most nearly consistent focus is upon a lifesmanship that preserves and celebrates humanity in the face of impossible odds. In regard to himself, Hughes is the most modest of persons. Even his apparent frankness in *The Big Sea* and *I Wonder as I Wander* is deceptive, since his emotional responses are frequently understated or their nuances undramatized. Missing is the close-up focus of the protracted relationship that threatens to reveal the soul or the total person. Thus there are unforgettable pictures—Hughes's relationship to his father and mother, his brief companionship with a refugee girl while down and out in Paris, his conflict with Russian officials over the production of a movie on race relationships in America, etc. But the man behind the picture remains somewhat elusive.

What does emerge is transcendent moments amidst the chaos that society and human nature tend to create. Two or more people getting through to each other, the seizure of richness from surrounding rottenness or confusion, the sudden appearance of the rainbow after the storm, the individual retaining his focus upon the human—the foregoing comprise the stuff of the autobiographies, which are frequently comparable to the episodic experiences of lyrics and convey only the slimmest hint of the single broad meaning that would impose the illusion of unity upon human experience. In all the autobiographical approaches, Hughes is consistent with what I have called the *is-ness* of folk vision and tradition—life is lived from day to day and confronted by plans whose going astray may evoke the face twisted in pain or the mouth open in laughter. The triumph is in holding fast to dreams and maintaining, if only momentarily, the spirit of the self.

As to the folk, Hughes was early captivated by their stubborn lifesmanship. Through his grandmother he had early learned the heroic side of black life, and he had experienced the rituals of the black church and pretended to be saved. As he encountered the urban folk, he was taken in by the full-bodied warmth of their lives, the color, the bounce, the vitality. But he also knew the harshness of their existence in the huge city, since he had spent a summer during adolescence on South State Street in Chicago where his mother was employed by a dress shop. In *The Big Sea: An Autobiography,* he says:

> South State Street was in its glory then, a teeming Negro street with crowded theaters, restaurants, and cabarets. And excitement from noon to noon. Midnight was like day. The street was full of workers and gamblers, prostitutes and pimps, church folks and sinners. The tenements on either side were very congested. For neither love nor money could you find a decent place to live. Profiteers, thugs, and gangsters were coming into their own.

Like Sandy in *Not without Laughter,* Hughes walked bewildered among the new sights. But the harshness within the black community was not the sum of the situation. When he wandered beyond it, he was beaten by hostile whites.

This early awareness of the embattled situation of folk existence in the Northern city and direct brutality of the Southern life that drove blacks to urban questing probably protected Hughes from the falsification of folk life that James Weldon Johnson found in the poetry of Paul Laurence Dunbar (see his comments in the two prefaces in *The Book of American Negro Poetry*). Instead of the idyllic, Hughes could portray honestly a people caged within a machine culture, sometimes feeding upon each other, sometimes snarling at the forces without, and sometimes rising above tragedy by the sheer power of human spirit. A people responding to existence through cultural forms and traditions derived from so many terrible years of facing up and demanding, at the same time, a measure of joy and affirmation: the dance, jazz, blues, spirituals, the church. Across the water in France, he found:

> Blues in the rue Pigalle. Black and laughing, heartbreaking blues in the Paris dawn, pounding like a pulse-beat, moving like the Mississippi!

*Lawd, I looked and saw a spider*
*Goin' up de wall.*
*I say, I looked and saw a spider*
*Goin' up de wall.*
*I said where you goin', Mister Spider?*
*I'm goin' to get my ashes hauled!*

The variety of life and its relationship to the self were expressed in simple symbols that allowed for the whole gamut of stances toward existence.

Later, amidst the phoniness that he found in black middle-class Washington society, he was again to encounter the triumphant spirit of the "low-down folks." They served as an inspiration:

> I tried to write poems like the songs they sang on Seventh Street— gay songs, because you had to be gay or die; sad songs, because you couldn't help being sad sometimes. But gay or sad, you kept on living and you kept on going. Their songs—those of Seventh Street—had the pulse beat of the people who keep on going.

Hughes speaks of the "undertow of black music with its rhythm that never betrays you, its strength like the beat of the human heart, its humor, and its rooted power." On Seventh Street, he encountered both the "barrel houses," suppliers of the gay, naughty, and wise music, and the black churches full of song and intense religious experience. It is good to keep in mind the ceremonies of humanity which Hughes found in the folk even when reading of his nonblack experiences, since he seems to have sought the same qualities in all people.

The above approach applies to Hughes's writings that are not in folk forms and are not about the folk. He seldom takes up a form that could not express the folk or that expresses *forms of response* to existence that are foreign to their sensibility. This is to say that Hughes was sensitive to the implications of form. Thus he early allied himself with free verse forms. The blues form, with its sudden contrasts, varied repetitions, resolution areas, allows for the brief and intense expression of the ambiguities of life and the self, and for sharp wit and cynicism. The jazz, bebop, and boogie-woogie rhythms achieve a free swing away from Western constraints. One could add comments on the significance of the traditional work songs, the influence of spirituals, shouts, the gospel song, the prayer, the testimonial, and the sermon. Suffice it here to say that they move us into an immediate recognition of a black experience that is at the center of a long tradition, convey attitudes and forms of response to existence, and often give the illusion of confronting us, not merely with lines upon a page, but with a participant of a particular ritual.

Now as James A. Emanuel has ably pointed out in his book, *Langston Hughes,* it is difficult to gain the total blues experience or the musical experience of jazz and other rhythms from the printed page, since the writer is deprived of the embellishments used by the blues singer and the musician. However, the handicap of printed page should alert us to compensations available to the writer, to other dangers that bestride his path, and to Hughes's variation from the standard path of the Western artist. In the first place, it is seldom really of value simply to duplicate a folk form, since the folk artist has already pushed the form to its greatest heights of expressiveness. In mere repetition, the self-conscious artist usually runs the risk of merely echoing achievements that have had the advantage of generations of responsive audiences. His real opportunity is in capturing the spirit of the art, in adapting techniques, in adding to folk forms an articulation of assumptions which the folk artist merely had to hint at because his audience was so closely akin to him (or he was so closely akin to his audience). Thus the self-conscious artist is not necessarily being praised for a very high achievement when the critic points to his creation of a perfect blues or spiritual form.

The above principles regarding the folk artist and the self-conscious writer are true if the printed page is to be the sole basis of judgment, a handicap that Hughes often hurdled by reading his poems directly to audiences (with or without musical accompaniment) and by his close relationship to the black community. He, therefore, to a degree, evaded the confinement to the printed page that is the fate of the alienated or abstracted standard Western artist. Thus he could read the mulatto's statement in the poem "Cross" to an audience that had lived with the white enforced miscegenation that forms the subject of the poem, and deliver a powerful impact. He did not, for example, have to dramatize or explain the changes within the mulatto, who merely states them as conclusions. This kind of compensation, however, was not available for every poem by Hughes, and therefore, he must frequently face the question as to whether he is not operating too close to the folk form.

Any criticism of Hughes must thus also face the instances and the degree to which he varied from the traditional stance of the Western artist. Much of his work is very little reflective of a concern to be *universal* and *timeless.* Instead, the topicality of numerous pieces reflects Hughes's satisfaction in giving the issues of the community an immediate and striking voice.

## II

A more concrete demonstration of Hughes's relationship to folk and cultural tradition may be gained from selected fiction, poetry, and drama. Although he became famous during the 1920s as a poet, Hughes reveals the spread of his concerns and their hazards more clearly in literary types that provided considerable sweep, rather than brief lyrical intensity. *Not without Laughter,* Hughes's first novel, is therefore the starting point, for strategic reasons peculiar to this essay, and its discussion will be followed by an examination of representative poems and plays.

*Not without Laughter* portrays a family that is very close to the folk, and reveals styles of confronting the disorder and chaos that attempted to hammer their way into the precariously held sanctuary of black family life. The novel portrays the tensions of a generation that came to adulthood not long after the hopes of blacks for freedom had been fully brought low throughout the land. (The first reference to time is a letter postmarked June 13, 1912.) The mainstay and would-be shepherd of this generation is Aunt Hager, whose life is an epic of labor over the washtub. Getting ready to meet adulthood as the third generation is her grandson, Sandy, a witness to the perilous hold on life managed by his family: the grandmother; his mother, Anjee; his wandering father, Jimboy; and his aunts, Tempy and Harriett. Although the events controlling the life of each member of the family absorb a goodly portion of the novel, the development and fate of the boy Sandy and especially the extent to which the lives of his elders provide him with a usable resource, form the big question mark in the novel.

Aunt Hager, the grandmother, represents the religious tradition begun in the secret "praise" meetings of slavery and further developed in the little white washed churches that once dotted the countryside and the small towns.

And here we must be aware of the oversimplified versions of black religion, since the race's religious experience, like all other black experiences, requires reevaluation in its own terms, one which will release it from the oversimplified categories of escapism and otherworldliness that were developed by analogy with what is required in duplicating the Faustian quest of whites. Aunt Hager's religion, as Hughes presents it, reflects solemn moments, dogged persistence, and an ability to love and forgive, that gives magnitude to the humblest. It places man against the sky. It allows Aunt Hager, according to her report, to pray for whites that she doesn't like, but she is still pragmatic and unworshipful towards them (unlike Faulkner's Dilsey of *The Sound and the Fury*). In her eyesight, whites, in their relationship with blacks, are good as far as they *see* but they do not see far. This is not to say that Aunt Hager fully grasps or brings into a single focus the hard realities of a racially oppressive system that primarily values her as a work horse and twists the lives of her children into shapes that can grasp joy only by refusing to be stifled by disaster. Since Hughes is aware of her limitations, he counterpoints her determined optimism by the bitter and sinister reports of Jimboy, Sister Johnson, and Harriett, and by portraits of racial injustice.

What impresses Hughes and Sandy is the passionate spiritual power that sustains faith in life and in a day of overcoming. She would like for Sandy to be a Booker Washington and a Frederick Douglass: "I wants him to know all they is to know, so's he can help this black race of our'n to come up and see de light and take they places in de world. I wants him to be a Fred Douglass leadin' de people, that's what, an' not followin' in de tracks of his good-for-nothin' pappy."

This folk sense of making something out of oneself has a lasting impact upon Sandy, but there are also available to him the jazz and blues tradition through his father Jimboy and his Aunt Harriett. Hughes plays very warmly and lovingly the notes of the tradition that involves a bouncing vitality and a defiant celebration of the sweets, joys, and pains of life, and Sandy finds himself drawn to the people who demand that life yield its more soulful fruits. However, Hughes has a very complex awareness, one that he cannot fully render within the novel. He is also an honest and realistic writer. Therefore, he can not make of Jimboy's situation a very simple triumph and must report the cost of Jimboy's joy, charm, and exuberance. It is the increased deprivation of his family and some rather painful childhood experiences of Sandy that register the cost of Jimboy's bounce and spontaneity. Thus, despite Hughes's distancing of Jimboy's wide-ranging amours, explanations of the systematic oppression that tends to reduce black men, the portrayal of him as a "rounder" who works and holds good intentions, and dramatization of his ability to transform the atmosphere of his surroundings, Jimboy is never quite clear of the dubious stature which Aunt Hager very early in the novel confers upon him. Jimboy is, after all, *boy*.

Thus the sensitive youth Sandy can only share moments of the tradition represented by his father, can only feel that the swing and bounce that he represents ought, somehow, to be a part of the richness of any life.

Hughes's complex awareness of what the folk were up against in the attempt to assert the free life spirit is also apparent in his portrait of Harriett, who learns through her intermittent bouts with prostitution and utter destitution the price-tag placed by a machine culture upon spontaneity.

Near the end of the novel, she seems to be on the way to fame and fortune, but Hughes was too familiar with the instabilities that hovered about the success of the black actors, actresses, and entertainers of this period. For most, it was an up and down sort of life, and the "down" area was often slimy.

Since Aunt Tempy's choice of a bloodless imitation of white society represented for Hughes an obvious surrender of soul, her life represented little that could promise richness to Sandy.

In the end, Sandy is thrown back upon the dreams of Aunt Hager. Although the metaphor seems awkward when applied to her, she too was a dancer of the spirit and held dreams of his becoming the dancer who overshot the unambiguous hazards that, for the folk, skyrocketed the price of soul. Perhaps, one need not literally repeat the folk forms of dancing, the folk existence; perhaps one might achieve fulfillment if one could conceive of Booker Washington and Frederick Douglass as dancers of the spirit, too. Perhaps one could retain much of the folk spirit and attitude as one transformed their dances.

> A band of dancers. . . . Black dancers—captured in a white world. . . . Dancers of the spirit, too. Each black dreamer a captured dancer of the spirit. . . . Aunt Hager's dreams for Sandy dancing far beyond the limitations of their poverty, of their humble station in life, of their dark skins.

Other than folk responses to existence, the novel contains such forms as blues, folk aphorisms, slave narratives and a slave tall story, dances, and spirituals. Especially significant is the spiritual that comes at the very end, "By an' by when de mawnin' comes. . . ." The spiritual ends with the line, "An' we'll understand it better by an' by!" It tells of overcoming, suggests a determined struggle which cannot be easily conceptualized or understood, and is being sung in the big, raw city of Chicago. As Hughes has said, it is the music of a "people on the go," who are somehow to break free from their cage. The vague aspirations, but settled determination, of Sandy are a fitting part of the ending.

The novel, of course, has its problems. Sandy's consciousness does not develop dramatically, and there are contradictory statements about his degrees of innocence. Jimboy's moral lecture to Sandy comes abruptly, and, seemingly, out of character, and Harriett's insistence upon the vision of Aunt Hager needs stronger foreshadowing. Finally, the ending does not dramatically impose itself upon the reader, although it is logically the right one. Much of the source of the foregoing deficiencies seems to be Hughes's complex awareness of the hard and stubborn realities, which the characters will somehow have to overcome. He is almost too aware of the uncertainties of black life.

On the other hand, the novel makes clear the sensibility that created the poems which preceded it and followed it, and looks forward to the rough urban responses provided by his short stories, the Simple sketches, and the plays. For *Not without Laughter* emphasizes Hughes's awareness of the overwhelming oppression that dancers of the spirit faced in both rural and urban cages of the American machine culture, the limitations in the major forms of folk culture, and the increasing difficulty of asserting the triumph of the spirit, as will be reflected by the poems and plays that form the remainder of this discussion.

In his essay, "The Harlem of Langston Hughes' Poetry," in *Phylon,* Arthur P. Davis has cogently pointed out the increasing desperation and the decreasing emphasis upon joy in poems devoted to urban Harlem reflected in the major collections of poetry from *The Weary Blues* through *Montage of a Dream Deferred*. The volumes represent the adaptation of the folk spirit to the big urban surroundings, and the attempt to transform the threatening pressures of city machine culture into a poetry responsive to the spirit and often to transcend by defiant assertion of spirit. On the one hand are the tough and soulful blues, the cabarets and jazz bands, the singers, and sparkling personalities; on the other, the stark upcreep of weariness and the varieties of offenses to the human spirit unleashed by the city. To these may be added other urban poems that do not deal with Harlem, the more rural Southern poems, or poems on the general theme of the South, and poems on the general theme of the qualities and dilemmas of blacks. Finally, there are the poems that address themselves to life, without regard to race. The variety of categories makes possible a variety of notes and attitudes.

Hughes's most obvious and original innovation was the introduction of blues form and attitudes as part of the art of poetry as pointed out by Margaret Walker. The use of such blues devices as swift contrasts, sharp wit, voice tones, and folk imagery, frequently create striking effects, despite the lack of musical accompaniment and gesture that were available to the blues singer. "Midwinter Blues" which first appeared in *Fine Clothes to the Jew,* seems to me to catch the essential folk spirit adapted to an urban setting and to contain the literary possibilities of the form. The poem taken from *Selected Poems of Langston Hughes* begins:

> In the middle of the winter,
> Snow all over the ground.
> In the middle of the winter,

> Snow all over the ground—
> 'Twas the night befo' Christmas
> My good man turned me down.

The conjunction of the cold of the winter with the associations we have with Christmas and the contrasting actual response of "my good man" get the poem off to an incisive start and combine narrative and blues techniques. However, the second stanza has the sudden turn of wit and irony of attitude more closely associated with the blues.

> Don't know's I'd mind his goin'
> But he left me when the coal was low.
> Don't know's I'd mind his goin'
> But he left when the coal was low.
> Now, if a man loves a woman
> That ain't no time to go.

The third and fourth stanzas, unfortunately, lack the power of the first two, but the third stanza does bring in a new response of the *contradictory self*. Despite the somewhat snide remarks in the first two lines of the second stanza, the "good man" is acknowledged as "the only man I'll/Love till the day I die." The fourth stanza states a general attitude that requires the voice of the blues singer to maintain intensity and to assert the toughness of spirit characteristic of the blues. Frequently, the last stanza seems to lose intensity, simply because we do not have the ingenious use of triumphant tone that the actual blues singer is able to render.

Thus "Young Gal's Blues" has three closely knit stanzas by written literary standards. The fourth is related to the other three in an associational way, but an actual blues singer would bring home both its power and relatedness. On the other hand, "Down and Out," which first appeared in *Shakespeare in Harlem*, 1942, maintains its unity, sings itself, and provides an interesting effect by an *apparently* anticlimactic arrangement and the repetition of the last line.

> Baby, if you love me
> Help me when I'm down and out.
> If you love me, baby,
> Help me when I'm down and out,
> I'm a po' gal
> Nobody gives a damn about.

> The credit man's done took ma clothes
> And rent time's nearly here.
> I'd like to buy a straightenin' comb,
> An' I need a dime fo' beer.
>
> I need a dime fo' beer.

As a song, "Down and Out" would lend itself to a variety of singing styles. As a written work, the concision of the first verse and the suggestiveness regarding the blues attitudes in the second verse allow for the activity of the creative reader. Several poems provide both this unity and suggestiveness: "Lament over Love," "Stony Lonesome," "Miss Blues'es Child," and "Hard Daddy," for example. Obvious literary unity, however, does not always produce the powerfully expressed folk spirit, since, in its own style, the poem must compete with the folk blues poem whose black audiences hold assumptions in common with the singer—a fact that permits him to impose a unity not based upon simple logical structure but upon his total performance. The following lines by Blind Lemon Jefferson as I have been able to gather them from Samuel Charters's edited record, *The Country Blues,* will illustrate the non-logical structure with which the blues singer is free to operate. Jefferson gives it a powerful rendering by his damn-my-hard-luck-soul variations in tone:

> I'm gwine to de river
> Walk down by the sea (Repeated)
> I got those tadpoles and minnows
> Arguing over me.
>
> Settin' here wonderin'
> Will a match-box hold my clothes (Repeated)
> Ain't got so many matches
> But I got so far to go.
>
> Lord, mama, who may your manager be?
> Hey, hey, mama, who may your manager be?
> You ask so many questions, can't you
> Make 'rangements for me?
>
> I got a girl way cross town
> She crochet all the time (Repeated)
> Baby, if you don't stop crocheting
> You goin' lose your mind.

> I wouldn't mind marrying,
> But I can't stand settlin' down
> Wouldn't mind marryin'
> But, Lord, settlin' down
> I'm goin' act like a preacher
> An' ride from town to town.
>
> I'm leaving town
> Cryin' won't make me stay,
> I'm leavin' town, woo-oo
> Cryin' won't make me stay,
> The more you cry, baby,
> The more you drive me away.

The blues lyric has behind it enough audience assumptions regarding the singer's message to make a discussion for a separate essay: the gritty circumstances that inform the mood; the appearance of the prostitute in the third stanza; the implications concerning the girlfriend in the fourth stanza "crocheting" (sexual intercourse); views of marriage and the preacher; attitudes of lovers; the character of the roving "rounder," etc. I leave the analysis of imagery, the associational development, and *apparent* difficulty of the images of the *river* and the sea, to the reader.

My point is that the conscious literary artist runs the risk of appearing second-rate when he is compared with the blues artist at his best, if he simply tries to mine exactly the same ore. In the "Match-Box Blues," the challenge resides even in the blues poem as literary lyric, since its images and associational development allow it to penetrate so suggestively the privacy and complexity of a particular black experience. (This associational development is greatly admired when it appears in a poem by T. S. Eliot.) It is perhaps not too much to say that even on a purely literary basis Hughes has trouble matching the authority wielded here by Blind Lemon Jefferson, in the poems that follow strictly the validated blues form.

I would tentatively say that Hughes is best when he attempts to capture the blues spirit and varied forms of response to existence in a poem that uses non-blues devices. Among such poems would be "Reverie on the Harlem River," "Early Evening Quarrel," "Mama and Daughter," and especially, "Lover's Return." Such poems can combine the simplicities of free verse, the free dramatizing of concrete situations, the folk tendency to hold in suspension contradictory attitudes, the incisive folk definition, and various formal resources of literary technique, for the effective rendering that is more available to the self-conscious and relatively isolated artist.

In an overall way, it may also be said that Hughes gains a good deal from experimentation with blues form. One certainly could not imagine his having to buy a Bessie Smith record, as James Baldwin reports that he once did, in order to get back to how blacks actually express themselves or to recapture the sound patterns of their speech. Hughes seldom strikes a false note with black sound patterns, and these are apparent also in non-blues poems. His poems are also full of the hard complex attitudes of the people stubbornly "on the go," whom he mentions in his autobiography, *The Big Sea.* He is seldom at the mercy of forms that immediately evoke experiences whose essentials are not those of the black experience, a dilemma that sometimes catches up with Claude McKay as we hear him crowded by the romantic tradition and the sudden notes of Byron or Shelley.

It is, of course, possible to credit too much to his contact with a single form, and to overlook the fact that Hughes was drawing from the whole of black culture. Suffice it to say that the self confronting defiantly the enemy at home and abroad is amply evident in his blues and blues-toned poems.

There is evidence in Hughes's poetry of his capturing the forms of response of the folk implied by the religious tradition and its cultural modes of expression: the spirituals, gospel songs, and the sermon. In most of such poems the concentration is not on the close duplication of form that is sometimes encountered in the blues poems, but upon mood, definitions, motifs, and the determination and persistence provided by having a friend not made of earth. Such approaches to life can sometimes be rendered through dramatization of personalities who sometimes mention God—but not always. Such poems as "Aunt Sue's Stories," "The Negro Mother," "Mother to Son," and even the poem that strikes the blues note, "Stony Lonesome," convey a sense of standing erect upon the earth by means of a quiet but deep relationship to something more than this world.

Perhaps the closest that Hughes came to attempting to catch the immediate bounce and beat of a form is the emphasis upon the gospel music form and beat found in the poem, "Fire," which begins:

> Fire,
> Fire, Lord!
> Fire gonna burn ma soul!

The beat of the gospel music can be heard, and if one has been exposed to the musical accompaniment, it too can be heard. But it is only necessary to read a few gospel songs or to hear Mahalia Jackson render one in the ecstatic modulations that have made her famous to realize that Hughes is trying neither to mount to the heights nor to give the typical resolution of conflict that is usually essential to the form. In the spiritual tradition, Hughes is better at rendering the quieter moments, even when they involve desperation, which may be found in such poems as "Sinner," "Litany," "Feet of Jesus," and "Judgment Day," although he can mount to the ecstatic by combining well-established lines and images drawn from tradition with other literary resources as he does in "Spirituals."

Hughes's spectacular effort in the vein of the folk sermon is "Sunday Morning Prophecy," but he makes no effort to exploit the full sermon form: the conventional apology for ineptitude, the clear statement and explanation of text, and the movement into ecstatic seizure by the spirit. The ecstatic seizure and eloquent imagery characteristic of the folk sermon are utilized, but the emphasis is finally upon the powerful condemnation of things of this world and the minister's final plea:

> Come into the church this morning,
> Brothers and Sisters,
> And be saved—
> And give freely
> In the collection basket
> That I who am thy shepherd
> Might live.
>
> Amen!

The associations that people have with the urbanized folk minister of Cadillac fame can raise issues concerning the interpretation of the poem, if one is also acquainted with the rural or small town folk minister who was expected by the congregation to make the same plea for his meager remuneration. If Hughes is thinking of the Cadillac preacher, then the effect is irony, but somewhat grotesque and the means seem out of proportion to the effect. It seems more effective to consider the poem in line with the folk tendency to balance apparent contradiction without feeling the urge for logical symmetry.

More important for Hughes is his sense of the power to persist, and perhaps eventually to prevail, which the religious impulse and definitions provide. To persist, that is, with human personality and its full range, refusing to be destroyed and determined to overcome "some day." Here Hughes is dealing with a cultural dimension that deeply reflects the desperate history of a people caged in a machine culture. It is, in its urban setting, in accord with the ending of the novel *Not without Laughter,* in which Sandy finds in Chicago his people hard embattled but retaining that dance of the spirit which they insisted upon amidst the ravages of slavery. In the poetry of Hughes, the dance moves sometimes in a deeply contemplative slow drag, sometimes in the fast triumphal pace inescapable in gospel music.

In a modified folk tradition also are poems which fit into no particular category, but represent depths of lives, nonetheless. "Railroad Avenue" celebrates the transforming power and spirit of laughter; "Me and the Mule" expresses stubborn self-acceptance and defiance; and "Mama and Daughter," the male-female attraction and resentment. Other poems touch upon a wide range of topics: defiance in the face of discrimination, the potential sudden explosion of put-upon people, the African heritage, the on-the-go impulse in the face of oppression, police brutality, etc. And still others range over topics that cannot be said to have a direct relation to folk and cultural tradition.

Finally, there are the published plays, some of which yield their full depths only when related to folk and cultural tradition. The play version of "Mulatto" is a tragedy, whose title suggests a focus upon the mulatto Robert, the son of the white Georgia plantation owner Colonel Norwood and his black housekeeper, Cora. However, the deeper aspects of the play derive from Cora and the narrow range of choices within which the plantation folk have had to make their definition of the possibilities of life. After submitting to sexual advances by Norwood in a seduction involving both her fear and attraction, Cora, at the age of fifteen, received her plantation mother's definition of her situation:

> Then I cried and cried and told ma mother about it, but she didn't take it hard like I thought she'd take it. She said fine white mens like de young Colonel always took good care o' their colored womens. She said it was better than marryin' some black field hand and workin' all your life in de cotton and cane. Better even than havin' a job lik ma had, takin' care o' de white chilluns.

Within this narrow margin of something "better," Cora has tried to move her relationship with Norwood from that of simple sexual exploitation into one in which natural claims of fatherhood and motherhood could prevail. Norwood has been married, but Cora is the sole source of his fatherhood, his only resource for rising above the mere category of *whiteness*. Cora's deepest pride is in the potential magnitude of her role. Otherwise, she has to be content with the fact that by force of personality she has compelled Norwood to educate his children, an act that strains and goes beyond the customary code governing miscegenation in the Georgia county. Thus, on the one hand Norwood strains the white code until it and its compulsions overtake him; on the other, Cora has strained the folk code, which only promised, in the definition provided by her mother, relief from brute labor. The clash between the claims of whiteness and the claims of the rhythms of natural fatherhood produces Norwood's tragedy: in the final analysis, he cannot exist without the validation of whiteness, a situation expressed by his participation in a lynching and the remorseful aftermath, his beating of his son for publicly calling him father, and the line he draws between Cora and himself: "There was no touchin' Bert, just like there was no touchin' you [Norwood]. I could only love him, like I loved you." The situation collapses completely as the mulatto son Robert chokes his father to death and then destroys himself to prevent being lynched by the mob. Robert acted after Norwood had drawn a pistol, in an attempt to force Robert to act, not like the son he demanded to be, but like a plantation darky.

The one-act play *Soul Gone Home* presents a mother crushed by the pressures of the city and self-betrayals, one result of which is the death of her illegitimate son from undernourishment and tuberculosis. By allowing the dead son and the mother to argue the essential realities of their lives, Hughes breaks through the simple realistic form which would merely have rendered a picture of environmental determinism. The reader is kept off balance, since no simple categories will sum up the density of the folk reality in the urban city as rendered by the dramatic structure. The folk element may be summed up by the compulsions of the mother: the emphasis upon all aspects of the decorum demanded by death—passionate mourning, the proper appearance of the dead, the set role of the bereaved mother, and the motif of the uneasy and troubled spirit. Within this frame, we learn, unsentimentally, of the tragedy of the mother, who has been reduced to prostitution in her effort to survive, and that of the boy—both the child to whom she, in her own way, has been attached and partially the premature instrument of her efforts to survive.

The remaining published plays in *Five Plays by Langston Hughes* are comedies which deserve more comment than can here be given to them. *Little Ham, Tambourines to Glory,* and *Simply Heavenly* all have their settings in Harlem.

The world of *Little Ham* is a bit beyond the folk, but involves cultural traditions and adaptations: the hipster, the actress who engages in high-level prostitution, the numbers men, the operators of shoe-shine and beauty parlors, and the promoters of the latest dances. Hughes is interested in what his smart personalities retain from the blues and jazz traditions: the fierce vitality, the insistent celebration of joy, and the frank and skilled seizing upon the fruits of existence. Laughter. Hughes gives effective rendering to those qualities by allowing nothing to become too serious: guns are drawn but do not kill, women begin to fight but do not maim, a disgruntled lover is comically locked away, and two-timing mates cast new and warm glances upon each other. Then, too, the pressures of the white world are cooled out before being released. One does not, however, escape entirely the awareness that a few touches of hard realism would turn the celebrators into sullen puppets of the gangsters and corrupt police who control the fat that permits the celebration. The play, nonetheless, has power and charm.

In the play *Tambourines to Glory* Hughes again keeps the white world on the periphery while he unites the traditions of the blues and the spirituals in the struggles of Laura and Essie, who, from different motives, become religious evangelists. Laura requires money and the presence of a flesh and blood comforter right here on earth, who can minister to her loneliness. She engages in a struggle to control the affections of Big-Eyed Buddy Lomax, a pimp-like figure with contacts that reach into the underworld. In the course of her losing struggles, she evokes the man-woman struggle that harks back to the folk ballads and folklore. Her struggle finally ends in her murdering Lomax, since her bouncing energy does not provide her with the power over the rampaging male that she admired in her North Carolina mother. Essie, on the other hand, triumphs through a simple Christian love and her desire to uplift the people. She is able also to bring forward representatives of a newer generation with brighter hopes and dreams. The play is filled with gospel songs, spirituals, folk and hipsterish definitions.

In a quieter vein, Simple of *Simply Heavenly,* more famous as the Southern migrant and curbstone philosopher of Hughes's sketches, manages finally to get his divorce from his first wife and prepares to marry his church-going, respectable girl-friend, Joyce. The play is filled with the varieties of song and character. Simple does not have quite the salty wit that he displays in the sketches, but retains his character as Hughes's ordinary black man with uncommon common sense and perception.

The works discussed offer a wide range of the manner and methods of Langston Hughes with black folk and cultural tradition, and they reflect a good deal of his achievement as a writer. It is difficult to imagine having to conceive both the battles and the joys of black life without him. His great value is in the range of notes that he was able to play regarding the souls and strivings of black folks. Moving so frequently with a strong sense of definitions and responses derived from the intense struggles that cryptically flash from folk and cultural traditions, his representations of black life usually carry the ring of the true metal, whether he is responding to the topic of the day or trying to reach deeply into the heart of being. His gift was also to catch the shifting tones of the times and to sense the continuity of old things among the new. Thus he always seems current with the newer forces that arise with each decade. Like the folk in their assertion of spirit over circumstance, he usually gives the impression of being "on top of it," an achievement that actually came from constant experimentation and work.

Now it is a commonplace that Hughes is uneven. I have suggested that a part of this "unevenness" derives from his lack of the concentrated Western concern about the immortality of the writer and his works. Hughes was often the social poet, committed to the tasks of the time. Perhaps a more serious criticism is that his awareness on many occasions seems more complex than the art which he can command to render it. His works in the folk area remain closer to the folk definitions in their original form than the self-conscious artist can afford to be, since he lacks the folk artist's well-defined audience. The consequence is that we look in vain for a few works that radiate with the big vision. On the other hand, it is apparent today that he almost always worked the right ground and broke and tilled it. So that today those who follow will find a field clearly marked out and in readiness for deeper harvesting.

# ROGER ROSENBLATT

# Not without Laughter

> *"Cross, you aint never said how come you was reading all them books," Joe pointed out.*
> *"I was looking for something," Cross said quietly.*
> *"What?" Pink asked.*
> *"I don't know," Cross confessed gloomily.*
> *"Did you find it?" Joe asked.*
> *"No."*
>
> —RICHARD WRIGHT, *The Outsider*

In *Not without Laughter,* despite the implication of the title, the potential means of breaking a cyclical pattern is education, education both in a formal sense and as it applies to the acquisition of an intelligence capable of dealing with a system which regularly works to domesticate it. Sandy Williams is a boy of promise, like John Grimes or Big Boy, who in the hopes of his family is supposed to get somewhere, to rise, which in fact he does. At the end of the novel, with the help of his mother and sister, Sandy is set to go off to college and save his soul. But until he reaches that point, he has already been educated by a number of looser forces, which have attended him with greater constancy and strength than his school curriculum. The questions which Hughes implies in this book are whether the two kinds of education, the academic and worldly, are equally valuable to a black child, whether they are equally valid, whether either one alone is valid or valuable, whether they are compatible, antithetical, or mutually exclusive.

These questions arise continually in black fiction, and are not easily answered. Du Bois's John ("Of the Coming of John"), Johnson's Ex-Colored

From *Black Fiction.* © 1974 by the President and Fellows of Harvard College. Harvard University Press, 1974.

Man, Ellison's Invisible Man, Himes's Bob Jones, Kabnis, Thurman's Emma Lou Morgan (*The Blacker the Berry*), and others all try college with painful results; yet the untutored intelligences of these characters, which they demonstrated either to show themselves worthy of college, or after they had been disillusioned by it, proved to be no more useful or satisfying to them than the academies. The crisis of their education, and of Sandy's, comes down to the fundamental problem in this literature of whether the act of learning, formal or otherwise, is an act of improvement. If the answer to that question seems to be no, the absence of an alternative suggests a terrible kind of self-denial. In order to survive in a white situation, a black character will often deliberately demean or minimize his intellectual capabilities, and eventually isolate himself from his own mind.

The three forces which influence Sandy before his schooling begins are Christianity, music, and laughter, all of which interrelate and occasionally become confused. The spokesman for Christianity in the book is Aunt Hager Williams, Sandy's grandmother and the mother of his mother, Anjee. Hager is a former slave whose enormous strength of will provides the novel with its force of gravity. There is no doubt or ambiguity in her Christian devotion. Of all the book's characters it is she who has had the most difficult time, yet she only speaks of doing the Lord's work, being the Lord's help, and praising His name, basing her faith firmly on the negative principle that as bad as things may be, they would be worse without religion. Her youngest daughter, Harriet, Sandy's aunt, remains unconvinced of this principle, and eventually deserts the household to keep company with other young people of the town, whom Hager considers godless. When Hager pleads, "I just want you to grow up decent, chile," Harriet cries, "lemme go! You old Christian fool!" and accuses her grandmother of trusting in a white Jesus, He who "don't like niggers."

Whether or not Hager understands the accusation, the hallmarks of her Christianity are all oriented toward a white world. Expressing an inherited white sense of aesthetics, she continually speaks in terms of achieving the light of God, and refers to cleansing one's soul in preparation for salvation. Her occupation is washing clothes; yet she also seems forever to be scrubbing and polishing, as if in an effort to make amends for her own blackness. Hager has fully absorbed the Protestant ethic. She disapproves of the intellectual and social pretensions of her well-heeled daughter Tempy, yet she equally disapproves of Anjee's husband, Jimboy, of his singing, freedom, and lack of seriousness. Hager believes in joylessness and obedience, and will work herself to death, as indeed she does, in order to get to heaven. One night when Harriet has sneaked out to a dance, Hager waits up for her holding in her hands a Bible and a switch, the two symbols of her faith.

Sandy observes Hager's religiosity as he observes everything in the first half of the novel, without comment. He functions largely as a photographic plate, on which a number of different impressions are made, but gives no sign of what effect those impressions may be having. He has only two direct run-ins with Christianity himself: once when he gets out of attending a revival meeting so that he can go to a carnival; and again when he pockets a nickel given to him for the Sunday School collection basket in order to buy candy. Hager exclaims, "de idee o' withholdin' yo' Sunday School money from de Lawd," but Sandy's deeper punishment comes from his father's "I'm ashamed of you." Sandy suffers because he violated human ethics, not because he stole from the Lord. By the time he enters school, he does not really know if he is Christian or not.

Sandy gets his music from the blues which Jimboy and Harriet sing and dance to. Music in *Not without Laughter* functions partly as a narcotic, but each of the songs in the book, like the original slave songs, contains a sober or practical undercurrent. Occasionally the music gets out of control, and the undercurrent overwhelms the sound. At the dance Harriet attends, the four black men in "Benbow's wandering band" were

> exploring depths to which mere sound had no business to go.
> Cruel, desolate, unadorned was their music now, like the body
> of a ravished woman on the sun-baked earth; violent and hard,
> like a giant standing over his bleeding mate in the blazing sun.
> The odors of bodies, the stings of flesh, and the utter emptiness
> of soul when all is done—these things the piano and the drums,
> the cornet and the twanging banjo insisted on hoarsely to a beat
> that made the dancers move, in that little hall, like pawns on a
> frenetic checker board.

The music is described in similes of violence and fate, both of which usually play beneath the surface of blues lyrics, and which attend Jimboy's and Harriet's lives throughout the story. Sandy merely listens pleased to the music around him, and does not participate in it, but in the first pages of the book, Hughes hints at the more sinister effects of music on the boy. In the wake of the opening hurricane, "Sandy saw a piano flat on its back in the grass. Its ivory keys gleamed in the moonlight like grinning teeth, and the strange sight made his little body shiver."

Laughter, the third force which operates on Sandy, is the most conspicuous and consistent of the three. There is always a great deal of laughing going on in this novel, Jimboy's and Harriet's especially. Harriet's boyfriend is described in terms of his grin; Maudel, the town madame, is forever laughing; during the dance "a ribbon of laughter swirled round the hall." There is much ridiculous activity in the story as well, particularly the absurd projects of Hager's church, which presents a pageant called "The Drill of All Nations," in which Anjee plays Sweden. Laughter is also connected with music, as in the image of the grinning piano. In Hughes's description of the band, the banjo is cynical, the drums are flippant, and the cornet laughs.

The reason for this connection is that both laughter and music are instruments of desolation in the novel, the more so for their conventional and hypothetical associations with joy. The townspeople's amusement at the antics of the freaks in the carnival is hollow and mirthless, as was the reaction of the audience to the boxing dwarfs in *Cane*. Here, as in *Cane*, as in Eliot's "Hysteria," there is a fierce desperation behind everything which is theoretically funny. Jimboy finds momentary companionship with the carnival's Fat Lady because he knows that in another context he too is a freak. He also senses that he and Sandy in the audience have a kinship with the act they watch: Sambo and Rastus, "the world's funniest comedians," who perform on a plantation set accompanied by women in bandanas singing "longingly about Dixie." Sambo and Rastus go through their act with wooden razors and dice as their props. They argue over money until a ghost suddenly appears and scares the two of them away. This the white audience finds "screamingly funny—and just like niggers." The act ends with a black banjo player picking the blues; "to Sandy it seemed like the saddest music in the world—but the white people around him laughed."

In LeRoi Jones's "A Poem for Willie Best" there is the same sense of comedy as a concealment of, or excuse for, horror. The poem takes the heart and life out of the comedian, leaving on display only a disembodied grin like the Cheshire Cat's. What Willie Best meant to his audience was an aggregation of stereotyped characteristics, which were funny in him, and therefore posed no threat: "Lazy/Frightened/Thieving/Very potent sexually/Scars/Generally inferior/but natural/rhythms." At the end of the poem Willie has been reduced to a "hideous mindless grin," like the one which sustained his success. This, in *Not without Laughter,* is the piano's grin and the grin of the carnival on-lookers. In both cases laughter is a means of punishment. When Harriet is driven out of her school, the children who chase her are laughing.

All three forces, laughter, music, and Christianity, descend on Sandy in a single night. He dreams of a carnival where he hears "sad raggedy music playing while a woman shouted for Jesus in the Gospel Tent." At the time when he enters the white school, these forces are inarticulate, and it is his formal education which makes them clear. Until the fifth grade he had not gone to school with white children. Stanton schools operated under a system by which in the early grades the black children were kept in separate rooms, and were taught only by black teachers. On the first day of the integrated school, the children are seated according to the alphabetic order of their names, but Sandy and the two other black children in the class are told to sit in the back. This is the first time Sandy has been told to sit apart, and he has been told this in the same context which he has also been told will make his life happy and successful.

For as long as he has lived, Sandy has been taught that education will make the difference between getting somewhere and nowhere, between freedom and dependence, and primarily between acceptability and rejection. One of Hager's great regrets is that Sandy's mother discontinued her education, while Tempy, for whom she has less affection, is nevertheless admired for having completed high school. Sandy is a "bright boy," and Hager tells him that he could become another Booker T. Washington or Frederick Douglass. She also teaches him that hate is ugly, that slavery was not so bad, that love is the essential force in the world, that white folks need black, and that therefore black folks ought not to hate white. When Hager dies, Tempy continues his education. First, she corrects his English, and teaches him to speak properly. She shifts his attention from Booker T. Washington to Du Bois, favoring the latter not for his conception of black equality but because he was an officially accomplished black man, a Harvard Ph.D. She teaches him to admire *The House behind the Cedars,* though she respects Chesnutt's fame more than his use of dialect, and to aspire to the Talented Tenth, and become a black gentleman. She also teaches him that money buys respect.

With such encouragement and advice, Sandy decides that he does indeed wish to become a great and educated man. He quickly becomes the star pupil in his class, and dreams one night that a Christmas book Tempy had given him had turned into a chariot, and "that he was riding through the sky with Tempy standing very dignified beside him as he drove." Yet, as he ponders his future, he also wonders "if he washed and washed his face and hands, he would ever be white," as if the ability to become white would be the end and justification of his learning. Cleaning spittoons in the local hotel, he takes pride in the fact that his spittoons are beautiful because they are bright. He too is called bright, and as he cleans his spittoons he wonders "how people made themselves great," perceiving no correspondence between himself and the object of his cleaning.

Yet gradually Sandy begins to acquire an education outside of school.

This "dreamy-eyed boy who had grown to his present age largely under the dominant influence of women" now enters the "men's world" through a job shining shoes in a barber shop. Kidded by the customers about his sandy-colored hair, he learns to exchange insults and play the "dozens," discovering "that so-called jokes are not really jokes at all, but rather unpleasant realities." In the barber shop he also learns that Harriet has become one of Stanton's most notorious loose women, and he learns what loose women are. In his hotel job he sees a naked woman for the first time, a prostitute, and he learns that if you do not feel like dancing when a drunken Mississippi red neck tells you to, you will be fired. Later, watching his high school girlfriend turn slut in the company of a less innocent boy, he learns disappointment in love. On the Chicago streets he learns about predatory desperation.

At the end of the novel Sandy, having left Tempy and Stanton, is reunited with his mother and sister in Chicago. He has learned something about books and something about "life," and now he is headed back to school. "He's gotta be what his grandma Hager wanted him to be," says Harriet, "—able to help the black race." Yet, despite the celebration and happy prospects, the ending of the book seems tacked on and unconvincing. There is a much more realistic conclusion earlier when Sandy takes a job running an elevator, just as Richard does in *Go Tell It on the Mountain* before he kills himself, because an elevator, like a formal education, is the perfect vehicle for providing the illusion of progress without the fact. As Ralph Ellison points out, it is also a vehicle for continually moving up and down between the levels of a social hierarchy.

Nothing in Sandy's past indicates that his learning or even his native intelligence will make any difference to his future. He has quietly looked about him—at Tempy, Hager, his mother and father, and Harriet—and among them all he has chosen Harriet as the ideal, because Harriet was honest with herself. Between forfeit and endurance he has chosen the latter, just as Harriet did, and in her own way, as Hager did as well. The question which Hughes leaves open is whether Sandy's endurance in pursuit of knowledge will be of any more use to him, or to "the black race," than Hager's endurance through Christianity, Harriet's endurance through music, or Jimboy's endurance through laughter. The feeling is that in education Sandy may have hit on a means of self-respect, but nobody else's.

It is a common practice in all literature, black and white, to demonstrate the penalties of learning on a sensitive and gifted child: the pain attached to a loss of innocence and increase of sophistication whereby the child's natural gifts are stunted, or the pain attached to the process of thought itself, and the accompanying discovery of the world's wickedness, or one's own. Hardy and Dickens explored this theme regularly, as did Wordsworth, Tennyson, and even Genesis. But the treatment of the theme differs in black and white writing. In the latter the implication of conflicts involving the questionable value of education, indeed the center of the drama, is that the protagonist always had a choice. If he (Pip or Adam) had not partaken of his particular apple, and maintained his innocence, then all would have been well. But in black fiction this is not so, because there is no distinction between ignorance and innocence, and no social benefit to either. For Sandy, as for John Grimes, the option of denying his abilities seems a greater evil than attempting to fulfill them to no advantage, but the choice is really Hobson's and not his own.

RAYMOND SMITH

# Hughes: Evolution of the Poetic Persona

Langston Hughes's career as a poet began with the publication of "The Negro Speaks of Rivers" in the June 1921 issue of *The Crisis,* the journal of Negro life and opinion edited by W. E. B. Du Bois. By 1926, before the poet had reached the age of twenty-five, he had published his first volume of poems, *The Weary Blues.* Of this volume Alain Locke, the leading exponent of "The New Negro," announced that the black masses had found their voice: "A true people's poet has their balladry in his veins; and to me many of these poems seem based on rhythms as seasoned as folksongs and on moods as deep-seated as folk-ballads. Dunbar is supposed to have expressed the peasant heart of the people. But Dunbar was the showman of the Negro masses; here is their spokesman." With the publication of his second volume of poems, *Fine Clothes to the Jew* (1927), Hughes was being referred to as the "Poet Laureate of the American Negro." During a visit to Haiti in 1932, he was introduced to the noted Haitian poet Jacques Roumain, who referred to Hughes as "the greatest Negro poet who had ever come to honor Haitian soil." When the noted Senegalese poet and exponent of African Negritude, Léopold Senghor, was asked in a 1967 interview "In which poems of our, American, literature [do] you find evidence of Negritude?" his reply was "Ah, in Langston Hughes; Langston Hughes is the most spontaneous as a poet and the blackest in expression!" Before his death in 1967, Hughes had published more than a dozen volumes of poetry, in addition to a great number of anthologies, translations, short

From *Studies in the Literary Imagination* 7, no. 2 (Fall 1974). © 1974 by the Department of English, Georgia State University.

45

stories, essays, novels, plays, and histories dealing with the spectrum of Afro-American life.

Of the major black writers who first made their appearance during the exciting period of the twenties commonly referred to as "the Harlem Renaissance," Langston Hughes was the most prolific and the most successful. As the Harlem Renaissance gave way to the Depression, Hughes determined to sustain his career as a poet by bringing his poetry to the people. At the suggestion of Mary McLeod Bethune, he launched his career as a public speaker by embarking on an extensive lecture tour of the South. As he wrote in his autobiography [*I Wonder as I Wander*]: "Propelled by the backwash of the 'Harlem Renaissance' of the early 'twenties, I had been drifting along pleasantly on the delightful rewards of my poems which seemed to please the fancy of kindhearted New York ladies with money to help young writers. . . . There was one other dilemma—how to make a living from *the kind of writing I wanted to do*. . . . I wanted to write seriously and as well as I knew how about the Negro people, and make *that* kind of writing earn me a *living*." The Depression forced Hughes to reconsider the relation between his poetry and his people: "I wanted to continue to be a poet. Yet sometimes I wondered if I was barking up the wrong tree. I determined to find out by taking poetry, *my* poetry, to *my* people. After all, I wrote about Negroes, and primarily *for* Negroes. Would they have me? Did they want me?"

Though much of the poetry Hughes was to write in the thirties and afterward was to differ markedly in terms of social content from the poetry he was producing in the twenties, a careful examination of his early work will reveal, in germinal form, the basic themes which were to preoccupy him throughout his career. These themes, pertaining to certain attitudes towards America and vis-à-vis his own blackness, had in fact been in the process of formulation since childhood. Hughes's evolution as a poet cannot be seen apart from the circumstances of his life which thrust him into the role of poet. Indeed, it was Hughes's awareness of what he personally regarded as a rather unique childhood which determined him in his drive to express, through poetry, the feelings of the black masses. Hughes's decision to embark on the lecture tour of Southern colleges in the thirties is not to be taken as a rejection of his earlier work; it was merely a redirection of energies towards the purpose of reaching his audience. Hughes regarded his poetry written during the height of the Harlem Renaissance as a valid statement on Negro life in America. The heavily marked volumes of *The Weary Blues, Fine Clothes to the Jew,* and *The Dream Keeper* (published in 1932 but consisting largely of selections from the two earlier volumes), used by Hughes for poetry readings during the thirties and forties and now in the James Weldon Johnson Collection at Yale University, indicate that Hughes relied heavily on this early work and in no way rejected it as socially irrelevant.

Hughes's efforts to create a poetry that truly evoked the spirit of Black America involved a resolution of conflicts centering around the problem of identity. For Hughes, like W. E. B. Du Bois, saw the black man's situation in America as a question of dual-consciousness. As Du Bois wrote in his *The Souls of Black Folk* (1903): "It is a peculiar sensation, this double-consciousness, this sense of always looking at oneself through the eyes of others, of measuring one's soul by the tape of a world that looks on in amused contempt and pity. One ever feels his twoness,—an American, a Negro; two souls, two thoughts, two unreconciled strivings; two warring ideals in one body, whose dogged strength alone keeps it from being torn asunder." Hughes was to speak of this same dilemma in his famous essay, published in 1927, concerning the problems of the black writer in America, "The Negro Artist and the Racial Mountain": "But this is the mountain standing in the way of any true Negro art in America—this urge within the race toward whiteness, the desire to pour racial individuality into the mold of American standardization, and to be as little Negro and as much American as possible." In *The Weary Blues* (1926), Hughes presented the problem of dual-consciousness quite cleverly by placing two parenthetical statements of identity as the opening and closing poems, and titling them "Proem" and "Epilogue." Their opening lines suggest the polarities of consciousness between which the poet located his own persona: "I am a Negro" and "I, Too, Sing America." Within each of these poems, Hughes suggests the interrelatedness of the two identities: the line "I am a Negro" is echoed as "I am the darker brother" in the closing poem. Between the American and the Negro, a third identity is suggested: that of the poet or "singer." It is this latter persona which Hughes had assumed for himself in his attempt to resolve the dilemma of divided consciousness. Thus, within the confines of these two poems revolving around identity, Hughes is presenting his poetry as a kind of salvation. If one looks more closely at Hughes's organization of poems in the book, one finds that his true opening and closing poems are concerned not with identity but with patterns of cyclical time. "The Weary Blues" (the first poem) is about a black piano man who plays deep into the night until at last he falls into sleep "like a rock or a man that's dead." The last poem, on the other hand, suggests a rebirth, an awakening, after the long night of weary blues: "We have tomorrow/Bright before us/Like a flame." This pattern of cyclical time was adopted in the opening and closing poems of *Fine Clothes to the Jew,* which begins in sunset and ends in sunrise. Again, it is the blues singer (or poet) who recites the song: "Sun's a risin',/This is gonna be ma song." The poet's song, then, is Hughes's resolution to the problem of double-consciousness, of being an American and being black.

Hughes viewed the poet's role as one of responsibility: the poet must strive to maintain his objectivity and artistic distance, while at the same time speaking with passion through the medium he has selected for himself. In a speech given before the American Society of African Culture in 1960, Hughes urged his fellow black writers to cultivate objectivity in dealing with blackness: "Advice to Negro writers: Step *outside yourself,* then look back—and you will see how human, yet how beautiful and black you are. How very black—even when you're integrated." In another part of the speech, Hughes stressed art over race: "In the great sense of the word, anytime, any place, good art transcends land, race, or nationality, and color drops away. If you are a good writer, in the end neither blackness nor whiteness makes a difference to readers." This philosophy of artistic distance was integral to Hughes's argument in the much earlier essay "The Negro Artist and the Racial Mountain," which became a rallying call to young black writers of the twenties concerned with reconciling artistic freedom with racial expression: "It is the duty of the younger Negro artist if he accepts any duties at all from outsiders, to change through the force of his art that old whispering 'I want to be white' hidden in the aspirations of his people, to 'Why should I want to be white? I am a Negro—and beautiful!' " Hughes urged other black writers to express freely, without regard to the displeasure of whites *or* blacks, their "individual dark-skinned selves." "If white people are glad, we are glad. If they are not, it doesn't matter. We know we are beautiful. And ugly too. If colored people are pleased we are glad. If they are not, their displeasure doesn't matter either. We build our temples for tomorrow, strong as we know how, and we stand on top of the mountain, free within ourselves." In this carefully thought-out manifesto, Hughes attempted to integrate the two facets of double-consciousness (the American and the Negro) into a single vision—that of the poet. His poetry had reflected this idea from the beginning, when he published "The Negro Speaks of Rivers" at the age of nineteen. Arna Bontemps, in a retrospective glance at the Harlem Renaissance from the distance of almost fifty years, was referring to "The Negro Speaks of Rivers" when he commented: "And almost the first utterance of the revival struck a note that *disturbed* poetic tradition." (Italics mine)

In Hughes's poetry, the central element of importance is the affirmation of blackness. Everything that distinguished Hughes's poetry from the white avant-garde poets of the twenties revolved around this important affirmation. Musical idioms, jazz rhythms, Hughes's special brand of "black-white" irony, and dialect were all dependent on the priority of black selfhood:

> I am a Negro:
> Black as the night is black
> Black like the depths of my Africa.

Like Walt Whitman, Hughes began his career as a poet confident of his power. Unlike Whitman, however, who celebrated particular self ("Walt Whitman, the cosmos"), Hughes celebrated racial, rather than individual, self. Hughes tended to suppress the personal element in his poetry, appropriating the first person singular as the fitting epitome of universal human tendencies embodied in race. "The Negro Speaks of Rivers" seems almost mystical in comparison to Whitman's physicality:

> I've known rivers:
> Ancient, dusky rivers.
> My soul has grown deep like the rivers.

One could venture too far in this comparison; of course, Whitman declared himself the poet of the soul as well as the body. Few would deny he had mystical tendencies.

In Hughes, however, there is little hint of the egotism in which Whitman so frequently indulged. Indeed, Hughes was hesitant to introduce the element of the personal into his poetry. In an essay published in the journal *Phylon* in 1947 on his "adventures" as a social poet, Hughes remarked that his "earliest poems were social poems in that they were about people's problems—whole groups of people's problems—rather than my own personal difficulties." Hughes's autobiographical account of the writing of "The Negro Speaks of Rivers" confirms this point, and sheds light on the process by which Hughes transformed personal experiences into archetypal racial memories. The poem had evolved out of personal difficulties with his father, who had emigrated to Mexico when Langston was a child, and had not seen his son in over a decade. Hughes had been summoned unexpectedly by his father to join him in the summer of 1919, hoping to persuade the son to enter into the business world. The elder Hughes felt nothing but contempt for the country and the race he had left behind. The following conversation, recorded in Hughes's autobiography *The Big Sea,* suggests the irreconcilable differences between the two:

"What do you want to be?"

"I don't know. But I think a writer."

"A writer?" my father said. "A writer? . . . Do they make any money? . . . Learn something you can make a living from anywhere in the world, in Europe or South America, and don't stay in the States, where you have to live like a nigger with niggers."

"But I like Negroes," I said.

The following summer, on a train trip to Mexico, Hughes's dread of the eventual confrontation with his father over his future vocation led to the writing of the poem: "All day on the train I had been thinking about my father, and his strange dislike of his own people. I didn't understand it, because I was Negro, and I liked Negroes very much." Despite Hughes's severe emotional state, the poem itself displays little hint of the personal anxiety that led to its creation.

Perhaps the closest Hughes ever came to incorporating his personal anxiety into a poem was his "As I Grew Older," published initially in 1925, and later included in The Weary Blues. The poem is almost reduced to abstractions; it is a landscape of nightmare, a bleak and existential examination of blackness. The poet begins by recalling his "dream," once "bright like a sun," but now only a memory. A wall which separates the poet from his dream suddenly appears, causing him severe anxiety. It is at this point that the poet is thrust back upon himself and forced to seek an explanation for his dilemma:

> Shadow.
> I am black.

These two lines appearing at the center of the poem provide the key to his despair and to his salvation. As he begins to realize that his blackness is the cause of his being separated from his dream, he simultaneously realizes that blackness is central to his ontology. It is as much a physical reality as it is a metaphysical state of mind. In order for the dream to be restored, the spiritual and the physical blackness must be reintegrated. As the poet examines his hands, which are black, he discovers the source of his regeneration as a full person:

> My hands!
> My dark hands!
> Break through the wall!

Find my dream!
Help me to shatter this darkness,
To smash this night,
To break this shadow
Into a thousand lights of sun,
Into a thousand whirling dreams
Of sun!

In order for the poet to transcend his temporal despair, he must accept the condition of his blackness completely and unequivocally. The poem thus ends, not in despair, but rather in a quest for self-liberation, dependent on the affirmation "I am black!"

The words had been used much earlier by another poet, W. E. B. Du Bois, far better known as the founder of the NAACP, editor of *The Crisis,* and lifelong champion of black pride. His poem "The Song of the Smoke," published in the magazine *Horizon* in 1899, opened with the words:

I am the smoke king,
I am black.

Later in the poem, Du Bois wrote these ringing lines:

I will be black as blackness can,
The blacker the mantle the mightier the man,
My purpl'ing midnights no day may ban.

I am carving God in night,
I am painting hell in white.
I am the smoke king.
I am black.

The poem, published when Hughes was five years old, prefigures the point in time, fifteen years later, when the careers of the two—Du Bois and Hughes—would converge, with the publication of Hughes's poem "The Negro Speaks of Rivers," in Du Bois's journal *The Crisis,* with the poem's dedication also going to Du Bois.

This early connection between Hughes and Du Bois is important, for it was Du Bois who was calling for a renaissance of black culture as early as 1913, in an essay on "The Negro in Literature and Art": "Never in the world has a richer mass of material been accumulated by a people than that which the Negroes possess today and are becoming conscious of. Slowly but surely they are developing artists of technic who will be able to use this material." By 1920, Du Bois was actually using the word "renaissance" in referring to the new awakening of black creativity in the arts: "A renaissance of Negro literature is due; the material about us in the strange, heartrending race tangle is rich beyond dream and only we can tell the tale and sing the song from the heart." This editorial in *The Crisis,* almost certainly read by Hughes, must have encouraged him to submit the poem for publication. In his autobiography, Hughes credited Du Bois and *The Crisis* for publishing his first poems and thus giving his literary career its first official boost: "For the next few years my poems appeared often (and solely) in *The Crisis.* And to that magazine, certainly, I owe my literary beginnings, insofar as publication is concerned."

While Hughes certainly owed Du Bois a debt of gratitude for his official entrance upon the literary scene, it seems that Hughes's very special sensitivity as a budding young poet developed organically from his experiences as a child. Though he did credit Dunbar and Sandburg among his influences, these literary mentors pale in light of what Hughes had to say about his method of poem-writing: "Generally, the first two or three lines come to me from something I'm thinking about, or looking at, or doing, and the rest of the poem (if there is to be a poem) flows from those first few lines, usually right away." This spontaneity of approach worked both for and against Hughes. Many of his poems, written in hasty response to some event reported in yesterday's newspaper, for example, have badly dated. The spontaneity that resulted in his best poetry came from the depths of his own experiences as a black man in America, though these personal experiences often were disguised as archetypal ones.

The tension between his awareness of growing up black and his acceptance of the "dream" of America, however tenuously defined, provided the dynamic for his poetry. From an early age, Hughes developed the distinction between the social versus the physical implications of black identity in America: "You see, unfortunately, I am not black. There are lots of different kinds of blood in our family. But here in the United States, the word 'Negro' is used to mean anyone who has *any* Negro blood at all in his veins. In Africa, the word is more pure. It means *all* Negro, therefore *black.*" During a trip to Africa as a merchant seaman in 1922, he discovered that the Africans who "looked at me . . . would not believe I was a Negro." The semantic confusion was of American origin. Whatever the semantic distinctions, Hughes desired to be accepted as Negro by the Africans, and was disappointed with their reaction to him.

Hughes's middle American background (he grew up in Lawrence, Kansas) sheltered him from some of the more blatant forms of racial prejudice toward Negroes in other regions of the country. When he lived in Topeka, he attended a white school, his mother having successfully challenged the school board to have him admitted. Most of his teachers were pleasant, but there was one "who sometimes used to make remarks about my being colored. And after such remarks, occasionally the kids would grab stones and tin cans out of the alley and chase me home." For a while he lived with his maternal grandmother, from whom he heard "beautiful stories about people who wanted to make the Negroes free, and how her father had apprenticed to him many slaves ... so that they could work out their freedom. ... Through my grandmother's stories always life moved, moved heroically toward an end. ... Something about my grandmother's stories ... taught me the uselessness of crying about anything." Hughes's poem "Aunt Sue's Stories," published in *The Crisis* in July of 1921, furnishes an example of how Hughes transformed such memories into poetry. His childhood was not a happy one in Lawrence, as he related in his autobiography, and he turned to books for solace. Parallels between his childhood experiences and later poems abound. Many of his poems focused on unhappy or wrongly treated children, for whom the American dream had no relevance. This empathy with wronged children had its origins in Hughes's own unhappiness as a child.

Many of his poems about black laborers originated out of his difficulties in finding work while in school. A job he had in a hotel, cleaning toilets and spittoons, while only in the seventh grade, was to result in one of his more well-known poems, "Brass Spittoons," included in his second volume of poetry *Fine Clothes to the Jew* (1927). Four decades after a local theatre owner put up a sign "NO COLORED ADMITTED" in Lawrence, Kansas, Hughes would recall the event in *ASK YOUR MAMA:*

> IN THE QUARTER OF THE NEGROES
> WHERE THE RAILROAD AND THE RIVER
> HAVE DOORS THAT FACE EACH WAY
> AND THE ENTRANCE TO THE MOVIE'S
> UP AN ALLEY UP THE SIDE

A beating administered by a group of white toughs in Chicago the summer before the Chicago riots would be transformed into "The White Ones" seven years later:

> I do not hate you,
> For your faces are beautiful, too.
> I do not hate you,

> Your faces are whirling lights of loveliness
> and splendor, too.
> Yet why do you torture me,
> O, white strong ones,
> Why do you torture me?

These parallels between Hughes's early life and his later poetry indicate that he had formulated certain attitudes towards his race and towards white America before he had ever considered the idea of becoming a poet.

It was only by accident that he became a poet. He was elected to the position of class poet at Cleveland's Central High because, as he humorously recalled, he was a Negro, and Negroes were supposed to have "rhythm." "In America most white people think, of course, that *all* Negroes can sing and dance, and have a sense of rhythm. So my classmates, knowing that a poem had to have rhythm, elected me unanimously—thinking, no doubt, that I had some, being a Negro. . . . It had never occurred to me to be a poet before, or indeed a writer of any kind." Thus the role of poet was thrust upon Hughes by accident, or perhaps, by design, because he was Negro in a white society. It was the social implications of his blackness, however, that fitted him for the role. The incidents of his childhood and youth had marked Langston Hughes as a black man, and his poetry would affirm his acceptance of the mission, to be a spokesman for the black masses.

At the same time, Hughes could not deny the double nature, the dual-consciousness of being an American as well as a black. The very fact that he had been chosen by his classmates as class poet *because* he was Negro only accentuated his separateness from them. By the same token, he had never completely been exposed to the full brunt of prejudice, American-style, during his youth. Up until the time of his Southern lecture tour of 1931, his acquaintance with Southern mores had been merely peripheral. Indeed, he often began these programs by explaining how truly "American" his upbringing had been: "I began my programs by telling where I was born in Missouri, that I grew up in Kansas in the geographical heart of the country, and was, therefore, very American." His audiences, which consisted largely of Southern Negroes, must have found his initial declaration of Americanism rather disorienting. As Hughes himself explained in his autobiography [*I Wonder as I Wander*], this first-hand encounter with racial prejudice in the South provided an introduction to an important aspect of racial heritage to which he had never been fully exposed: "I found a great social and cultural gulf between the races in the South, astonishing to one who, like myself, from the North, had never known such uncompromising prejudices."

In a poem published in *The Crisis* in 1922, Hughes outlined his ambivalence towards the region in rather chilling imagery:

> The child-minded South
> Scratching in the dead fire's ashes
> For a Negro's bones.

He indicated in the poem's conclusion that the South had a strong attraction, but that he was more comfortable in resisting its allure:

> And I, who am black, would love her
> But she spits in my face.
> And I, who am black,
> Would give her many rare gifts
> But she turns her back upon me.

In the same year that Hughes published "The South," Jean Toomer published *Cane*. One of the poems in *Cane*, "Georgia Dusk," evoked similar imagery:

> A feast of moon and men and barking hounds,
>     An orgy for some genius of the South
>         With blood-hot eyes and cane-lipped scented mouth,
>     Surprised in making folk-songs from soul sounds.

Where Toomer's *Cane* was the product of direct experience (a six-month sojourn in Georgia as a rural schoolteacher), Hughes's South was an imaginatively evoked nightmare. The last lines of Hughes's poem suggest that he was not yet ready to embrace the Southern experience as Toomer had done. Hughes's Gothic South was a far cry from Toomer's seductive lines in "Carma":

> Wind is in the cane. Come along.
> Cane leaves swaying, rusty with talk,
> Scratching choruses above the guinea's squawk,
> Wind is in the cane. Come along.

If Hughes feared the direct Southern confrontation during the twenties, he found much to admire in those Southern blacks who came to settle in the teeming cities of the North, and from them he derived material for his poetry. In seeking communal identity through them, Hughes overemphasized the exotic, as this passage from *The Big Sea* indicates: "I never tired of hearing them talk, listening to the thunderclaps of their laughter, to their troubles, to their discussions of the war and the men who had gone to Europe from the Jim Crow South. . . . They seemed to me like the gayest

and the bravest people possible—these Negroes from the Southern ghet-
toes—facing tremendous odds, working and laughing and trying to get
somewhere in the world." The passage suggests the attitude of a sympathetic
observer rather than that of an engaged participant. In some ways, Hughes's
attitude towards Southern Negroes was directly counter to that of his father's. According to Langston, the elder Hughes "hated Negroes. I think
he hated himself, too, for being a Negro. He disliked all of his family because
they were Negroes and remained in the United States." Hughes, on the
other hand, proudly affirmed his racial heritage. Where his father rejected
both race and country, Hughes could reject neither.

At the end of his lecture programs in the South, Hughes would recite
his poem "I, Too, Sing America." As often as he invoked this poem, he
would be reaffirming his faith in the American dream. Some of Hughes's
earliest poems reveal an almost childlike faith in the American ideal, as in
the opening lines of the following, first published in 1925:

> America is seeking the stars,
> America is seeking tomorrow,
> You are America,
> I am America
> America—the dream,
> America—the vision.
> America—the star-seeking I.

The same poem affirmed the unity of black and white America:

> You of the blue eyes
> And the blond hair,
> I of the dark eyes
> And the crinkly hair,
> You and I
> Offering hands.

This affirmation of racial unity had a direct relation to Hughes's experience
with racial integration at Cleveland's Central High, where he was often
elected to important class positions because of his acceptability to various
white ethnic factions: "Since it was during the war, and Americanism was
being stressed, many of our students, including myself, were then called
down to the principal's office and questioned about our belief in Americanism. . . . After that, the principal organized an Americanism Club in our
school, and . . . I was elected President" (*The Big Sea*). While this experience
might serve to strengthen his faith in an ideal America, it also, paradoxically,

reinforced his sense of separateness as a Negro. His race was clearly an advantage in terms of popularity among his peers; still, it was his color which marked him as different.

At the same time, Hughes's experience in racial integration set him apart from the experience of those Negroes from the South whose life-style he so admired. Hughes must have realized that his experience vis-à-vis that of most black Americans was rather unique. Though he claimed at times to have had a typical Negro upbringing, it was nevertheless different, as he pointed out in this passage from *The Big Sea:* "Mine was not a typical Negro family. My grandmother never took in washing or worked in service or went to church. She had lived in Oberlin and spoke perfect English, without a trace of dialect. She looked like an Indian. My mother was a newspaper woman and a stenographer then. My father lived in Mexico City. My grandfather had been a congressman." In addition, Hughes harbored no grudges against white society: "I learned early in life not to hate *all* white people. And ever since, it has seemed to me that *most* people are generally good, in every race and in every country where I have been."

Hughes often sought to dispel the distinction between American and Negro by affirming his nationality in no uncertain terms. The following incident from his autobiography illustrates this point. He had been teaching English to Mexicans during his final summer in Mexico with his father. The teacher who was to replace him was a white American woman who found it incredible that a Negro could be capable of teaching anything:

> When she was introduced to me, her mouth fell open, and she said: "Why, Ah-Ah thought you was an American."
> I said: "I am American!"
> She said: "Oh, Ah mean a white American."
> Her voice had a Southern drawl.
> I grinned.

Another incident from his autobiography concerns his refusal to deny his race. On the return trip to the United States from Mexico after his first summer there, Hughes attempted to purchase an ice cream soda in St. Louis. The following exchange took place:

> The clerk said: "Are you a Mexican or a Negro?"
> I said: "Why?"
> "Because if you're a Mexican, I'll serve you," he said. "If you're colored, I won't."
> "I'm colored," I replied. The clerk turned to wait on someone else. I knew I was home in the U. S. A.

These incidents were to have their counterparts in his poetry, where he could affirm with equal assurance his two credos of identity: "I am a Negro" and "I, Too, Sing America." But while affirming these polar commitments, Hughes was alienated from both of them. As a black man, he was aware that his race had never been granted full participation in the American dream. His exposure to the possibilities of that dream, however, through his experience with racial integration, and his relative innocence (this was to disappear, of course) in matters of Southern mores, would distinguish his circumstances from the lot of the black masses, with whom he sought to identify to the extent of becoming their spokesman. This peculiar set of conditions allowed Hughes to assume a degree of sophistication in racial matters quite unusual among his contemporaries, white or black. This sophistication, coupled with his insistence on maintaining the necessary aesthetic distance of the artist, provided the stimulus for his poetry and endowed the poet with a sense of mission. He was absolutely confident of his self-imposed mission as a poet of the black masses. His familiarity with white Bohemian intellectual circles in New York during the twenties provided him with the additional stimulus of communicating his message across racial lines. Thus two kinds of poetry emerged in the twenties: the black vernacular poetry, utilizing dialect, jazz talk, and everyday subject matter; and "message" poetry, which concentrated on the position of the black man in white America. *The Weary Blues,* Hughes's first book, contained much of this message poetry, besides some experiments in jazz poetry ("The Cat and the Saxophone," "Blues Fantasy," "Negro Dancers"), and additional nonracial lyrics. The second book, *Fine Clothes to the Jew,* concentrated almost entirely on the vernacular subject matter, and contained many poems written in blues dialect. These two tendencies in Hughes's early work were to predominate throughout his career.

*Shakespeare in Harlem* (1942), for example, may be considered a sequel to *Fine Clothes,* while *Montage of a Dream Deferred* (1951) integrated the vernacular subject matter with the thematic concerns introduced in *The Weary Blues. Montage,* along with *ASK YOUR MAMA* (1961), will probably remain Hughes's most important achievements in poetry since his work of the twenties. *ASK YOUR MAMA,* permeated with humor, irony, and exciting imagery, contains echoes of "The Negro Speaks of Rivers," "As I Grew Older," and "The Cat and the Saxophone." As in these earlier poems, Hughes transforms personal experiences and observations into distillations of the Black American condition.

Hughes wrote in his autobiography: "My best poems were all written when I felt the worst. When I was happy, I didn't write anything." When he first began writing poetry, he felt his lyrics were too personal to reveal to others: "Poems came to me now spontaneously, from somewhere inside. . . . I put the poems down quickly on anything I had at hand when they came into my head, and later I copied them into a notebook. But I began to be afraid to show my poems to anybody, because they had become very serious and very much a part of me. And I was afraid other people might not like them or understand them." These two statements regarding his poetry suggest deep underlying emotional tensions as being the source of his creativity. And yet the personal element in Hughes's poetry is almost entirely submerged beneath the persona of the "Negro Poet Laureate." If, as Hughes suggested, personal unhappiness was the groundstone for his best work, it then follows that, in order to maintain the singleness of purpose and devotion to his art, he would be required to sacrifice some degree of emotional stability. Thus poetry became a kind of therapy, masking deeper emotional tensions. We know from his autobiography that Hughes experienced two severe emotional breakdowns. The first one had to do with a break with his father over the course of his vocation; the second followed upon a break with his wealthy white patroness in the late twenties over the kind of poetry he was writing. Both of these emotional traumas were directly related to his decision to become a poet of his people.

The persona of the poet was the role Hughes adopted in his very first published poem, as *the Negro* in "The Negro Speaks of Rivers." It was a persona to which he would remain faithful throughout his lengthy career. The link between his personal experiences and his poetry has been suggested in this paper. It cannot be defined because it seems clear that Hughes suppressed the more frightening excursions into his own personal void. Poetry was an outlet as well as a salvation. Only occasionally, as in the poem "As I Grew Older," does Hughes provide a window upon his inner anxieties, and even in this poem the real root of these anxieties is hidden, and the poem becomes an allegory of the black man's alienation in white America.

Hughes's early attempts in the twenties to fill the role of Poet Laureate of the Negro led him to create a body of work that was organic in nature. The traditional literary sources of inspiration were for the most part bypassed. The source of his poetry was to be found in the anonymous, unheard black masses: their rhythms, their dialect, their lifestyles. Hughes sought to incorporate this untapped resource of black folk language into a new kind of poetry. His personal experiences, as related in his autobiography, combined with this folk material to provide thematic dimension to his work. The basic themes regarding the American dream and its possibilities for the black man were always present in his poetry. The tension between the unrealized dream and the realities of the black experience in America provided the dynamic. This tension between material and theme laid the groundwork for the irony which characterized Hughes's work at its best.

# ONWUCHEKWA JEMIE

## *Jazz, Jive, and Jam*

Unlike classic blues, the jazz poem has no fixed form: it is a species of
free verse which attempts to approximate some of the qualities of jazz. The
dynamic energy of jazz is to be contrasted with the relatively low-keyed
and generally elegiac tone of the blues. Blues is for the most part vocal and
mellow, jazz for the most part instrumental and aggressive. The jazz poem
attempts to capture that instrumental vigor.

In the free verse of Walt Whitman, and its modernist sequel in Pound,
Eliot, and others, the language is formal and literary, with long, complex
sentences and well-made phrases, or informal but not conversational; or,
when it is conversational, it is in the idiom of the educated middle class.
Jazz poetry, on the other hand, moves with the bouncy rhythms and exuberance that characterize the music. The sentences are casual and short-
winded; the phrases are short, tumbling after one another in rapid
succession:

> Dusk dark
> On Railroad Avenue.
> Lights in the fish joints,
> Lights in the pool rooms.
> A box-car some train
> Has forgotten
> In the middle of the
> Block.

From *Langston Hughes: An Introduction to the Poetry.* © 1973, 1976 by Columbia
University Press.

> A player piano,
> A victrola.
>     942
>     Was the number.
> A boy
> Lounging on a corner.
> A passing girl
> With purple powdered skin.

The jazz poem derives from oral performance and music. Its relaxed attitude reflects the informal atmosphere in which the music thrives, and its open verse form is reminiscent of the improvisational latitude of the music. Its language—swift-paced, informal talk—aids the impression of spontaneity. The language is most often colloquial, sometimes the hip talk of the musicians, almost always the language of the common people, rarely the language of the academies.

Jazz poetry might be viewed as a stage in that search for native American rhythms begun by Walt Whitman and carried forward in the early twentieth century by such poets as Vachel Lindsay and Carl Sandburg. Its ancestor on the black side is the dialect poetry of Paul Laurence Dunbar which was built on black speech rhythms of the rural South. Of Hughes's contemporaries, Lindsay especially had established a reputation as a jazz poet with his "General William Booth Enters into Heaven" (1913), a rhythmic adaptation of black folk sermons, with built-in leader-choral antiphony and the accompaniment of drums, banjos, flutes, and tambourines; and with his racist "The Congo: A Study of the Negro Race"(1914), which came with precise marginal notes on mood and musical accompaniment. "The Congo" is a rehearsal of fantastic events in black lands of the white imagination, and a panegyric on the white man's so-called "civilizing mission" in Africa.

> THEN I had religion, THEN I had a vision.
> I could not turn from their revel in derision.
> THEN I SAW THE CONGO, CREEPING THROUGH THE
>     BLACK,
> CUTTING THROUGH THE FOREST WITH A GOLDEN
>     TRACK. . . .

> "Be careful what you do,
> Or Mumbo-Jumbo, God of the Congo . . .
> Mumbo-Jumbo will hoo-doo you,

Mumbo-Jumbo will hoo-doo you,
Mumbo-Jumbo will hoo-doo you. . . .

Boomlay, boomlay, boomlay, boom.
Boomlay, boomlay, boomlay, boom.
Boomlay, boomlay, boomlay, boom.
Boomlay, boomlay, boomlay,
BOOM."

Much of the poem's strength is in its rhythmic energy, its repetitions and imitative sounds, the vivid detail in which the varied scenes are painted, and the terror of the experience which is so vitally captured and dramatized. In his ability to recount the experience, Lindsay's spiritual voyager is Coleridge's Ancient Mariner, Sindbad the Sailor, and a convert testifying at a Holy Roller church all in one. Hughes himself has acknowledged the debt he owes to Dunbar, Sandburg, and Lindsay, among others. His "Song for a Banjo Dance" could be read as a version of Dunbar's "A Negro Love Song." His "Harlem Night Club" and "Jazz Band in a Parisian Cabaret" remind us of Sandburg's "Jazz Fantasia" (1920). And his *Ask Your Mama* is closely related in form and manner to Lindsay's "The Congo."

Dunbar's dialect poetry, and the dialect stories of Charles Waddell Chesnutt, together constituted the fullest flowering in black literature of a nineteenth-century tradition which was popularized by the white minstrel stage and by white writers of the Southern local color school such as George Washington Cable, Thomas Nelson Page, Joel Chandler Harris, and Irwin Russell. Both Chesnutt and Dunbar attempted to turn dialect inside out, to purge it of its all too familiar stereotypes of the happy-go-lucky, chicken-stealing, comic Sambo, but with limited success (with Dunbar the less successful). Chesnutt's last published novel in 1905, and Dunbar's death in 1906, might be said to have brought to a close the nineteenth century in black literature. The next fifteen to twenty years saw a dramatic shift in black population from the rural South to the urban North; and as it turned out, the transition in literature from nineteenth to twentieth century, and from dialect poetry to jazz poetry and blues, paralleled that Great Migration. As might be expected, the younger generation of writers took their cues from Dunbar and Chesnutt, but they soon discovered that dialect was too old and crumbly to survive a face lift. It was impossible to use dialect and avoid the stereotypes. But fortunately for them, their coming of age coincided with the boisterous jazz and blues age, and it was in the contemporary life, language, and music of the city, rather than in the South and the past, that they found what James Weldon Johnson has called "form[s] that will express the racial spirit by symbols from within rather than by symbols from without (such as the mere mutilation of English spelling and pronunciation)."

The jazz poem was such a form; and while Hughes did not invent it, he carried it to a high level of development. He manages to suggest the frenetic energy of instrumental jazz in the breathless enumerations of "Railroad Avenue," "Jitney," "Man into Men," "Brass Spittoons," and "Laughers," and the complex interplay of instruments in the counterpoint of voices in "Mulatto," "Closing Time," and "The Cat and the Saxophone":

> EVERYBODY
> Half-pint,—
> Gin?
> No, make it
> LOVES MY BABY
> corn. You like
> liquor,
> don't you, honey?
> BUT MY BABY
> Sure. Kiss me,
> DON'T LOVE NOBODY
> daddy.
> BUT ME.
> Say!
> EVERYBODY
> Yes?
> WANTS MY BABY
> I'm your
> BUT MY BABY
> sweetie, ain't I?
> DON'T WANT NOBODY
> Sure.
> BUT
> Then let's
> ME,
> do it!
> SWEET ME.
> Charleston,
> mamma!
> !

Of "The Cat and the Saxophone" Countee Cullen wrote: "This creation is a *tour de force* of its kind, but is it a poem?"—a question not to be asked.

In "Death in Harlem" Hughes builds an extended jazz narrative on the structure of the black folk epic or toast, adding exhortative asides ("Do it, Arabella!/Honey baby, sock it!"). The setting is Dixie's, a Harlem basement nightclub. The Texas Kid, " a dumb little jigaboo from/Somewhere South," has a thick bill roll in his hands, and Arabella Johnson has her hands on him. Dixie's musician whips that piano. "Aw, play it, Miss Lucy!/ Lawd!/Ain't you shame?" They drink and dance and laugh. "Everybody's happy. It's a spending crowd—/ Big time sports and girls who know/Dixie's ain't no place for a crowd that's slow." Then Arabella goes to the "LADIES' ROOM" and comes back to find another good-time woman has taken her place. ("It was just as if somebody/Kicked her in the face.") She drew her pistol and the shots rang out. "Take me,/Jesus, take me/Home today." Bessie falls and Arabella is taken to jail. And the Texas Kid—he "picked up another woman and/Went to bed."

"Death in Harlem" is a record of one of the meanings of Harlem nightlife. Dixie's pleasure cellar is a den of death. Dixie is an eager Tom who wants money—bootleg money, sex money, blood money, any money. He rubs his hands and grins and bows as his white customers enter. In this nightspot the contraries meet and merge: black and white, poor and rich, pleasure and pain, laughter and death. The white presence presages death: the white women look at the blacks and think of rape, a rope, a flame. They dream of sex and violence, anticipating the sexual rivalry that will force the evening to a shuddering climax. Down south in Dixie it would have been death from a white mob; but up north at Dixie's it is death from the self-destructiveness of blacks, as it were activated by the white presence, actualizing the hidden white wish.

Death is so close to the heightened moments of life that it is almost impossible to avoid. Danger and death are expected and accepted parts of the evening's entertainment. The line, "Everybody's happy," describing the music and dancing, is intimately related to "Stand back folkses, let us/Have our fun"—where the fun is with guns and knives. The ambiguity of the evening's experience is summed up in the closing image of night slipping away like a reefer-man, an image that captures the compulsion, pleasure, pain, and final death of the experience—of the addiction, whether to drugs, which the reefer-man dispenses, or to life's reckless pleasures (liquor, music, sex, and money), which Dixie in his nightclub dispenses.

The story is elaborately but briskly told, detailed but terse, in the classic folk manner. In conception and delivery, "Death in Harlem" is a literary child of the great epic cycles such as "The Signifying Monkey," "Shine and the Sinking of the Titanic," and "Stagolee." The mastery which Hughes developed in this and other jazz poems is to be fully utilized in *Montage of a Dream Deferred* and *Ask Your Mama*.

*Montage of a Dream Deferred* (1951) is more carefully orchestrated than Hughes's earlier volumes because conceived as a unity, as one continuous poem, although it is organized in sections and subtitles just like the others, and uses single poems previously published in periodicals. In *Montage* the days of our black lives are telescoped into one day and one night. Montage is primarily a technique of the motion picture, its camera eye sweeping swiftly from scene to scene, juxtaposing disparate scenes in rapid succession or superimposing one scene (layer of film) over another until the last fades into the next. In literature, montage provides a technical shortcut, a means of avoiding the sometimes long-winded "logical" transitions demanded by the conventional story line. Through montage, the reader/viewer is able to traverse vast spaces and times (and consciousness) in a relatively brief moment. Hughes in his prefatory note prepares the reader for this mode of seeing:

> In terms of current Afro-American popular music and the sources from which it has progressed—jazz, ragtime, swing, blues, boogie-woogie, and be-bop—this poem on contemporary Harlem, like be-bop, is marked by conflicting changes, sudden nuances, sharp and impudent interjections, broken rhythms, and passages sometimes in the manner of the jam session, sometimes the popular song, punctuated by the riffs, runs, breaks, and disc-tortions of the music of a community in transition.

The theme is the dream deferred. The vehicle is primarily be-bop but also boogie-woogie and other black music. And the mode is montage, which has its musical equivalent in be-bop and its literary equivalent in free association (stream of consciousness). Be-bop, montage, and free association parallel one another so closely in technique (rapid shifts) that the mode could be thought of as all three simultaneously. However, free association is used sparingly, as in the "Dig and Be Dug" section when talk of death leads to talk of war. (Free association will see full service in *Ask Your Mama*.) Some sections open and close with the musical motif (boogie or bop), and each is sprinkled with musical references and phrases, including the "nonsense syllables" or "scat singing" ("Oop-pop-a-da!/Skee! Daddle-de-do!/Be-bop!") which especially characterized bop. In "Dive," for instance, while there is no mention of music, it is the music that is picking up rhythm "faster. . ./faster," lending its speed to the nightlife on Lenox Avenue. Similarly, "Up-Beat" describes a speeding up of the beat as well as a possible metamorphosis of black youth—their emergence from the gutter, up from the dead into the quick—the kind of process by which the youngsters of "Flatted Fifths," "Jam Session," "Be-Bop Boys," and "Tag" are transformed from jail-birds into musical celebrities.

The poem could be viewed as a ritual drama, but without the stiffness that the term usually connotes. It is a vibrant seriocomic ceremony in which a community of voices is orchestrated from a multiset or multilevel stage, the speakers meanwhile engaged in their normal chores or pleasures. The setting is Harlem, with a close awareness of its connection with downtown Manhattan and its place as a magnetic mecca for refugees from the South. The time: the continuous present on which the burden of times past is heavy, with brief projections into the future. The poem opens in the morning and progresses through daytime into evening, into late night, and on to the following dawn. *Harlem, a microcosm of the black presence in America,* is the victim of an economic blight, relieved only sporadically by the wartime boom. This is hardly the joy-filled night-town of the 1920s. Money, or more precisely the lack of money, determines many of the human relationships presented to our view especially in the opening section. Money is the main riff, the musical current flowing steadily just below the surface and surfacing from time to time, bearing the theme of the dream deferred. A few situations transcend the terms and boundaries of the economic imperative, as in "Juke Box Love Song," where love unlocks and lets fly softness and beauty amidst the discordant, dissatisfied voices of poverty, creating a harmony that money could not by itself accomplish; in "Projection," where unity and peace are described in terms of a harmonious orchestration of disparate types; and in "College Formal," where the youthful couples, wrapped in love and melody, lend transcendence to the audience as a whole.

The deferred dream is examined through a variety of human agencies, of interlocking and recurring voices and motifs fragmented and scattered throughout the six sections of the poem. Much as in bebop, the pattern is one of constant reversals and contrasts. Frequently the poems are placed in thematic clusters, with poems within the cluster arranged in contrasting pairs. *Montage* does not move in a straight line; its component poems move off in invisible directions, reappear and touch, creating a complex tapestry or mosaic.

The dream theme itself is carried in the musical motifs. It is especially characterized by the rumble ("The boogie-woogie rumble/Of a dream deferred")—that rapid thumping and tumbling of notes which so powerfully drives to the bottom of the emotions, stirring feelings too deep to be touched by the normal successions of notes and common rhythms. The rumble is an atomic explosion of musical energy, an articulate confusion, a moment of epiphany, a flash of blinding light in which all things are suddenly made clear. The theme is sounded at strategic times, culminating in the final section where all the instruments beat out their versions of the theme. The energy level is brilliantly high in the windup: music as structure and metaphor succeeds in holding the poem together and moving it to the end, creating continuity in depth. Music is preeminently the medium that can hold so many sides and dimensions, that can bring to the front similarities among things apparently dissimilar—the similarities between church music and jazz; between the lives of the good folk and of the good time folk; between the lives of pimps, whores, mothers, children, musicians, and the folks that sit on stoops—similarities even to the point of desperation where they all cry out, "Great God!" ("Sliver of Sermon"). Jazz, above all, is the music that can hold so much simultaneous motion, melody, and meaning.

The first section, "Boogie Segue to Bop," opens with the theme question: "You think/It's a happy beat?"—this rumble of the boogie-woogie and pata-pata of the feet of the dance? And toward the end of the book the question is posed again in what is to become its classic form: "What happens to a dream deferred?" ("Harlem"). Hughes first made the point in *The Weary Blues* ("Does a jazz band ever sob?") that it may all sound like a happy beat but it ain't. Behind and beneath the gaiety is something sad and ominous, something that some day might explode. Hughes is usually explicit and direct, but often enough he chooses to deliver his insights and warnings veiled in hints or wrapped in questions: "I wonder where I'm gonna die,/Being neither white nor black"; "Who but the Lord/can protect me?"; "Or does it explode?" Or he gives an answer that momentarily deflects our attention from the question and amounts to no answer at all. For instance, to the question "You think/It's a happy beat?" he replies: "Sure,/I'm happy." Or, as in "Projection," he forecasts that the day black unity is achieved—what would happen? According to the poem, nothing more momentous than Father Divine declaring: "Peace!/It's truly/wonderful!"—which is momentous enough but not quite the point. In each case the weight of the question demands something more, and the reader is thrown back upon his own resources, is forced to confront the deeper implications of the question.

After the opening question comes "Parade," hauling out the whole cast, a concentration of blackness shocking in its vastness and vivacity ("I never knew/that many Negroes/were on earth,/did you?"). Cops stand alert when so many blacks come together, anticipating the unity that does not yet exist—"Solid black,/Can't be right"—and would speed them out of sight if they could. A festive atmosphere prevails. Harlem has seen some colorful parades, starting back in Marcus Garvey's days. As with Father Divine's declaration, Hughes chooses to give the parade a human significance and in the black folk style, instead of a political /rhetorical significance. The parade, he says, is just "a chance to let/. . . the whole world see/. . . old black me!"—which is what *Montage* itself is, with its variegated presentation of Harlem and Harlemites.

The rest of the opening section progresses from childhood to youth to adulthood. The youngsters of "Children's Rhymes" and "Sister" are in process of discovering the world and learning to cope with it. In "Children's Rhymes" the adult voice serves as counterpoint and foil to the young voices. Times have changed, and innocent rhymes have given way to verses fraught with precocious knowledge.

> By what sends
> the white kids
> I ain't sent:
> I know I can't
> be President.

This early, the children already understand their racial situation and the ceiling placed on their aspirations. They can distinguish rhetoric from reality. White kids are fired by political and other ambitions; black kids can't afford to be. This early their dream is already deferred—they can hardly afford to dream. So young, and so cynical, "living 20 years in 10," as Hughes will put it in *Ask Your Mama*. The letter of the law and the promise of the Constitution to them is meaningless: "Liberty And Justice—/Huh—For All."

Cynicism and disillusionment with America is nothing new, of course, but perhaps not until the generation of the 1960s was it so pervasive and complete among black youth, and even among a significant portion of white youth. Hughes may be said to have anticipated it in "Children's Rhymes."

In "Sister" the tables are turned. Here it is youth that is innocent and age that is realistic or cynical. If Marie runs around with trash it is because she needs cash; and "decent folks" (the unmarried gentleman ideal) usually have none to give. Poverty is generated by the limited opportunities outlined in "Children's Rhymes." Things being as they are, black women—and men too, as the voice on the stoop reminds us—do the best they can. Black men and women are equally trapped.

The truth of the voice on the stoop is immediately tested in "Preference." The young man prefers older women because they give more and ask for less. Like Marie, he too is doing the best he can. But the young man of "Necessity" is not so lucky: he has to work, if only to pay his high rent.

The common problem is economic. Love and money are closely intertwined, and in "Question" and "Ultimatum," as in "Sister" and "Preference," the choice of partners and the nature of the relationship is determined by economics. The question of "Question" is: can a man in these circumstances both love his woman and feed her (the familial ideal)? And if he cannot, what happens to their relationship, and their family? In "Buddy" the young man is doing his best to save his mother from the question of "Question" and its predictable answer ("De-bop!"—the answer is in the music, an answer too painful for words) by giving her ten of his twelve dollars a week. But we know it won't last: he is left only two dollars a week for clothes and carfare. In "Croon" and "New Yorkers" the economic situation is summed up: North or South, black folks "never own no parts/ of earth nor sky."

The scene now modulates into night, the phrases "in the dark" ("New Yorkers") and "early blue evening" ("Wonder") serving as time indicators. "Easy Boogie" ushers in the nightlife and ends the opening section. It's been a short day, but it's going to be a long night. Daytime will not return until the closing section.

In summary, the opening poem, "Dream Boogie," poses the question, and the rest of *Montage* attempts to answer it. In *Montage* we see some of the things that happen to a dream deferred. "Parade" presents the people: this is Harlem, "I'm talking about/Harlem to you." The rest of the poems in the section exhibit the institutional limitations to black aspirations and the effects of economic deprivation on black life and love. As usual with Hughes, there is no moralizing; each poem delivers the picture starkly and without comment.

The second section, "Dig and Be Dug," opens with a juxtaposition of art ("Movies") and life ("Not a Movie"). Movies spin non-stop on celluloid the American Dream—while the KKK beat up one more black man who tried to make that Dream real. Because of its divorce from reality, movie art is "crocodile art" evoking "crocodile tears." Harlem sees it for what it is—and laughs "in all the wrong places." What is serious to Hollywood is funny to black folks and vice versa. "Hollywood/laughs at me": when black people appear in the movies, it is in the service of white fantasies (stereotypes). But Hollywood refuses to deal with the brutality of the South or the economic constrictions on life on 133rd Street, which is no laughing matter. On 133rd Street you may not have the KKK at your back, but you have the police; and you still don't own a thing. "Why should it be *my* dream/deferred/overlong?" ("Tell Me").

"Neon Signs" is a roll call of the night spots where black music reigns, the genius of "re-bop/sound" in such sharp contrast to Hollywood's sterile crocodile art on the one hand, and to the dilapidated physical environment ("broken glass," "smears") of black night spots on the other. The poet's camera and microphone make the rounds, recording the scene and reporting the conversation. Survival savvy in this night world is "play it cool/And dig all jive." Know the environment and be at home in it, be part of its swing. Live and let live: "Dig And Be Dug/In Return" ("Motto"). Gambling ("Numbers") is one way to get some money, entertainment ("Dancer") is another. Both are subject to rare and uncertain chances. Especially with gambling, too much luck among the luckless can be worse than too little: "When I rolled three 7's/in a row/ I was scared to walk out/with the dough" ("Situation"). Death stalks. One of the inset progressions is from birth ("What? So Soon?") through survival/life ("Motto") to death ("Dead in There"). "Advice" pinpoints the lesson:

> Folks, I'm telling you,
> birthing is hard
> and dying is mean—
> so get yourself
> a little loving
> in between.

Talk of death brings back memories of the war. "Green Memory" is one of several excursions into history. As the red blood rolled out the green money rolled in. Blood money, as it were, is all that Harlem has ever been permitted. *But* even for this alone, let the white folks fight another war, "or even two" if they wish; "the one to stop 'em won't be me" ("Relief"). The issue is survival.

Memories of the depression and war time clear the stage for "Ballad of the Landlord," which is one of the high points of *Montage*. First collected in *Jim Crow's Last Stand* (1943), this poem is likely to remain contemporary for a long time to come. It is not for nothing that as recently as 1965 the public school system of a major American city dismissed a teacher for assigning "Ballad of the Landlord" to his class.

In a few bold strokes Hughes paints a picture of a slum dwelling broken from roof to bottom step; of the callous landlord who will not make repairs but will evict if rent is not paid on time; and, most importantly, of the forces of law and order who are ranged on the landlord's side and who, like the landlord, equate the assertion of tenant rights with revolution, for the tenant's refusal to accept and pay for substandard and dangerous living conditions is a threat to a society which grows fat from tenant abuse. Their reprisal is swift and smooth: landlord, police, judge, and press have rehearsed and acted out this scenario so many times before.

The poem is tightly constructed, and in the black idiom. The first half follows the form of the conventional English folk ballad: quatrains of alternating tetrameter and trimeter lines, rhyming *abcb*. The last half is irregular, the short, broken lines recreating the curtness of the police arrest, the precipitousness with which the judge assigns a jail term, and the brevity with which the press dismisses the incident. The rhymes are conventional until we get to "land" and "man," "press" and "arrest," which rhyme as they would in black folk dialect.

In the first half of the poem a balance is maintained between landlord and tenant with claims and counterclaims, threats and counterthreats, "I" and "you." The landlord is comfortable issuing threats, but he can't take them; and he quickly upsets the balance of words by yelling for the police. His hysterical "Police! Police!" is in violent contrast to the even tone of the tenant's "Landlord, landlord." But, ironically, the landlord's power is as great as his terror. The tenant calls on the landlord twice and gets no action; the landlord calls on the police once and gets immediate action. Against the landlord's organized might, the tenant's fearless manhood is ineffectual; his individual resistance is hopeless. And it is to gather organizational strength that the orator of the next poem, "Corner Meeting," mounts his ladder. His message is contained in "Projection"—that were disparate black factions to unite and work together in their own self-interest, it would be "truly/wonderful," for then would black power emerge, and only then would the problems of the ghetto, symbolized by the slumlord, begin to find solutions.

Thus, this second section, which opened with the nighttime escapes from and makeshift solutions to the frustrations aired in the preceding section, closes with a vision of a dependable vehicle of redress: *black unity, the prerequisite for black power.* Hughes of course does not spell it all out. He does not need to.

The third section, "Early Bright," is the late night, hard bop section. Here are the hard-core night people in their milieu: the music makers, the "little cullud boys" whose early encounters with "bail" and "jail" ("Jam Session") and "fear" ("Flatted Fifths," "Tag") erupt into be-bop; black celebrities ("Mellow") into whose laps "white girls fall," defying the taboos;

drug pushers who find the people no obstacle (survival savvy: "Live and Let Live," "Dig And Be Dug"); "the vice squad/with weary sadistic eyes" sniffing out the degenerates ("Cafe: 3 A.M."); drunkards, rounders, and assorted faces. Ironically, the "Be-Bop Boys" implore "Mecca/to achieve/ six discs/with Decca"—which, among other things, is Hughes's recognition of the non-Western forces at work in the community.

The first half of the fourth section, "Vice Versa to Bach," offers a thematic contrast to the preceding section. Here the poet touches on the world of the educated and middle class aspiring after white culture—Bach, not bop.

> See that lady
> Dressed so fine?
> She ain't got boogie-woogie
> On her mind—
>
> ("Lady's Boogie")

But even they, he says, if they would listen, they too would hear the music of a dream deferred even in the Bach.

> But if she was to listen
> I bet she'd hear,
> Way up in the treble
> The tingle of a tear.
>
> Be-Bach!
> ("Lady's Boogie")

The delicate treble "tingle" is at the opposite end of the musical scale from the deep "rumble," but the dream, encompassing life itself, is broad enough to touch both. The music of the dream is inescapable: it is heard by high and low, by blacks everywhere and in all circumstances.

"Theme for English B" is one of Hughes's most nearly autobiographical poems. There is relatively little distance between him and the experience recounted in the poem. The "college on the hill above Harlem" is of course Columbia University, where he spent an unsatisfactory year in 1921–22, and the poem evidently grew out of an incident there. The poem reiterates one of his leading themes, first enunciated at the close of The Weary Blues: that "I, too, am America." American identity of necessity embraces equally the white and the black experience. Those two experiences interpenetrate, are defined one by the other, even though neither group relishes the idea. "Sometimes perhaps you don't want to be a part of me./Nor do I want to be a part of you./But we are, that's true."

The quarrel between black and white finds an echo in the argument between the "black bourgeoisie" and the "common element" in "Low to High" and "High to Low." The "low" accuse the "high" of turning their backs on them, the masses. The "high," who are "trying to uphold the race" in the eyes of white folks, regard the masses as a liability because they "talk too loud,/cuss too loud,/look too black/don't get anywhere,/ and sometimes it seems/you don't even care." The argument is a classic and familiar one. And Hughes in his usual way is content to dramatize it, with no comment, although his manner of presentation leaves no doubt where his sympathies are.

"Freedom Train" and "Deferred" constitute the climax of this section and are among the most strategic poems in *Montage*. Each is a poem of considerable scope, permitting the varied illustration of the essential theme. "Freedom Train" is a response to the patriotic train which toured the United States in 1947–48 carrying historical documents and mementoes. The Free- dom Train symbolizes the promise of America. For the black man, freedom has so far been a fantasy; he has heard the word but never experienced the reality. Past experience makes him skeptical: this train might be just another piece of pompous propaganda—unreal, in contrast to the very real deaths of black soldiers who helped make and keep America free. In his inventory of the things which should not be found on a Freedom Train (segregated facilities, job discrimination, denial of franchise) the poet gives an accurate description of racial abuses, of the United States as it is. The Freedom Train is long enough to encompass past, present and future, from the grandmother in Atlanta trying to board the train and some white man yelling "Get back!/ A Negra's got no business on the Freedom Track!" to the children in their innocent questioning trying to make sense of senseless Jim Crow.

The train as metaphor comes out of Afro-American secular and reli- gious traditions: it is the heaven-bound train and chariot of the spirituals, the northbound train of the Underground Railroad, and the out-bound trains carrying unhappy lovers and restless wanderers to fresh scenes and new hopes in the blues. Further, as a mode of speedy and comfortable travel, impressive with its sharp whistle, grinding wheels, and many cars rolling along at a swift and noisy pace, the train joins place to place and people to people in a vast and varied land, abbreviating space and time and consciousness and thereby serving as an intimation of America's ability to fuse the many into one, as in its motto "E Pluribus Unum." But that fusion cannot be complete, America's unity train cannot run full steam until a "coal black man," his color and strength in unison with earth's great energy source, is also free to drive that train.

The poem has the amplitude and rhetorical sweep of a folk sermon, with its familiar and effective parallelisms and forceful repetitions:

> No back door entrance to the Freedom Train,
> No signs FOR COLORED on the Freedom Train,
> No WHITE FOLKS ONLY on the Freedom Train.

The lead voice is the preacher's, with the congregation providing a choral counterpoint in the lines, "I'm gonna check up on this/Freedom Train," "But maybe they'll explain it on the/Freedom Train," "But, Mister, I thought it were the/Freedom Train!" etc. The sermon-poem is delivered in a smooth, driving rhythm, building up to a screaming crescendo in the italicized lines at the end. Religion is not isolated from politics and daily life; on the contrary, the poem achieves a happy union of secular matter and religious manner. Even the racial harmony envisioned at the end is given as a goal achievable here on earth, not in a religious afterworld.

From the collective political dream of "Freedom Train" Hughes turns to fragments of individual dreams, so intimately connected with the political, in "Deferred." The poem opens with a sustained discourse by three whose long-deferred dreams are now about to be fulfilled, followed by a flurry of voices rapidly listing dreams whose fulfillment is still deferred to some vague future time. The dreams are low-keyed and not at all extraordinary, ranging from the tangible and material (housewares, furniture, clothing, radio and television sets) to the intangible (a place in heaven, a good wife); from economic ambitions (to pass the civil service) to educational and cultural ambitions (leisure to study French, leisure to discover and enjoy Bach). Most of the dreams are of necessities and minor luxuries, of things which a little money and leisure would buy. For those who have nothing, the little things are everything.

The section closes with another excursion into history. John Brown, who died fighting to stop the dream being deferred any longer, is now as forgotten as the "unknown soldier" ("Shame on You"). To black people in particular—"Black people don't remember/any better than white"— Hughes says "shame on you." But here again he avoids direct statement, pretends he is saying something else: "If you're not alive and kicking,/ shame on you." The same people who so readily forget John Brown so readily remember "World War II" as a time of fun—"What a grand time was the war!"—till the Echo asks: "Did/Somebody/Die?" True, the war brought relief, which was a good thing; but to call the war fun is the thoughtless side of "Green Memory." "Shame on you!"

In the fifth section, "Dream Deferred," the dream is viewed through the monocle of the religious experience. Religion is a major segment of the black experience in America, over the centuries providing breeding ground for some of the greatest black poetry and music, incubating revolts, and serving for consolation. Even pimps and whores reach a point where they are forced to cry out to God ("Sliver of Sermon"). Those who have made it, those whose dreams have come true and who now live downtown or in the suburbs, all miss Harlem, with its bitter, unfulfilled dreams, especially on sunny, summer, Sunday afternoons when the crowded sidewalks, stoops, and windows resound with cheerful chatter ("Passing"). Deracinated, isolated from the vital nourishment of their people and culture, their fulfilled dream has become a nightmare of "faces/Turned dead white" ("Nightmare Boogie")—the faces of their now white neighborhoods. So that their dreams have not really come true since, unlike other ethnic groups, they are forced to abandon their own people in their movement upwards. Their dreams will not come true till they come true for the masses of black folk.

Amidst the disparate voices of the community gossiping and commenting on various matters, the money motif returns in "Dime," "Fact," and "Hope." The child asking for a dime—and "Granny aint got no dime"—will reappear at the close of Ask Your Mama, crying "Show fare, Mama. . . . /Show fare!" his young dream still deferred. "Hope" is one of Hughes's many epigrammatic successes, succinct little statements carrying fantastic power:

> He rose up on his dying bed
> and asked for fish.
> His wife looked it up in her dream book
> and played it.

This is one of Hughes's most pointed comments on the erosion of black emotions, the dehumanization of people by poverty. Here Hughes is at his coldest and most brutal. W. C. Handy once said of this poem that in four lines Hughes says "what it would have taken Shakespeare two acts and three scenes to say."

One of the closing themes of the section is the relationship of the different ethnic groups in the urban community. "Subway Rush Hour" forces a type of brotherhood: black and white are crowded so close there is "no room for fear." "Brothers" stresses pan-African unity: the Afro-American, Afro-Caribbean, and African are brothers. And in "Likewise" Hughes declares that Jews are not alone to blame for the ghetto's ills, and that they are likewise brothers, especially since they too, with their history of persecution, must have heard that same music of a dream deferred. The hostilities between black and white, Jew and Gentile, are symptomized by the "cheap little rhymes" deplored in "Sliver."

The poet has taken us on a guided tour of microcosmic Harlem, day and night, past and present. And as a new day dawns and the poem moves into a summing up in the final section, he again poses the question and examines the possibilities:

> What happens to a dream
> deferred?
>
> Does it dry up
> like a raisin in the sun?
> Or fester like a sore—
> And then run?
> Does it stink like rotten meat?
> Or crust and sugar over—
> like a syrupy sweet?
>
> Maybe it just sags
> like a heavy load.
>
> *Or does it explode?*
> ("Harlem")

The images are sensory, domestic, earthy, like blues images. The stress is on deterioration—drying, rotting, festering, souring—on loss of essential natural quality. The raisin has fallen from a fresh, juicy grape to a dehydrated but still edible raisin to a sun-baked and inedible dead bone of itself. The Afro-American is not unlike the raisin, for he is in a sense a desiccated trunk of his original African self, used and abandoned in the American wilderness with the stipulation that he rot and disappear. Like the raisin lying neglected in the scorching sun, the black man is treated as a thing of no consequence. But the raisin refuses the fate assigned to it, metamorphoses instead into a malignant living sore that will not heal or disappear. Like the raisin, a sore is but a little thing, inconsequential on the surface but in fact symptomatic of a serious disorder. Its stink is like the stink of the rotten meat sold to black folks in so many ghetto groceries; meat no longer suitable for human use, deathly. And while a syrupy sweet is not central to the diet as meat might be, still it is a rounding-off final pleasure (dessert) at the end of a meal, or a delicious surprise that a child looks forward to at Halloween or Christmas. But that final pleasure turns out to be a pain. Aged, spoiled candy leaves a sickly taste in the mouth; sweetness gone bad turns a treat into a trick.

The elements of the deferred dream are, like the raisin, sore, meat, and candy, little things of no great consequence in themselves. But their unrelieved accretion packs together considerable pressure. Their combined weight becomes too great to carry about indefinitely: not only does the weight increase from continued accumulation, but the longer it is carried the heavier it feels. The load sags from its own weight, and the carrier sags with it; and if he should drop it, it just might explode from all its strange, tortured, and compressed energies.

In short, a dream deferred can be a terrifying thing. Its greatest threat is its unpredictability, and for this reason the question format is especially fitting. Questions demand the reader's participation, corner and sweep him headlong to the final, inescapable conclusion.

Each object (raisin, sore, meat, candy, load) is seen from the outside and therefore not fully apprehended. Each conceals a mystery; each generates its own threat. The question starts with the relatively innocuous raisin and, aided by the relentless repetition of "Does it . . . ?" intensifies until the violent crescendo at the end. With the explosion comes the ultimate epiphany: that the deadly poison of the deferred dream, which had seemed so neatly localized (the raisin drying up in a corner harmless and unnoticed; the sore that hurt only the man that had it; the rotten meat and sour candy that poisoned only those that ate it), does in fact seep into the mainstream from which the larger society drinks. The load, so characterless except for its weight, conceals sticks of dynamite whose shattering power none can escape.

Rotten meat is a lynched black man rotting on the tree. A sweet gone bad is all of the broken promises of Emancipation and Reconstruction, of the Great Migration, integration and voter registration, of Black Studies and Equal Opportunity. It might even be possible to identify each of the key images with a generation or historical period, but this is not necessary: the deferred dream appears in these and similar guises in every generation and in the experience of individuals as well as of the group. The poem is the "Lenox Avenue Mural" of the closing section title, painted in bold letters up high and billboard-size for all to see. To step into or drive through Harlem is at once to be confronted with its message or question. The closing line is Hughes's final answer/threat and will return with some frequency in *The Panther and the Lash*.

Each of the five other poems of the final section takes the question and plays with it, incorporating variations of it from earlier sections. All sorts of things are liable to happen "when a dream gets kicked around." And, sure, they kick dreams around downtown, too, even on Wall Street, not to speak of Appalachia or the Indian Reservations. But right now, one thing at a time, first things first: "I'm talking about/Harlem to you!" ("Comment on Curb").

*Ask Your Mama* (1961) is another montage of a dream deferred, but this time the controlling mechanism, the instrument of seeing is not the camera eye but the free-wheeling mind and memory (free association) of the poet. Accordingly, the shift from scene to scene is much more rapid than in *Montage*. In *Montage* scene shifts took place at the end of a poem; here they take place in the middle of a sentence or end of a line. In place of the neat set pieces of *Montage,* we find here an almost nonstop flow of recall, allusion, and juxtaposition of distant objects, events, and ideas. In *Montage* themes recurred in the form of single poems. Here the leading motifs—Santa Claus and Christmas; white snow and dark shadows; mother, grandmother, and grandfather; river and railroad; quarter (time, money, living space, breathing space, violent death—"a lynched tomorrow . . . tarred and feathered," drawn and quartered)—recur quite often as single words or phrases embedded in alien contexts. These together with the book's design—its album shape, pastel colored pages, abstract cubist illustrations, two-tone lettering, and the capital letters in which the whole poem is printed—underline the fact that *Ask Your Mama* is an avant-garde experiment. Remarkably, the linguistic idiom is not primarily black, though of course the title, rhythm, music, and ethos are. Chiefly as a result of its total immersion in free association, there is a distinct "disorganization" about *Ask Your Mama.* Compared to the electric clarity of his other books, *Ask Your Mama* is Hughes's one and only difficult book. It is his sop to academia, his answer to those readers who demand complex surfaces to puzzle over. This is the kind of poetry Hughes might have written all his life had he not had such a clear conception of his goals and of the light years of difference between formal complexity and literary worth.

*Ask Your Mama* is intended to be performed. Hughes wrote mood and musical accompaniment into one earlier volume, *The Negro Mother and Other Dramatic Recitations* (1931), and of course over the years he frequently read his poems to jazz accompaniment. *Ask Your Mama* is his most elaborate effort along this line, and a climax of the life-long intimacy between his poetry and black music. In reading poetry to music, he insisted that

> the music should not only be background to the poetry, but should comment on it. I tell the musicians—and I've worked with several different modern and traditional groups—to im-

provise as much as they care to around what I read. Whatever they bring of themselves to the poetry is welcome to me. I merely suggest the mood of each piece as a general orientation. Then I listen to what they say in their playing, and that affects my own rhythms when I read. We listen to each other.

The poetry of *Ask Your Mama* does indeed "listen" to jazz rhythms. The step-rhythm of the following, for instance, recreates the cumulative repetition of instrumental jazz:

> IN THE
> IN THE QUARTER
> IN THE QUARTER OF THE NEGROES
>
> SINGERS
> SINGERS LIKE O-
> SINGERS LIKE ODETTA—AND THAT STATUE
>
> DE-
> DELIGHT-
> DELIGHTED! INTRODUCE ME TO EARTHA

In each example, the musician/poet returns again and again to the mother-note, reaches back into that vast source of the music's energy, and pulls, each time dragging out a larger chunk of that energy, and in the process driving his audience into ecstasy. In the trail-off of the finale, the movement is reversed:

> IN THE QUARTER OF THE NEGROES
> WHERE NEGROES SING SO WELL
> NEGROES SING SO WELL
> SING SO WELL
> SO WELL,
> WELL?
>
> SHOW FARE, MAMA, PLEASE.
> SHOW FARE, MAMA. . . .
> SHOW FARE!

The jazz instrumentalist's predilection for picking on a note or phrase and playing with it, repeating it over and over and over and weaving it into changes on a theme, thereby creating unexpected intensities, is paralleled in the above repetitions as well as in the many reduplications: "Nasser Nasser"; "Manger Manger";

GRANDPA, DID YOU HEAR THE
HEAR THE OLD FOLKS SAY HOW
HOW TALL HOW TALL THE CANE GREW
SAY HOW WHITE THE COTTON COTTON

The book's title comes from the sassy black tradition of the dozens, a
form of verbal contest commonest among adolescents. The contestants trade
insults (mostly sexual) on relatives (mostly female). The dozens is a mean
game because, as H. Rap Brown has said, "what you try to do is totally
destroy somebody else with words. . . . The real aim of the Dozens was to
get a dude so mad that he'd cry or get mad enough to fight."

—Let's get off the subject of mothers, 'cause I just got
  off of yours.

—I did it to your mama on the railroad track,
  And when her ass went up the trains went back.

—Your mother is a doorknob, everybody gets a turn.

—Your mama has so many wrinkles in her head she has
  to screw her hat on.

—I saw your mother on a bench trying to screw a cock
  with a monkey wrench.

Compared to this brutal comedy, Hughes might seem like a gentle and
inhibited player. But his gentleness is deceptive. As in his love blues, he has
chosen to avoid the strong sexual imagery of the folk original; instead, he
has adapted the form, transforming it from an adolescent game of abuse
and bravado confined to the ghetto, into an adult weapon of offense and
defense in the sophisticated combats of the national and interracial arena.
He has lifted the dozens out of the school yard into the boardroom and
onto the floor of the Congress. To the white neighbors who ring his bell
and ask if he would recommend a maid, Hughes's black suburbanite replies:
"Yes, your mama." To the creditor's threat of legal action, the debtor
retorts: "Tell your ma." And to the question, "Did I vote for Nixon?/I
said, Voted for your mama." Even on the two occasions when the question
is left hanging fire: "They asked me right at Christmas,/Would I marry
Pocahontas?"—a variant of "would I marry a white woman?"; and "Asked
me right at Christmas/Did I want to eat with white folks?" the retort is
the same, "Ask your mama." Hughes twice approaches the suggestiveness
of the popular dozens: "They asked me at the PTA/Is it true that Negroes—?

[have the most fun? as he explains in his notes]/I said, Ask your mama";
"And they asked me right at Christmas/If my blackness, would it rub off?/
I said, Ask your mama"—because in both cases your mama ought to know,
seeing as how I've been her backdoor man from way back since slavery
time.

To these questions Hughes might have added the standard one heard
after every ghetto riot: "What do you people want?" And the answer would
have been the same: "Ask your mama," which is less an answer than a
question (your mama knows what we want, she's got what we want, and
don't ask what is it?). Oppression, Hughes says, "makes of almost every
answer a question, and of men of every race or religion questioners."

IN THE QUARTER OF THE NEGROES
ANSWER QUESTIONS ANSWER
AND ANSWERS WITH A QUESTION

Hughes is a relentless questioner. In *Montage* it was: "What happens
to a dream deferred?" And for answer he offered a series of questions, with
an ominous closer: "Or does it explode?" In *Ask Your Mama* the key
question is contained in the musical accompaniment, the "Hesitation
Blues": "How long must I wait?/Can I get it now?/. . . Or must I hesitate?"
To this question the "gentleman in expensive shoes/Made from the hides
of blacks," builder of twenty-story housing projects covered with "chocolate
gangrenous icing," and representative of white American power, replies:
"Just wait." His answer is transparent with irony: go slow, be patient, you
can't have it now, just wait, he says; just wait, Hughes says (explicit in a
later book), you got something coming, something "upon the breeze/As yet
unfelt among magnolia trees." Just wait:

> You're the one,
> Yes, you're the one
> Will have the blues.

Hughes varies the question: "Tell me, pretty papa,/What time is it
now?" And the frivolous non-answer: "Don't care what time it is—/Gonna
love you anyhow." But it is late, very late. It is the "last quarter of Cen-
tennial/100-years Emancipation"—and still I must hesitate, can't have it
now, got to wait. Time ("how long must I wait?") and money (quarter;
show fare) are the dominant images in *Ask Your Mama,* just as they were
in *Montage of a Dream* (money) *Deferred* (time).

Appropriately, the book is dedicated to Louis Armstrong, "the greatest
horn blower of them all." And musicians and singers—Dinah Washington,

Charlie Parker, and Leontyne Price among them—constitute the majority of the celebrities presented or alluded to. As a black singer of white opera Leontyne represents a particular kind of bridge between black and white culture. In her the two cultures ("collard greens," "lieder") coexist. Her experience is the "cultural exchange" of the opening section. "Culture, they say, is a two-way street"; and it should therefore be possible for whites who are so inclined to participate in black culture the way the Leontynes participate in white culture. However, important as such exchange is, it is in the final analysis peripheral to Hughes's particular concern, which is the black community, "the quarter of the Negroes," its life and its woes. The book may be viewed as a historical pageant, recreating, in its zig-zag manner, significant scenes of Afro-American history from the villages by the Congo, their integrity unsullied by the white presence down through slavery to the present day.

The "quarter of the Negroes" is beleaguered. Its doors are "doors of paper," fragile against white lawlessness. The "amorphous jack-o'-lanterns" of the Ku Klux Klan "won't wait for midnight/For fun to blow doors down." And their lawlessness is protected by the law, whether in its constitutional instruments ("filibuster versus veto"), or in its cynical ventriloquisms ("with all deliberate speed"). White violence goes back to earliest American history when "the Tom dogs of the cabin/The cocoa and the cane brake/The chain gang and the slave block" made black life a daily death. The river and the railroad, staples of the blues and spirituals, "have doors that face each way"—one for whites and one for blacks; but more fundamentally, one facing south, through which many were sold further down the river into harder labor territory, and one facing north toward freedom, following the routes of the Underground Railroad, the archetypal northward movement of the black experience, and of the Great Migration, its modern analogue.

The movement north receives the attention it deserves as one of the most important ongoing processes of Afro-American life. Hughes celebrates the Underground Railroad, together with its most flamboyant conductor, tough, irrepressible Harriet Tubman, "a woman with two pistols/On a train that lost no passengers/On the line whose route was freedom." He contrasts its destination and dignity (freedom) with the ghetto terminal of the Great Migration. The Underground Railroad was made possible by the existence of a sense of human community among certain whites (Quakers, Abolitionists), a sense of community which extended to blacks. Slaves fled "through the jungle of white danger/To the haven of white Quakers/Whose haymow was a manger manger/Where the Christ child once had lain."

Paradoxically, the danger was white, and so was the haven, each finding its rationale in the same Christian religion. The Quakers were truly their brothers' keepers; but now, with slavery abolished, the rulers of the nation have assumed the office of brother's keeper, and they perform it gracelessly, with neither charity nor warmth. The depersonalized ghetto housing project, which is the haven they have constructed for modern fugitives from the Southern terror, is a mockery of that original Quaker haven, a mockery of the communal idea and African communal past:

> TRIBAL NOW NO LONGER ONE FOR ALL
> AND ALL FOR ONE NO LONGER
> EXCEPT IN MEMORIES OF HATE
> UMBILICAL IN SULPHUROUS CHOCOLATE

Locked in the project and supported by welfare, it is no longer possible for a man to be his brother's keeper, nor even keeper to his child. Welfare "generosity" is a mockery of Quaker generosity, for the welfare system is created to perpetuate poverty and destroy dignity.

> SANTA CLAUS, FORGIVE ME,
> BUT BABIES BORN IN SHADOWS
> IN THE SHADOW OF THE WELFARE
> IF BORN PREMATURE
> BRING WELFARE CHECKS MUCH SOONER
> YET NO PRESENTS DOWN THE CHIMNEY

Santa Claus, the snowy northern liberal father-figure who brings gifts to children, brings no gifts to "chocolate babies" born "in the shadow of the welfare." Rather, ghetto money enables white folks to live in comfort and to afford gifts (play Santa Claus) for their children at Christmas. The "million pools of quarters/ . . . Sucked in by fat jukeboxes" are "carted off by Brink's." And children born "in the shadow of the welfare" grow old before their time and die rapid early deaths,

> LIVING 20 YEARS IN 10
> BETTER HURRY, BETTER HURRY
> BEFORE THE PRESENT BECOMES WHEN
> AND YOU'RE 50
> WHEN YOU'RE 40
> 40 WHEN YOU'RE 30
> 30 WHEN YOU'RE 20
> 20 WHEN YOU'RE 10

You may dream "your number's coming out," but the chances are most uncertain. "In the quarter of the Negroes," "Even when you're winning/ There's no way not to lose." Hughes sums it all up in the couplet: "White folks' recession/Is colored folks' depression."

But those who have "made it," the few who have been showered by the "horn of plenty," those whose dreams have come true (and who will miss Harlem on sunny summer Sunday afternoons), live only a little less precariously in suburbia, surrounded by manicured lawns and suspicious neighbors. Hughes surrounds their names (famous athletes, entertainers) with dollars and cents (money talks). They are the ones who have managed

TO MOVE OUT TO ST. ALBANS     $ $ $ $ $ $ $ $
WHERE THE GRASS IS GREENER     $ $ $ $ $ $ $
SCHOOLS ARE BETTER FOR THEIR CHILDREN $
AND OTHER KIDS LESS MEANER THAN
IN THE QUARTER OF THE NEGROES

But racial attitudes pursue them there. They all achieved fame the hard way, and are known across the country and abroad.

YET THEY ASKED ME OUT ON MY PATIO
WHERE DID I GET MY MONEY?
I SAID, FROM YOUR MAMA!

However, even they do not want too many blacks to move into their neighborhood:

HIGHLY INTEGRATED
MEANS TOO MANY NEGROES
EVEN FOR THE NEGROES—
ESPECIALLY FOR THE FIRST ONES

Those left behind "in the quarter of the Negroes," those who never owned "$40,000 houses," who can't even keep up payments on their furniture: these have-nots sometimes find consolation in religious ecstasy, celebrated in the "Gospel Cha-Cha" section. Religion is offered as a contrast to the comforts of the financially successful. It is what the successful do not need, but since it is also a part of the total culture which they miss when they move out of the black community, it hovers unacknowledged in the background of their nostalgia. It is no accident therefore that Hughes places "Gospel Cha-Cha" immediately after "Horn of Plenty," or that in *Montage*, "the ones who've crossed the line/to live downtown" miss Harlem most on sunny Sunday afternoons when the folks crowd the streets in their Sunday best and grandma can't get her gospel hymns on the radio because of the ball games.

"Gospel Cha-Cha" is an account of the syncretic religions of the black Americas. It is a dramatized fragment of a sermon, prayer, vision, testimony, and ritual possession all in one, starting with Haitian voodoo (cha-cha) and moving to the Holy Roller churches (gospel) of North America. The horse and its white tourist rider laboring up the mountain to the "citadelle" metamorphose into the statue of Toussaint L'Ouverture mounted on his stone horse, then into the possessed votary and the divine horseman that rides him in the voodoo ceremony, and finally into the black Christian reenacting Christ's journey lugging his heavy cross up the hill to Calvary. The believer arrives at the hill-top to find that Christ has already been crucified. Christ has already died for him; he does not now need to die, only to endure the pain. The ritual of atonement is complete when he suffers as Christ suffered, bearing his own cross through life. Of the three crucified on the hill, he says, "One/Was black as me"; and the one is Jesus himself rather than one of the two thieves, not only because that belief has some basis in history, but more importantly, because only a black Christ (or a syncretized, non-racial Christ) could know the agonies of the black man in the New World and therefore serve for identification.

The matter of identification with a member of the trinity recurs at the end of the book:

> THE HEADS ON THESE TWO QUARTERS
> ARE *THIS* OR *THAT*
> OR *LESS* OR *MOST*—
> SINCE BUT TWO EXIST
> BEYOND THE HOLY GHOST.
> OF THESE THREE,
> IS ONE
> ME?

These disparate and incongruent images are held together by the centripetal force of free association. In the passage immediately preceding, blacks are portrayed as making a way out of no way, "ten Negroes/Weaving metal from two quarters/Into cloth of dollars/For a suit of good-time wearing." The poet then makes an associational leap to the image of George Washington's head engraved on the two quarters, and from that to the segregated living quarters which characterize the nation. The mottos "In God We Trust" and "E Pluribus Unum" inscribed on the coin provide a bridge to the three-in-one principle of the Christian godhead, which parallels the ethnic multiplicity of the nation. Since whites and blacks occupy the poles of American consciousness, they could be identified with the first and second persons of the trinity, and all other groups with the ghostly third. More specifically, Washington, as "father of his country," is Father and Head in that trinity, and his white progeny partake of his primacy. Blacks in their lesser status are "this" and "less," whites "that" and "most." As a citizen, even if second-class, the black man ("me") is a child of Washington in his capacity as father of his country; and as a mulatto, he is the unacknowledged and disinherited son of Washington and Jefferson and other "Founding Fathers" and their white brothers. He is the "holy bastard," the "nigger Christ" who in "Christ in Alabama" is rejected, cast out, crucified. The dream of "E Pluribus Unum"—that out of the welter of nationalities a single whole American nation might arise—is still deferred.

Around and through the black ghetto and even integrated suburbia whip the heady winds of change, carrying rumors of revolutions in faraway lands. "Ça ira! Ça ira!" cried the French Revolutionary crowds at the aristocrats on their way to the guillotine; and Hughes incorporates their cry into the "Hesitation Blues." Europe's colonial empires disintegrate, but their "ghosts cast shadows"—the shadows of neocolonialism. New nations rise in Africa and the Caribbean. African leaders, diplomats, and students flood the scene, bringing to the "quarter of the Negroes" ancestral memories:

> THERE, FORBID US TO REMEMBER,
> COMES AN AFRICAN IN MID-DECEMBER
> SENT BY THE STATE DEPARTMENT
> AMONG THE SHACKS TO MEET THE BLACKS

The activities of communists and revolutionaries ("Ride, Red, Ride") on the international scene reverberate on the domestic scene. Conservative public opinion blames social unrest and the civil rights movement on communist agitators, New York niggers, and Yankee liberals:

> THOSE SIT-IN KIDS, HE SAID,
> MUST BE RED!
> KENYATTA RED! CASTRO RED!
> NKRUMAH RED!
> RALPH BUNCHE INVESTIGATED!

Witch-hunt flames burn as fiercely in the House Un-American Activities Committee as they ever did in colonial New England.

SANTA CLAUS, FORGIVE ME,
BUT YOUR GIFT BOOKS ARE SUBVERSIVE,
YOUR DOLLS ARE INTERRACIAL.
YOU'LL BE CALLED BY EASTLAND.
WHEN THEY ASK YOU IF YOU KNOW ME,
DON'T TAKE THE FIFTH AMENDMENT.

Martin Luther King and his followers, on their nonviolent boycotts, sit-ins, and freedom rides, are met head-on with violence. But King preaches love and dreams on his impossible dream:

THE REVEREND MARTIN LUTHER
KING MOUNTS HIS UNICORN
OBLIVIOUS TO BLOOD

The unicorn is a figure of imagination and mythology said to be accessible only to virgins, the "pure at heart." It represents the vast faith which sustained Martin Luther King and his followers in their massive programs of civil disobedience. The unicorn is King's belief that the deferred dream could be made reality, that racial justice, brotherhood, and peace were possible in America. The poem precedes King's famous oration, "I Have a Dream," by two years, but of course King's program had been in operation since his Montgomery, Alabama, bus boycott of 1955. When King in his idealism and innocence mounts his unicorn, he appears suspended in air, above reality, for his dream-horse is invisible, inaccessible to the multitude.

The image of the unicorn is deliberately ambiguous: King's idealism makes him a hero but also makes him blind to reality, "oblivious to blood." And, historically speaking, it was not long before he himself publicly admitted that his program was inadequate to demolish the stone walls of America's racist realities, and that his dream had turned into a nightmare.

King is not the only one in the poem who holds commerce with the unicorn, for his dream is but an articulation of his people's individual dreams and collective dream:

IN THE QUARTER OF THE NEGROES
WHERE NO SHADOW WALKS ALONE
LITTLE MULES AND DONKEYS SHARE
THEIR GRASS WITH UNICORNS

Communal living in the original African style has disappeared among black people, but not completely. A considerable sense of relatedness, of community, survives, and the people even in their poverty share their material goods, their dreams, and their dream-producing drugs.

In and out of the scenes of turmoil glides the unobtrusive figure of Santa Claus, the liberal northerner. He is a philanthropist, a giver of gifts, and he gives to blacks as well as whites (his dolls are interracial). He is a nice fellow—except that he has no gifts for the children of the welfare poor. Because he is so friendly-seeming to blacks, he is not well liked in the South. Yet, as holder and exerciser of American power, he is different from his Southern peers chiefly in his smoothness and sophistication. He welcomes black participation, but only a token participation which permits blacks no share of real power. Adam Clayton Powell, as paradigmatic black Congressman, loaded with seniority and an outstanding record as sponsor of important social legislation, nevertheless rides the American power chariot only as a chauffeur rides a limousine:

> IN THE QUARTER OF THE NEGROES
> RIDING IN A JAGUAR, SANTA CLAUS,
> SEEMS LIKE ONCE I MET YOU
> WITH ADAM POWELL FOR CHAUFFEUR
> AND YOUR HAIR WAS BLOWING BACK
> IN THE WIND.

Santa Claus in his bohemian aspect, and his well-fed sons and daughters, come to black life as observers or limited participants, with romantic notions and protections, with boots far too deep for the shallow waters where they choose to wade:

> HIP BOOTS
> DEEP IN THE BLUES
> (AND I NEVER HAD A HIP BOOT ON). . . .
> DIAMONDS IN PAWN
> (AND I NEVER HAD A DIAMOND
> IN MY NATURAL LIFE)

For blacks, there is no protection from the harshness of ghetto life, the harshness which explodes into blues and into revolutionary struggle. Santa's protective boots (American prosperity), like the shoes of the gentleman "who tips among the shadows/Soaking up the music," were made from the hides of blacks.

The most poignant figure in *Ask Your Mama* is the Black Mother or Grandmother, she who watched helpless as her children were sold down the river (or as they meet early deaths or go to prison in the modern context):

> I LOOK AT THE STARS
> AND THEY LOOK AT THE STARS,
> AND THEY WONDER WHERE I BE
> AND I WONDER WHERE THEY BE

Grandpa and Grandma are the Black Archives, the experiencers and re-memberers of our oldest history. All questions ("Ask Your Mama") eventually filter back to them.

> GRANDPA, WHERE DID YOU MEET MY GRANDMA?
> AT MOTHER BETHEL'S IN THE MORNING?
> I'M ASKING, GRANDPA, ASKING. . . .
> GRANDPA, DID YOU HEAR THE
> HEAR THE OLD FOLKS SAY HOW
> HOW TALL HOW TALL THE CANE GREW
> SAY HOW WHITE THE COTTON COTTON
> SPEAK OF RICE DOWN IN THE MARSHLAND

But all too often they and their history are lost in the shuffle, in the confusion of the dream deferred, in the revolutionary struggle:

> IN THE QUARTER OF THE NEGROES
> TU ABUELA, ¿DÓNDE ESTÁ?
> LOST IN CASTRO'S BEARD
> TU ABUELA, ¿DÓNDE ESTÁ?
> BLOWN SKY HIGH BY MONT PELÉE?
> ¿DÓNDE ESTÁ? ¿DÓNDE ESTÁ?
> WAS SHE FLEEING WITH LUMUMBA?

Wherever Grandma ("abuela") is, that is where the answers are. But Hughes tells us in his notes that "grandma lost her apron with all the answers in her pocket (perhaps consumed by fire)"—the fire that leaps "From the wing tip of a match tip/On the breath of Ornette Coleman." Ornette and the new black music, signifying the spirit of the age, deliver "consternation," burn "like dry ice against the ear." And this is the spirit which in its relentless progression produces freedom rides, sit-ins, riots and fires, the Black Panthers, and the Black Esthetic. History, in other words, has made Grandma's answers inadequate. Her answers were in her apron; and her apron, the badge of black servitude in white kitchens, has been consumed by the flaming spirit of the age.

Grandma's answers are unacceptable to the modern generation. Yet the adequate and proper answers are nowhere to be found. The dream of social and economic well-being remains a dream, almost as distant and fantastic as the dream "that the Negroes/Of the South have take over—/ Voted all the Dixiecrats/Right out of power" and reversed the racial hierarchy:

> WEALTHY NEGROES HAVE WHITE SERVANTS,
> WHITE SHARECROPPERS WORK THE BLACK
>     PLANTATIONS,
> AND COLORED CHILDREN HAVE WHITE
>     MAMMIES:
>     MAMMY FAUBUS
>     MAMMY EASTLAND
>     MAMMY PATTERSON.
> DEAR, DEAR DARLING OLD WHITE MAMMIES—
> SOMETIMES EVEN BURIED WITH OUR FAMILY!

This dream, with its variations, is a longstanding one in black literature, and Hughes uses it again in his Simple tales. The drastic reversal of racial/ social roles is as startling and effective as the reversal of man and horse in Swift's *Gulliver's Travels:* it enables the author to show how ridiculous the society's beliefs and behavior really are. But the fantasy does not last. A rude awakening soon follows, and *Ask Your Mama* ends with the frustrated dream of black youth (our future) still asking mama for "show fare," and mama saying:

> NO SHOW FARE, BABY—
> NOT THESE DAYS

"Ask your mamma": and this is mama's final answer. Things didn't get better, they got worse ("Not these days"). The dream is still deferred.

R. BAXTER MILLER

# "No Crystal Stair": Unity, Archetype, and Symbol in Hughes's Poems on Women

Of the four major Black American writers—Richard Wright, Ralph Ellison, James Baldwin and Langston Hughes—the latter is probably the most highly regarded, and one would wonder why. He gave us no single work which aroused public scorn or sympathy, as did Richard Wright's *Native Son,* nor did he write any masterpiece which rivals Ralph Ellison's *Invisible Man* in overall unity and structure. Similarly, Hughes left us no literary production which considered alone equals *Invisible Man* in philosophical profundity. Moreover, we fail to enjoy Hughes's art for the reasons for which we enjoy James Baldwin's. In Hughes no liberation from repressed carnal urges leads to sincere revelation and to candid truth. Yet who among these other three attempted as much as Langston Hughes?

From the 1920s to the 1960s, Hughes's changing vision mirrored the changing times. During that period the writer tried many diverse modes: poetry, fiction, drama, critical essays, social essays, and editing. In comparing him with or to other black writers, one concludes by remembering Faulkner. Asked to name the greatest American novelist, the Mississippian answered Thomas Wolfe. Faulkner added that Hemingway succeeded best at what he tried, but attempted the least. Wolfe, Faulkner expressed further, succeeded the least, but tried the most.

Hughes, too, tried the most. I do not mean that he, like Wolfe, set about trying to express the unsayable or the ineffable. I mean, instead, that he was most concerned with finding the proper medium to range with his literary ability. To the archetype of woman, Hughes could graft his own

From *Negro American Literature Forum* 9, no. 4 (Winter 1975). © 1975 by Indiana State University.

ethnic vision; indeed, he could build upon it his most captivating themes: heroic endurance, human mortality, marital desertion, and enduring art. In a statement by Maud Bodkin, one of the best critics of Hughes's time, one finds a key to some of his best poems. Bodkin explains here the function of the female image in literature:

> Following the associations of the figure of the muse as com-municated in Milton's poetry, we have reached a representation of yet wider significance—the figure of the divine mother ap-pearing in varied forms, as Thetis mourning for Achilles, or Ishtar mourning and seeking for Tammuz. In this mother and child pattern the figure of the child, or youth, is not distinctively of either sex, though the male youth appears the older form. In historical times, the pattern as it enters poetry may be present, either as beautiful boy or warrior—Adonis, Achilles—or as maiden—Prosperine, Kore—an embodiment of youth's bloom and transient splendor. In either case, the figure appears as the type—object of a distinctive emotion—a complex emotion within which we may recognize something of fear, pity and tender admiration, such as a parent may feel, but "distanced," as by relation to an object universal, an event inevitable.

I intend to show here that different transformations of this archetypal image are essential to the thematic unity and image structure of many of Hughes's poems. First the archetypal image underlying the unity of his best two matriarchal verses, "Mother to Son" and "The Negro Mother," is demonstrated. Next, Hughes's concern with women is extended to other poems. Finally, the last section uses Hughes's religious (women) poems to introduce a discussion of the theme of faith and redemption in American letters.

James Emanuel perceptively notes that "Mother to Son" begins the strong matriarchal portraits found in Hughes's poetry and fiction. The plot of this poem is simple. For twenty lines a black mother addresses her son in a dramatic monologue. First (ll. 1–7), she makes clear the hardships of black life and thus suggests the paradox of the American mythmakers, who assert that all Americans are equal. Second (ll. 8–13), the mother acknowl-edges the personal and racial progress represented by her metaphor of ascent. Last (ll. 14–20), she teaches the child in a powerful refrain her moral of endurance: "And life for me ain't been no crystal stair."

Structurally, the poem provides the folk diction and rhythm that make the woman real. The individual lines skillfully blend anapestic, iambic, and trochaic cadences to simulate the inflections of black colloquialisms. Thus, the lines have varying syllabic length: ten, nine, eight, seven, four, three, and one. Although the last line is iambic, the rhythm of the poem depends more on the noted simulation of black rhetoric than on meter.

Thematically the complex of Christian myth unifies around the portrait of the mother. Being related to mythic ascent, she becomes one with the Virgil of the *Divine Comedy* or with the Christ of the New Testament. But she is neither a great and ancient poet, nor a God Incarnate. Rather, she is Woman struggling to merge with Godhead. This black woman therefore does more than make her way from failure to success; indeed, she moves from a worldly vision to a religious one. We find in her less a progression of the body than an evolution of the soul. Her last line—"And life for me ain't been no crystal stair"—reinforces her second. In the interim, she cautions her son, "Don't you fall now" (l. 17). She admonishes against a falling away from self-realization and racial struggle. Because she associates these two quests with her Divine Vision, human separation from them suggests a descent from Heavenly Grace.

Thus the female figure in "Mother to Son" reveals three themes besides that of Christian myth: a demand to continue questing; a self-realization, personally and racially; a perseverance on both levels. Using the past participle of the durative verb *be,* she tells her offspring, "I'se been a-climbin' on" (l. 9). The vertical ascent here anticipates her continued ascent. It also looks forward to temporary success or to a respite from future quest ("reachin' landin's" [l. 10] and "turnin' corners" [l. 13]). Through this woman, two complementary perspectives of distance prepare for a final heroic determination: "I's still goin' " (l. 18).

This black woman shrouded in religious myth must confront secular reality. When her image opposes this grim reality, a fourth theme emerges: black oppression. The mother addresses her son metaphorically. In her monologue, torn-up boards and bare feet indicate deprivation. Moreover, the metaphorical bareness of the poem mainly serves to complement the suffering which the verse also communicates symbolically. Literally, the mother lived in houses that had loose tacks (l. 3) and splinters (l. 4). Thus, throughout her life, she risked having bodily penetration and, hence, bodily infection. Symbolically, however, she is speaking about having withstood a possible injury to the black American soul. The imagery of light and dark leads to conjecture: Has not this woman successfully faced the darkness of outer reality by having inner illumination? Such an interpretation would explain her ability to go in the dark, where "there ain't been no light" (l. 13).

The "Negro Mother" resembles "Mother to Son" in theme but differs from it in form. As in the earlier poem, one finds here a mixture of iambic and anapestic feet. Again, the rhythm results in a simulation of black rhetoric. Here, however, tetrameter and pentameter lines give more of a formal consistency. One can divide "Negro Mother" into three parts. Part 1 (ll. 1–16) introduces the reader to the spirit of ghost of the black mother, who represents the racial and historical consciousness of blacks. Addressing her children, black posterity, the mother identifies herself. Part 2 (ll. 17–21) shows that the mother's religious faith enabled her to endure adversity. Here she stands aside from the monologue. This moment thus becomes her awed reminiscence of personal accomplishment more than a speaking to any person. In spirit the mother merges with her racial children and thus encourages the reader to foresee continued racial success. Part 2 skillfully prepares for part 3 (ll. 22–52), in which the mother returns from introspection and again expresses herself in direct monologue. In this last section, she cautions black youth against the barriers which still lie ahead.

The myth, imagery, theme, and unity of "Negro Mother" cohere around the image of the black woman. By "myth" I mean the religious overtones which cloak the parent-child monologue and which imply pilgrimage. At the beginning of "Negro Mother," one becomes aware of its religious tone. This tone, opposing the secular reality of the mother's being stolen from Africa, creates tension. In part 1, the mother also remembers the selling of her children, with the biblical tone possibly reminding the reader of the human wanderings found in Exodus.

Part 2 shows a shift in emphasis from the mother to the children. They must continue the sacred quest. She prepares them by using metaphor, simile, and echo to express her belief in Right: "But God put a song and a prayer in my mouth. God put a dream like steel in my soul" (ll. 18–19). By again empathizing with a Christian woman, Hughes demonstrates his talent for creating an autonomous persona. His more personal poems, such as "Who But the Lord," indicate his own humanism, as opposed to the black mother's Christianity. Nevertheless, the faith of the mother in part 2 prepares for her lines near the end of part 3: "Oh, my dark children may my dream and my prayers/Impel you forever up the great stairs."

Christian images relate to the black woman and help to develop the theme of heroic sacrifice associated with her. Hughes concentrates Christian images in the second and final sections. One finds, for instance, a valley related to a journey (l. 25). Moreover, one encounters the goal (l. 20) and blessings (l. 22) that the mother realizes through her children (l. 21) and the forward march that the mother urges the children to take. Her urging them to "Look ever upward" during the journey again suggests spatial duality.

As in "Mother to Son," linear and vertical distances merge in the Christian metaphor of travel. The mother's encouraging the children to climb the "great stairs" (l. 50) adds to the reader's sense of vertical distance. Like the dilapidated stair in "Mother to Son," the stairs here imply racial quest. Unlike the earlier stair, however, these are not an explicit symbol of life.

The female figure in "Negro Mother" functions similarly to the one in "Mother to Son": being religiously mythic, it becomes a foil to secular reality. From an opposition of divine quest and earthly limitation emerges a theme of social restriction. The reader becomes aware of the longevity of black suffering in America—three hundred years (l. 17). During this period, unmentioned experiences forged the "dream like steel" in the mother's soul. The fervor of this dream gave birth to adamance. Consequently, the dream also inspired her to survive a valley "filled with tears" (l. 25) and a road "hot with sun" (l. 27). Although she has been beaten and mistreated (part 1), and warns her offspring that racial restrictions still exist, her spirit has endured. We do not know the strength of the bars that represent this restriction in part three. Nevertheless, the tone suggests that these surpass neither the will of the mother, nor the potential strength of the children whom she inspires. That the mother overcame her inability to read and write in part 2 further supports this reading. So do the sweat, pain, and despair which she remembers in part 3, after having transcended them. She has withstood the whip of the slaver's lash. When combining social restriction with Christian myth, Hughes uses his alliterative skill in fusing liquids and plosives. The result is a powerfully memorable statement: "Remember how the strong in struggle and strife/still bar you the way and deny you life" (ll. 45–46).

While helping to illuminate the theme of social restriction, the black woman serves a third and equally important function, for the theme and imagery of Nature rely on her presence. Images of light and dark, plants which grow, or seeds which imply growth are all Nature images, as is any place of growth. Hughes distributes his important images throughout by putting five in part 1 and three in parts 2 and 3. This distributive method helps unify the different parts as sections and as a whole. For example, the "long dark way" (l. 2) of which the mother speaks anticipates her self-reminiscence as the "dark girl" (l. 9). In the latter instance she becomes the collective or archetypal image of the black race transported across the sea. The darkness of the travelled way and the female figure, who must travel it through time, fuse with the diurnal cycle. Consequently, the black woman expresses the past in cyclic metaphor: "I had nothing, back there in the night" (l. 24). The mother's advice to others will make for a different future, one of heroic progress due to a complementary opposition of woman and her posterity: "Out of the darkness, the ignorance, the night,/Lift high my banner out of the dust" (ll. 40–41). We find again the echo of Christian myth, with dust alluding to Ecclesiastes and suggesting mortality. In part 3 the mother instructs her children to make of her past a "torch for to-morrow" (l. 38). With this advice, she teaches them the secret of black art: the ability to transform suffering into good. The torch which lights the way, like the stars overhead, becomes positive by being related to moral pro-gression. Neither, however, completely agrees in image with the "Dark ones of today" (l. 34).

Additional parts of a natural complex unify parts 1 and 2 in "The Negro Mother." Like corn and cotton, the black race grows. But the analogy is subtly ambiguous. The products described grow for the purpose of human consumption or to be used, literally. Hughes implies, on the other hand, that the black race grows in order to end exploitation, or one's being "used," metaphorically. Corn and cotton grew in the field that the mother worked; suffering enhanced her spirit and wisdom. Tending the field outside herself, she also nourished within the dream and seed of the free. The latter is the more important fruition, for woman's spiritual evolution takes precedence over the physical growth of plants.

Considered together, other natural icons show that the thematic unity of the poem depends upon the maternal portrait. One finds early the moth-er's general delineation as woman (l. 11). This description of her sex pre-pares for a particular depiction of her as the Negro Mother in parts 2 and 3. By coming last, her figure receives emphasis. We have observed that in part 2 the woman is the seed of an emerging free race. Thus, she becomes one with her children, who are young and free. Similarly, the black woman's advice in part 3 displays both her courage and the tie between a woman and her descendants: "Stand like free men" (l. 42). The banner that she urges her offspring to lift shares the firmness of her imperative verb: "stand." Part 1 also makes clear the mother's place in the lineage of black people. Through internal rhyme, the color of her face (l. 5) blends with the history of the race (l. 4).

Several of Hughes's other poems about women preceded or followed "The Negro Mother." "Mother to Son" is probably the most famous of the early poems and the "Madam Poems" the most memorable of the later ones. The image of woman operates throughout these poems in at least eleven different ways, which are not always separable:

1. Signalling stories about yesterday and about surviving adversity
2. Presenting an opportunity to admire the splendor of youth now departed
3. Characterizing a folk life-style full of flare and color
4. Offering a portrait of trouble, when the woman portrayed cannot transcend adversity
5. Indicating absorption which becomes a means of transcendence
6. Working to create a heavy but affirmative tone in which character sublimates suffering into art
7. Making clear a character's comically serious confrontation with mortality
8. Emphasizing the situation of a deserted wife and of a matriarchal society
9. Communicating heroic determination
10. Becoming a tool for expressing weariness with the racial struggle
11. Functioning as a means for presenting racial themes either by comic recollections of character or by dramatic dialogue

The poems themselves illustrate these different functions. Within Hughes's complete poetic edifice, the title characters in "Aunt Sue's Stories" and "Mexican Market Woman" are foils. Having survived adversity, Aunt Sue tells a black boy stories about the past. Although she tells them as fiction, he knows that they are true. Unlike Aunt Sue, Mexican Market Woman remembers the joy of her past. The female figure in "Troubled Woman" is not as transcendent as Aunt Sue. Nevertheless, Hughes achieves rhythmic success in "Troubled Woman" by combining iambic, anapestic, and trochaic feet. The effect is a religious chant which suggests a subdued form of the black folk sermon.

In other poems by Hughes, the female image serves to reveal major motifs. At first, the figure in "Strange Hurt" probably strikes the reader as being masochistic. Apparently, some man has deserted this woman. Having lost love, or a part of spiritual reality, she becomes indifferent to physical reality. She finds, therefore, ". . . rain better/Than shelter from the rain" (ll. 4–5) and seeks the ". . . burning sunlight/Rather than the shade" (ll. 9–10). Her wandering naked in the cold at the end of the poem intensifies a sense of loss.

This poem becomes a remarkable display of absorption: the ability to take on the fear of suffering but to transcend it through confrontation. Burning sunlight and snowy winter become metaphors of the bodily harm which black Americans face. To stand without fear against the elements, therefore, is to be free of spirit. One could probably infer from our discussion thus far that Hughes often dresses in varying tones the archetypal image of woman: interrogative but affirmative, comic, sad, uncertain, and angry. In "Midnight Dancer" the tone is affirmative and heavy, although the narrator asks the dancer, "Who crushed/The grapes of joy/And dripped their juice/On you" (ll. 7–10). Lighter in tone, "Widow Woman" presents a character's comic, but also serious, confrontation with mortality. This persona does not want anyone to replace her late husband. If we believe her, moreover, nobody wants to marry her either. Still, the lady humorously raises doubt at the end: "*Yet you never can tell/When a woman like me is free.*"

For contrast, one should juxtapose "Widow Woman" and "Cora." If the former shows Hughes's comic spirit, the latter lays bare his tragic one. In one reading, indeed, "Cora" becomes an allegorical treatment of the racial dilemma: Is a chance at true love worth the risk of renewed despair? In blues rhythm, Cora realistically tells the story of her love-life. Allegorically, however, she represents her race. A man broke Cora's heart this morning, and she denies the possibility of her trying love again. Yet her tone suggests a tantrum more than a certitude. Hughes's analogy to the black race here is subtle, but sure. Like Cora, it pouts. It tires, moreover, from an irreparable hurt or the burden of seeking humanity. But perhaps blacks will try again. The secret lies in Cora's tone. Is this a tantrum or a resolution?

> Next time a man comes near me
> gonna shut an lock my door
> Cause they treat me mean—
> The ones I love.
> They always treat me mean.
>
> (ll. 3–7)

Hughes incorporated in his poetic treatment of women the traditional archetype of the Divine Mother. Through the years he transformed this, with major or minor revisions, into diverse female portraits: heroic, comic, and despairing. By observing Hughes's various transformations of the female archetype, one can understand why the quality of his poetry deteriorated. As the years wore on, the poet could no longer wrap the figure of woman in religious myth. To him, woman became more secular.

In part, the change is owing to Hughes's own diminishing optimism. "Southern Mammy" (1940s) bridges "Mother to Son" (1920s) and "Down Where I Am" (1950s–1960s). The movement is from energetic hope to overpowering fatigue. Note, for instance, that the tone and sense of "Down Where I Am" differs from that of the two poems with which we began. The persona's sex here is neutral:

> Too many years
> Climbin that hill
> 'Bout out of breath
> I got my fill
> I'm gonna plant my feet
> On solid ground
> If you want to see me
> Come down.
>
> (ll. 9–16)

Thus ends Hughes's black presentation of the mythic archetype. To some despairing and comic transformations of a traditional figure, the poet has sacrificed his folk version of a religious image. "Southern Mammy" again marks the turning point, for Hughes uses the female figure here to express a motif of spiritual exhaustion. The black character is disillusioned because whites hanged a "colored boy." The child's only crime was stating that people should be free.

"Southern Mammy" unifies this poem by being a foil to "Miss Gardner," "Miss Yardman," and "Miss Michaelmas." Each of these last three women personifies her place of habitation. But having no place, the black woman is alienated. Racially and symbolically, she has seen the death of her sons; literally, she has witnessed the needless murder of one black youth. Her tone lacks the determination that the Black Mother had in the nineteen twenties and thirties. Thus disenchanted, the Southern Mammy prefaces an atmosphere of war and death: "I am gettin tired!/Lawd/I am gettin tired" (ll. 5–6).

The "Madam Poems" restore a comic sense to the archetype, but they eliminate the mythic level. Often the Madam verses embody folk themes in dialogue. At least one, "Madam and the Phone Bill," uses dramatic monologue. The thematic range of the collection includes the following: nationalism, self-reliance, and self-doubt. Here humor and worldly vision supplant myth.

Langston Hughes's "Mother to Son" and "Negro Mother," however, combine Christian myth and folk experience. In them the poet deals with a problem of religious belief and thus becomes one of several American poets to do so. Our literary artists have believed (or disbelieved) in God, the American Dream, the Power of Transcendence, or the American Myth. Edward Taylor and William Cullen Bryant believed in God. Emerson believed in transcendence, and his contemporary, Whitman, believed in himself. Whitman also had faith in a poetic power that could rejuvenate the world or that could at least reinvigorate the world through enthusiastic perception. Wallace Stevens, humanistic like Whitman, believed more in man than in External Divinity. To Stevens, indeed, man *was* divinity, since divinity must "live within herself." Closer still to our time, T. S. Eliot has restored to our poetry a sense of the Externally Divine. Even more recently, Allen Ginsberg has laughed at American myth by saying that he is putting his "queer shoulder" to the country's wheel.

But no American poet, I think, combines myth and pragmatism better than Hughes does in the poems presenting matriarchal archetypes. Indeed, Hughes himself will never do so again. In the 1950s he will turn his attention more to prose than to poetry. Returning to the writing of verse in the sixties, he will miss his once lyrical gift. Slowly but surely social injustice whittles away hopeful vision.

Fortunately Hughes left to posterity his earlier image of the black woman who can tell stories about her yesterdays. She sometimes becomes a means of discoursing on youth, which is gone forever, while at other times, unable to transcend adversity, she becomes a personified portrait of trouble, occasionally sublimated into art. We must sometimes laugh at her confrontation with mortality, at her attempts to transcend adversity, if only to avoid crying at her weariness, at the bitterness surrounding the racial quest. But ultimately we must admire her incarnate heroic determination, the Black Spirit.

MARTHA COBB

# Langston Hughes

The literary career of Langston Hughes spans more than forty-five years of rich productivity. He was born in Joplin, Missouri, in 1902; his first poem, "The Negro Speaks of Rivers," appeared in *The Crisis* magazine in June, 1921, and his last works, including *The Panther and the Lash* and the collection *The Best Short Stories by Negro Writers*, were published in 1967, the year of his death. Although Hughes came of middle-class parentage, he had a lonely and difficult childhood. After his parents' divorce, he moved from place to place, his loyalties divided between them. Several summers were spent in Mexico with his father, who had settled there in order to avoid racial segregation in the United States. While in Mexico Hughes learned Spanish which became the foundation of his later proficiency in the language, both as a speaker and translator. He was fluent in both Spanish and French and as a consequence translated works of Nicolás Guillén and Jacques Roumain into English.

When Hughes was a young man he arrived in Washington, D.C., to live with members of his mother's family. In Washington he reacted negatively to the middle-class pretensions of many of its black citizens who lived, ironically, in the segregated neighborhoods of the nation's capital. By 1926 Langston Hughes had moved to New York City where his life and works became closely associated with the Negro, or Harlem, Renaissance. Of the many writers associated with the movement, Langston Hughes is without doubt one of the most significant. The feeling of its independence, its freedom from the need of white approval, and its thrust toward self-expression are underlined by Hughes: "We younger Negroes who create,"

From *Harlem, Haiti, and Havana.* © 1979 by Three Continents Press.

he asserted in 1926, "now intend to express our individual dark-skinned selves without fear of shame. If white people are pleased we are glad. If they are not, it doesn't matter. We know we are beautiful. And ugly, too. If colored people are pleased we are glad. If they are not, their displeasure doesn't matter either. We build our temples for tomorrow, strong as we know how, and we stand on top of the mountain, free within ourselves."

Remarkable for the time in which this statement was issued, it clearly defines Hughes's own position with respect to both his art and his race, one which he maintains throughout a long literary career. He experimented with forms and techniques, was successful in several literary genres, but never deviated from the centrality of presenting the black world from the point of view of a man speaking from within the many manifestations of its experiences.

When "The Negro Speaks of Rivers" appeared in print it projected a proud image of black life, that of a black man relating to African history with pride and to "soul," defined as African or black, that gave him a reassuring sense of identity. It ends with lines that leave no doubt concerning racial affirmation. As we see later, it can profitably be compared to Jacques Roumain's "Sur le chemin de Guinée" ("On the Road to Guinea") or to Nicolás Guillén's "Son Número 6," which begins "I am Yoruba. . . ." In this vein, Hughes writes:

> I bathed in the Euphratres when dawns were young.
> I built my hut near the Congo and it lulled me to sleep.
> I looked upon the Nile and raised the pyramids above it.
>
> . . . . . . . . . . . . . . . . . . . . . . . . .
> I've known rivers;
> Ancient, dusky rivers.
> My soul has grown deep like the rivers.

Other poems expanding on this theme appeared in his first published collection, *The Weary Blues*. One of them, "For the Portrait of an African Boy after the Manner of Gauguin," implicates a more primitive and, by poetic assumption, a superior way of life to whose appeal the poet admits responding:

> All the tom toms of the jungle beat in my blood.
> And all the wild hot moons of the jungle shine in my soul
> I am afraid of this civilization
>   So hard,
>     So strong
>       So cold.

The last lines introduce a mood that is reflected in much of the poetry written in this era, not only by black writers but by white. The search for a freer, more genuine and human way of life to counteract the cold abstractions of an industrial civilization had already appeared in European ninteenth-century Romantic poetry. The catastrophic First World War stimulated a search for new values which accounted for the interest in Negroes and Africa.

Black writers of the twentieth century reflected a similar dissatisfaction with their present life, but for different reasons. Racial humiliations, violence, and injustice, compounded by economic misery, caused them to romanticize a racial past centered in feelings for Africa as the only real home for black people. An expression of this interest was the Marcus Garvey movement to resettle black people in Africa, a plan that captured the imaginations of many in the 1920s, especially those in Eastern urban centers. Its antecedents reached back to the late eighteenth and early nineteenth centuries when free blacks called themselves *African* Americans and set up institutions with Africa in the title—the Free African Society (1787), Africa Free School (opened New York City, 1787), the African Methodist Episcopal Church (organized 1816), and so on. The back-to-Africa theme has persisted in African-American life, including its conception by mid-nineteenth-century leaders such as John B. Russwurm, Martin Delaney, Robert Campbell, Edward Blyden, many of whom became involved in the establishment and settling of Liberia. Whether in the eighteenth century or the twentieth century, among black people the persistent dream of Africa has been more than a romantic urge to find a primitive Garden of Eden. For many it has meant nothing less than the promise of liberation from the abrasive contact with the West.

For black writers the imaginative expression of the African theme has had several dimensions. Among them have been the rejection of European cultural values and lament for a land that slavery has robbed blacks of, thematic concepts also found in the poetry of Jacques Roumain and Nicolás Guillén. In a poem he called "Black Seed" Hughes describes "World-wide dusk/Of dear dark faces/Driven before an alien wind/Scattered like seed . . . /In another's garden." He underscores the violence of the diaspora in subsequent lines—"Cut by the shears/Of the white-faced gardeners/—Tell them to leave you alone."

Jacques Roumain, in his poetic description of "the long road to Guinée" employs similar imagery to emphasize the sense of loss, confrontation with an alien society, and the need to reject that society's imposition. Additionally, an "elegy" by Nicolás Guillén alludes with bitterness to the separation of black people from their ancestral home, pointedly describing the cruelty of the slave trade: "Along the sea roads/with the jasmin and the bull,/and with grain and iron/came the black man, to dig out the gold;/weeping in his exile/along the sea road."

To call the black point of view romantic in its nostalgia for a mythologized Africa, or unrealistic in its opposition to a culture that dominated it, is not to assess fully the obliquity of the perspective from which black poets could not escape as they looked out from within racial experiences onto a world that rejected their race. The poetry of alienation, lament, exile, and bitter memories which expresses a mythic image of Africa is part of a larger pattern which presents the black man as victim, outcast, and to a great extent scapegoat of Western civilization. Poetry on the subject of the slave trade embodies a racial memory which sings bitterly of blacks building a civilization whose benefits they do not share. Africa therefore becomes the *locus amoenus* where the victim/scapegoat becomes ideally reinstated as human being. This perception points to a major cleavage from the popular sentimental point of view, shared by most whites and some blacks, which sees the black as embodiment of either primitive innocence in its natural state, or of primitive—sometimes called "exotic"—passions whose jazz would release the industrialized West from the confinements of its inhibitions or from the madness of its wars. It was against this use of blacks as playthings and puppets that Guillén warned in "Pequeña oda a un negro boxeador" ("Small Ode to a Black Boxer") and that two other writers of Afro-Cuban poetry, Regino Pedroso and Marcelino Arozarena, denounced in "Hermano negro" ("Black Brother") and "Evohé" respectively.

In the first volume of his autobiography Hughes attacks the romantic view of the Negro as he describes the parting between himself and a wealthy patroness:

> She wanted me to be primitive and know and feel the intuitions
> of the primitive. But, unfortunately, I did not feel the rhythms
> of the primitive surging through me, and so I could not live and
> write as though I did. I was only an American Negro—who had
> loved the surface of Africa—but I was not Africa. I was Chicago
> and Kansas City and Broadway and Harlem. And I was not what
> she wanted me to be.

Other black writers during the era of the Harlem Renaissance were not as sure of their position on Africa and the cult of the primitive as Hughes, Roumain or Guillén. The dual pull between cultures is expressed in the contradictions that Countee Cullen finds within himself as he asks "What is Africa to me/Copper sun or scarlet sea/One three centuries removed/from the scenes his fathers loved,/Spicy grove, cinammon tree,/ What is Africa to me?" And Haitian poet Léon Laleau expresses ambivalences from a somewhat different point of view:

> And this despair like nothing else
> To tame, with words from France,
> This heart which came to me from Senegal.

Langston Hughes is less concerned with drums throbbing in his blood than with the black man's repossession of his own identity, when in "Afro-American Fragment" he recalls that "Subdued and time lost/Are the drums—and yet/Through some vast mist of race/There comes this song/I do not understand,/... So long,/So far away/Is Africa's/Dark face." Similar sensitivity to the need for both spiritual and geographical *place* for black people appears in one of Hughes's "dream variations."

> To fling my arms wide
> In some place of the sun,
> To whirl and to dance
> Till the white day is done.
> Then rest at cool evening
> Beneath a tall tree
> While night comes on gently,
>     Dark like me—
> That is my dream.

Although Africa is not named in the poem, the last four lines suggest its presence not merely as a place but as a symbol of idealized uncorrupted beauty that nature offers: "Rest at pale evening ... /A tall, slim tree ... / Night coming tenderly/Black like me." Here the poet has identified darkness and coolness and night with the beauty of a place, conceivably Africa, that is meant for black people.

In another poem images of a people that reflect the most compelling symbols of natural beauty are presented in six lines which anticipate by more than thirty years the "black is beautiful" concept that swept the 1960s:

> The night is beautiful,
> So the faces of my people
> The stars are beautiful
> So the eyes of my people
> Beautiful, also, is the sun.
> Beautiful, also, are the souls of my people.

Hughes experimented with poetic form in "When Sue Wears Red" with an interesting presentation of the beauty of a black woman in a blend of African imagery with gospel hymn refrain:

> Her face is like an ancient cameo
> Turned brown by the ages

Then the refrain:

> Come with a blast of trumpets,
> Jesus!

And:

> When Susanna Jones wears red
> A queen from some time-dead Egyptian night
> Walks once again
> Blow trumpets, Jesus!

He concludes with a lyrical evocation, "the beauty of Susanna Jones in red/ Burns in my heart a love-fire sharp like pain," which he emphasizes in the joyful gospel shout:

> Sweet silver trumpets,
> Jesus!

Interest in Africa and in racial origins led Hughes, as it did Roumain and Guillén, to a consideration of the mixed heritage, the mulatto theme that is so prevalent in literature written by blacks or about them. In the poem "Cross" Hughes's poetic narrator delivers a scathing denunciation of both branches of his ancestral tree, cursing his white father and black mother, then raising an ironic question:

> My old man died in a fine big house.
> My ma died in a shack.
> I wonder where I'm gonna die,
> Being neither white nor black.

This poem is one of the few in which Hughes explicitly raises the issue of duality, and where the mixed racial heritage creates bitter self-doubts. In dealing with the sense of dualism, Langston Hughes is more like Guillén than Roumain, who struggled with the duality of France and Haiti within himself before he reversed his position with an almost total rejection of European values. Hughes presents another aspect of the motif of duality which deals with the speaker's attitudes toward his country rather than with personal tensions. "I, Too, Sing America" serves as an example of his perspective:

> I am the darker brother.
> They send me to eat in the kitchen
> When company comes,
> But I laugh,
> And eat well,
> And grow strong.

Unlike "Cross," this poem is without rancor, and promises that "Tomorrow,/I'll sit at the table/When company comes." In the end the poet affirms a sense of racial dignity which rejects the dual tensions implicit in the word "too" of the title and the refrain:

> They'll see how beautiful I am
> And be ashamed,—
> I, too, am American.

Hughes's poetic exploration of black identity and racial pride led to a considerable, and quite understandable, romanticizing of Africa and the poetic themes connected with it. In his observation of the daily struggles of black people and their responses to life, Hughes found another thematic pattern for presenting the black experience—the use of blues, spirituals and jazz as poetic reference and poetic medium for describing the daily existence that black men and women confronted. Again Hughes's tendency was to stress the colorful aspects (an over-emphasis that appeared to characterize Harlem Renaissance writing) to the neglect of the plain, hard-pressed people of the working world, who came home too tired from cleaning and cooking and day labor to spend nights in Harlem clubs. Hughes was well aware of the workaday aspect of the urban scene, which poems like "Mother to Son," and "Brass Spittoons" present, and on which his poetry of social rebellion will elaborate. He chose, however, the material with which he was most familiar during the decade of the twenties, and described an equally valid aspect of Harlem, its streetlife and its night people, among whom were many of the young workers who could indeed labor all day and dance the charleston all night. Many of these people were new to Harlem, transplants from the rural South, a part of the great northern migration of black people that had gained increased momentum after the First World War. Hughes understood that in confronting a new kind of life these people soon realized they had not escaped the disease of racism from which they had fled. He understood their need for release in music and dance, and even as he describes the colorfulness and the noise, the movement, the slang, and the jazz horns, there is a note of sadness in his poetry, like the blues, which many of the titles convey: "Misery," "Suicide," "Death of Do Dirty," "Homesick Blues," "Midwinter Blues," "Po' Boy Blues," and many more.

In his autobiography *The Big Sea* Hughes describes his early interest in the black masses—the folk—whom he preferred to the elite few to whom he was connected by family ties. In relating his life in Washington, D.C., he tells of leaving the neighborhood where prominent Afro-Americans lived to search out the sights and sounds of Seventh Street where he knew he would find a more down-to-earth people:

> From all this pretentiousness Seventh Street was a sweet relief. Seventh Street is the long, old, dirty street, where the ordinary Negroes hang out, folks with practically no family tree at all, folks who draw no color line between mulattoes and deep dark-browns, folks who work hard for a living with their hands. On Seventh Street in 1924 they played the blues, ate watermelon, barbecue, and fish sandwiches, played pool, told tall tales, looked at the dome of the Capitol and laughed out loud. I listened to their blues:
>
> *Did you ever dream lucky—*
> *Wake up cold in hand?*
>
> And I went to their churches and heard the tambourines play and the little tinkling bells of the triangles adorn the gay shouting tunes that sent sisters dancing down the aisles for joy.

Hughes's ear for the sounds of the urban street and his eye for its sights were essential in the formation of his poetic tastes. An active curiosity which led him to mingle with people deepened his sensitivity toward those of the lowest strata of human society. He learned to respect the dynamism inherent in their struggle to survive. They had little control over the problematic in their lives since the real world they dealt with was imposed by a social system which all but dispossessed them of their humanity. Their experience was in the immediate and the concrete—meeting the landlord's rent, trying to find one of the menial jobs they were limited to, trying to scrape enough money for food, for liquor to take away some of the pain, dealing with the snubs and humiliations that the color of their skin drew on them. He heard their songs and knew that these were an accessible means of combatting the odds piled up against them:

I tried to write poems like the songs they sang on Seventh Street—
gay songs, because you had to be gay or die; sad songs, because
you couldn't help being sad sometimes. But gay or sad, you kept
on living and you kept on going. Their songs—those of Seventh
Street—had the pulse beat of people who keep on going.

Hughes's first collection of poems, *The Weary Blues,* is distinguished
for its use of blues, spirituals and jazz references in poetry. It set the tone
for an entire literary career. A second book appeared in 1927 under the
title *Fine Clothes to the Jew.* Here too the blues predominate and Hughes
has undertaken to translate the cadences, rhythms, and the measured beat
and off-beat of the blues song into the printed word. To make his intent
clear, in *Fine Clothes to the Jew* he writes "A Note on Blues" as preface
to his text:

The first eight and the last nine poems in this book are written
after the manner of the Negro folksongs known as Blues. The
Blues, unlike the *Spirituals,* have a strict poetic pattern: one long
line repeated and a third line to rhyme with the first two. Sometimes the second line in repetition is slightly changed and sometimes, but very seldom, it is omitted. The mood of the *Blues* is
almost despondency, but when they are sung people laugh.

The difficulty would appear insurmountable for bringing one mode of
artistic presentation (the musical instrument or the voice) into harmonious
relationship with another (the printed poem). The blues soloist surrounded
by an audience uses gesture, facial and body movements to draw meanings
from the simple and repetitive narration. Or, the saxophone solo is pure
sound whose music conveys the notes of despair or gaiety within the conventions agreed upon by both soloist and audience. However, fusions, syn-
aesthesia, correspondences were not new to poetry. Baudelaire, for instance,
suggested in his poetry that "Les parfums, les couleurs et les sons se ré-
pondent" (Perfumes, colors and sounds correspond). And Edgar Allan Poe,
whom Baudelaire admired, attempted a similar poetry of sounds, fused with
meanings, notably in "The Bells." Hughes was equally the experimenter.
He used the image-making powers of black speech, the rhythms of its
sounds, to bring a way of life into existence through the movements of a
song. For the blues, like the spirituals, was poetry set to music within the
confines of a circumscribed form, and he used the blues form—the phrasing,
the break in the line, the beat—to realize its effects. For him, "The rhythm
of life is a jazz rhythm."

Where Guillén was to use Africanisms, repetitive drum beats, alliter-ations and shouts in the short lines of Spanish popular art to effect the movements of his early poetry, which he called *son* poems, and Roumain was to evoke a poetry of creole speech through the blend of two languages, Hughes used the black idiom of the United States to reproduce the blue note of melancholy, or to shift to ironic laughter, while following the metric pattern of the song. Hughes, Roumain and Guillén achieved their singular success by allowing the narrator's voice to come through the poetry of blues, creole patois, and *son* in language that characterized the ordinary people of Harlem, Haiti, and Havana. An example of the design which identifies the blues in Hughes's poetry is "Young Gal's Blues":

> When love is gone what
> Can a young gal do?
> When love is gone, O,
> What can a young gal do?
> Keep on a-lovin' me, daddy,
> Cause I don't want to be blue.

We are reminded here of blues samplings from the oral-aural tradition pointed out earlier in this study, for instance, "I hate to hear my honey call me so lonesome an' sad . . ." in which the "blue note" carries the melancholy theme.

Other examples of poems inspired by the blues follow the same thematic arrangement of parts. The element of hope seldom finds expression except indirectly in steps taken to remove oneself from a familiar situation and head toward an unknown and presumably better life. Thus the "Bound No'th Blues," beginning:

> Goin' down de road, Lawd,
> Goin' down de road.
> Down de road, Lawd,
> Way, way down de road.
> Got to find somebody
> To help me carry dis load.

Concurrent with his blues poems, Hughes was writing poetry that expressed the feelings and the meaning of the Negro spirituals he admired. They can be identified on three levels: by the setting the poet designates, by the use of words within biblical context and imagery, and by language that suggests the religious sentiment of the spirituals. "Prayer Meeting" presents a more hopeful aspect of black life than the blues, greatly dependent on trust in the church and religion:

> Glory! Halleluiah!
> De dawn's a-comin'
> Glory! Halleluiah!
> A black woman croons
> In the amen-corner of the
> Ebecanezer Baptist Church
> A black old woman croons,
> De dawn's a-comin!

Or, in "Feet o' Jesus"—

> At de feet o' Jesus
> Sorrow like a sea
> Lordy, let yo' mercy
> Come driftin' down on me.

And sometimes his poetry captures the gospel shout that expresses the rapture of religious fervor, again comparable to the anonymous folk expression that this study has previously referred to. Hughes writes:

> Listen to yo' prophets
> Little Jesus!
> Listen to yo' saints!

This association of song and shout with religion, prevalent in black folk life in the United States, has its counterpart in the works of Jacques Roumain which present *Vaudou* in its Haitian setting and the works of Nicolás Guillén that deal with the African-based Santeria and the processions of the Nañigos in Cuba. In Hughes, Roumain and Guillén there is deep sensitivity toward religion, which has sustained black people in their respective countries. None of them subscribed personally to religious practice, but each perceived it as a valid life experience that they wanted to capture in their writing. Thus religion is one more common denominator in the poetry of Hughes, Roumain and Guillén as each recognized its significance in black life. Their poetry reflects its uses: it enabled blacks to confront the confusion and instability that they faced in their lives; it gave a sense of dignity and humanity through its link to an all-powerful Creator; it served as emotional release. The question of whether this is good or bad, palliative or stimulus, is not the concern of poetry except as the poet chooses to weave it into his theme, as Roumain did in his repudiation of Western culture.

With the appearance of *Fine Clothes to the Jew*, which included blues presentations of the struggles of poor blacks and jazz poetry about the life of urban blacks who frequented cabarets, street corners and bars, Hughes encountered strongly worded negative criticism, especially from the black press and the middle-class Negro. The gist of the critical reaction dealt with the poet's persistence in displaying what was designated the seamy side of the lowest class of black people in his poetry instead of the life of the self-proclaimed better class of Negroes. One black newspaper called Hughes's book "trash," another called the poet a "sewer dweller," still another named him "the poet lowrate of Harlem." Our interest in the controversy lies mainly in Hughes's response in the form of an imaginary interview, which informally states his poetic theory. He says, in response to those who attack him for not using conventional forms, that "I do not write chiefly because I'm interested in forms—in making a sonnet or a rondeau . . . I choose the form which seems to me best to express my thoughts . . . Certainly the Shakespearian sonnet would be no mould in which to express life on Beale Street or Lenox Avenue . . . I am not interested in doing tricks with rhymes. I am interested in reproducing the human soul if I can." And in response to the attack that Hughes dealt with low life, he replied, "Is life among the better classes cleaner or any more worthy of a poet's consideration?" Poems carrying the titles "Beale Street Love," "A Ruined Gal," "Minnie Sings Her Blues," are examples of the discredited subject matter. "Red Silk Stockings" especially angered Negro newspaper critics and many among the Negro professional classes:

> Put on yo' red silk stockings,
> Black gal.
> Go out and let the white boys
>     look at yo' legs.
> Ain't nothin' to do for you, nohow.
> Round this town—
> You's too pretty.
> Put on yo' red silk stockings, gal,
> An' tomorrow's chile'll
> Be a high yaller.

The poem is an early indication of Hughes's mastery of the ironic mode. Behind the image of a fun-loving girl in red silk stockings are the grim themes of poverty, racial discrimination, prostitution and illegitimacy.

Jazz poems, increasingly important in Hughes's works, first appeared in *Fine Clothes to the Jew*. Techniques for transferring musical forms, blues, spirituals and gospel, to the printed page are continued in Hughes's jazz poetry. In accordance with verbal devices he had worked out, Hughes handles black music as poetic resource in one of three ways, sometimes with formal arrangements overlapping each other in the same poem. First, music is recreated directly in verse—in phrasing, rhythms, metric beat, riffs and breaks. Next, the language of music and song is used as reference, such as "play that thing," "da-da-dee-da-da" (in spirituals—"at de feet o' Jesus"), or else music is announced in the title: "Young Singer," "Blues Fantasy," "Dream Boogie," and so on. Lastly, music is dramatically arranged by means of stage directions printed alongside the poem to indicate musical movements used, for instance, in "Ask Your Mama: 12 Moods for Jazz."

Whatever the musical resource used, the poetry generally treats of urban folk life. The setting of Hughes's music poems, in the manner of Roumain's recreation of *coumbite* songs and *Vaudou* chants, and Guillén's *son* poetry, is associated with a background of voices, noise, music, shouts, which imply that dancing is in progress. Music and dance ordinarily suggest a mood of excitement and a release of happy emotions connected with entertainment and pleasure, and on one level this is what Hughes's jazz poems reveal. However, they persistently maintain undertones that range from the ironic perception of self as victim (while dancing the charleston, for example) to the bitter recognition of another "dream deferred"—a poetic theme that permeates Hughes's jazz poetry as a low-key form of social criticism. The poems create images of black people who appear to personify the stereotypes that Western assumptions have postulated, but behind the jazz Hughes reveals the concerns of people caught in realities of the city milieu. Moods are conveyed in the asides and shouts, by explicit racial references, or in the commentary of the poet-observer. Four poems that combine verbal techniques and themes dealing with jazz aspects of the black experience are "Song for a Banjo Dance," "Jazz Band in a Parisian Cabaret," "Trumpet Player—52nd Street," and "Jazzonia."

The first poem opens in a jazz and dance setting:

> Shake your brown feet, honey,
> Shake 'em swift and wil'—
>   Get way back, honey,
>   Do that low-down step,
>   Walk on over, darling,

> Now! Come out
> With your left.
> Shake your brown feet, honey,
> Shake 'em, honey chile.

The second stanza suggests the *carpe diem* topos which is the theme of the poem:

> Sun's going down this evening—
> Might never rise no mo' (repeated with variations),
> So dance with swift feet, honey
> (The banjo's sobbing low)
> Dance with swift feet, honey—
> Might never dance no mo'.

And the poem ends in encouragement to dance with the idea implanted that there's very little future in sight (poetic motif which reinforces investigations on the brevity of ghetto life, especially for the black male):

> Shake your brown feet, Liza,
>     (the banjo's sobbing low)
> The sun's going down this very night—
>     Might never rise no mo'.

"Jazz Band in a Parisian Cabaret" evokes the essence of the Harlem Renaissance while interpreting a racial point of view in reaction to white enjoyment of jazz. The opening lines set the mood in the use of one of the favorite shouts of jazz enthusiasts: "Play that thing, Jazz band!" The narrative voice comments ironically on playing for "the dukes and counts,/For the whores and gigolos,/For the American millionaires,/and the school teachers/Out for a spree." Momentarily, the narrator reveals his assessment of the situation: "You know that tune/That laughs and cries at the same time." Then the speaker reverts to dialect—"Can I go home wid yuh, sweetie," obviously addressed to a white female onlooker—in a mocking reminder of the sexual taboos of racism, even in a foreign land where black men play to a white audience. The sardonic monosyllable that ends the poem both underlines this perception and serves as musical coda to the jazz structure of the total poem.

> Play it, jazz band!
> You've got seven languages to speak in
> And then some,
> Even if you do come from Georgia.

Can I go home wid yuh, sweetie?
Sure.

"Jazzonia" and "Trumpet Player—52nd Street" are less musical poems in verbal techniques than pictorial descriptions of the relationship of music and dance to the sensibilities of black people. "Jazzonia" begins, "Oh, silver tree!/Oh, shining rivers of the soul!" The poem then describes the "Six long-headed jazzers" who play "in a Harlem cabaret," while a dancing girl who "lifts high a dress of silken gold" is compared to Cleopatra in a "gown of gold . . ." However it is the variations on the refrain, one of which I have indicated begins the poem, that underscore Hughes's attempt to capture a current of black life that runs deep under the outer display of jazz skills: "Oh, singing tree!/Oh, shining rivers of the soul."

"Trumpet Player—52nd Street" uses images drawn from the real world of black life to create the sense of an inner world at odds with the noise and blare of night clubs. Thus it begins:

> The Negro
> With the trumpet at his lips
> Has dark moons of weariness
> Beneath his eyes
> Where the smoldering memory
> Of slave ships
> Blazed to the crack of whips
> About the thighs.

And concludes with the image of "The Negro/With the trumpet at his lips. . . ."

> Does not know upon what riff the music slips
> Its hypodermic needle
> To his soul—
>
> But softly
> As the tune comes from his throat
> Trouble
> Mellows to a golden note.

Two works mark a high point in Hughes's fusion of poetry and jazz, *Montage of a Dream Deferred*, and *Ask Your Mama: 12 Moods for Jazz*. The poem "Dream Boogie," which comes from the first work, translates a very special type of jazz and dance, popular in the 1940s, into poetic form which insinuates ironic commentary on the disillusionment of Black Americans after the Second World War. The poem begins,

> Good morning daddy!
> Ain't you heard,
> The boogie-woogie rumble
> of a dream deferred?

Despite the serious implications of the poem, Hughes maintains the fast rhythmic movement, the phrasing, and the break of the music:

> Listen closely:
> You'll hear their feet
> Beating out and beating out a—
>     You think
>         It's a happy beat?
> Listen to it closely:
> Ain't you heard
> Something underneath
> Like a—
>     What did I say?

The rhythmic structure adhering to a popular musical beat is designed to present the paradox of the stereotyped/song-and-dance black who understands perfectly what his life is really like.

> Sure,
> I'm happy!
> Take it away!
>     Hey, pop!
>     Be-Bop!
>     Mop
>     Y-e-a-h!

Musical rhythms are equally essential to *Ask Your Mama*. In this volume of poetry Hughes appears to pull together the many threads of his poetic experimentation in order to introduce a style that correlates the sounds and rhythms of music with the printed word. The first edition, 1961, is in the format of a colorful album in which the texts are printed in capitals. To make clear his intent, Hughes dedicated the book to Louis Armstrong. Its title comes out of the plain talk of black people, a method of denigrating, "putting down" or "bad talking" someone, "playing the dozens," which can lead to high emotional reaction. Like jazz music, "the dozens" follows a basic pattern, but much of its brilliance depends on a set style within the improvisation, the quick retort, and timing. Hughes thus draws on a particular in-group experience to present jazz moods which reflect responses to the deep inner anxieties of an always pressing outer reality. Stage directions in the manner of Vachel Lindsay accompany the poems in vertical columns. In the title poem, the opening lines set the scene for a confrontation:

> FROM THE SHADOWS OF THE QUARTER
> SHOUTS ARE WHISPERS CARRYING
> TO THE FARTHEREST CORNERS
> OF THE NOW KNOWN WORLD:
> 5TH AND MOUND IN CINCI, 63RD IN CHI,
> 23RD AND CENTRAL, 18TH STREET AND VINE.
> I'VE WRITTEN, CALLED REPEATEDLY,
> EVEN RUNG THIS BELL ON SUNDAY, YET
> YOUR THIRD-TENANT'S NEVER HOME.
> DID YOU TELL HER THAT OUR CREDIT
>          OFFICE
> HAS NO RECOURSE NOW BUT TO THE LAW?

And then the black retort to the exigency:

> YES, SIR, I TOLD HER.
> WHAT DID SHE SAY?
> SAID, TELL YOUR MA.

The problem is unresolved, the rent unpaid, but the response ("the dozens") comes quickly for dealing with a situation in which there is no solution because there is no money: "Tell your ma."

The close of the 1920s had marked the end of the popular vogue for Negro music, writing, dancing. On October 29, 1929, came the collapse of the stock market. By 1931 unemployment among black people was widespread. In his autobiography Hughes records his personal condition wryly. "When I was twenty-eight my personal crash came. . . . Now I found myself in the midst of a depression. I had just lost my patron. Scholarships, fellowships and literary prizes became scarce. . . . The WPA had not yet come into being." Other events of the 1930s moved Langston Hughes to write in an increasingly polemical vein both in poetry and in prose. In 1931 the Scottsboro trials became a *cause célèbre* in the United States. The unjust condemnation of nine black youths in an alleged rape incident on a freight train in Alabama aroused the indignation of leading writers in the United

States and of white and non-white people in many other parts of the world. Another disaster preoccupying Hughes was the Spanish Civil War, which began in 1936. In the company of Nicolás Guillén, he went to Spain as war correspondent, where what he observed and what he felt are described in some of his most bitter verse. From the 1930s onward into the 1950s, Hughes's poetry and prose focused on the concept of liberation. From his pen issued the poetry of social protest; his works increasingly reflected his sensitivity to the conditions around him. Moreover, caught in the despair of the times, he began to move away from racial materials and write about the class struggle from a largely communist-inspired perspective which stressed capitalist exploitation, unemployment, poverty.

During the decade of the thirties Hughes's published poetry was limited to three collections—*Dear Lovely Death, Scottsboro Limited,* and *A New Song.* The first of these appeared in 1931 and with the title poem set a mood in sharp contrast to his jazz poetry of the 1920s. "Dear lovely death" the speaking voice begins, "That taketh all things under wing, . . ." and somberly concludes ". . . Change is thy other name." Here one notes Hughes's change in theme and technique, no doubt reflecting the sensibility of the poet to the disasters of the 1930s, which Afro-Americans in particular had to confront.

*Scottsboro Limited,* published in 1932, consisted of four poems and a play which were more directly critical. The poems reflect his despair over Alabama justice, his criticism of the handling of the young black men in the case, and his cynicism with respect to the morality of the white girls who were allegedly violated. One of his poems, "Justice," illustrates his bitter expectations of injustice under Alabama law:

> Justice is a blind goddess
> To this we blacks are wise
> Her bandage hides two festering sores
> that once perhaps were eyes.

The economic depression, the issue of justice for Negroes, the burden of poverty were dominant themes now, affecting the tone and style of the poet in sharp contrast to the earlier writing of the 1920s. In an article "My Adventures as a Social Poet," Hughes makes his sentiments clear with respect to the predicament of black men and women as he recalled the sophisticated glitter of the Harlem Renaissance:

> But it was impossible for me to travel from hungry Harlem to
> the lovely homes on Park Avenue without feeling in my soul the
> great gulf between the very poor and the very rich in our society.

In 1931, after winning the Harmon Gold Award (and four hundred dollars) for literature, Hughes, on his way to Haiti where he would meet Jacques Roumain, stopped in Havana and was warmly received by writers and musicians, including Nicolás Guillén. He admits to his concern about capitalistic excesses—"I had written poems," he said, "about the exploitation of Cuba by sugar barons and I had translated many poems of Nicolás Guillén, among them 'Cane' ":

> Negro
> In the cane fields.
> White man above the cane fields
> Earth
> Beneath the cane fields.
> Blood
> That flows from us.

In a long dramatic poem "Advertisement for the Waldorf Astoria" Hughes uses irony to sustain the theme of the great gap between the rich and the poor:

> Say, you colored folks, hungry a long time
> in 135th Street, they got swell music
> at the Waldorf Astoria . . .
> Drop in at the Waldorf this afternoon for tea.
> Stay for dinner. Give Park Avenue a lot of
> darkie color—free for nothing!

And in many other poems he expands this theme to include the miserable conditions of the masses of the poor. Thematic variations appear in his third book of poetry of social criticism, *A New Song,* published by the International Workers Order. Titles range from "Park Bench," "Chant for May Day," "Song of Spain" to "Negro Ghetto" and "Lynching Song." In them the ironic undertone of plain folk addressing themselves to their condition, hallmark of Hughes's blues and jazz poetry, is gradually abandoned for a poet-spokesman whose eloquence speaks out against the injustices he observes around him. His scope soon became international. A speech made by Hughes as delegate from the United States to the Second International Writers Congress in Paris, July 1937, shows how he had added to his concerns the new political menace in Europe:

> It is because the reactionary and Fascist forces of the world know
> that writers like Anand and myself, leaders like Herndon, and

poets like Guillén and Roumain represent the great longing that
is in the hearts of the darker peoples of the world to reach out
their hands in friendship and brotherhood to all the white races
of the world.

Like Nicolás Guillén, Hughes envisions a universal justice embracing
all races. And his rejection of Western religion as an instrument of oppression foretells in a less abrasive fashion the theme of Roumain's "New Black
Sermon" (Nouveau sermon noir), as we shall see. For instance, Hughes
writes in "Good-bye Christ":

> Listen Christ,
> You did all right in your day, I reckon—
> But that day's gone now.
> They ghosted you up a swell story, too,
> Called it Bible—
> But it's dead now.

Hughes ends the poem in an outspoken repudiation of the church's relationship to the rich and powerful:

> The world is mine from now on—
> And nobody's gonna sell ME
> To a king, or a general,
> Or a millionaire.

His reassessment of religion continues in "Christ in Alabama," one of the
poems he wrote on the Scottsboro trials:

> Christ is a Nigger
> Beaten and black—
> O' bare your back.

Throughout the poem Hughes has interwoven social reality with the poetry
of black religious song. The third line takes us back to Hughes's gospel
music shout. Successive lines create images of Mary as black mammy of
the South and God the Father as white master, ending:

> Most holy bastard
> Of the bleeding mouth:
> Nigger Christ
> On the cross of the South.

An examination of a half dozen anthologies reveals that less attention
has been given to Hughes's poetry which handles social themes than to his

poems dealing with the African motif, the folk experience, or the Harlem ambiance. The social poetry, most of which appeared in magazines, has only recently been collected (1973). One senses that proletarian poems of the thirties—Hughes's as well as those of other writers—may have become dated for readers of the 1960s and 1970s, yet what marks much of his poetry in the decades of the thirties and early forties is not the fact that he is protesting injustice but the way in which he continues to adhere to racial styles—the spiritual, the gospel, the blues—and the unadorned direct speech he uses to evoke poetic images which drive home man's inhumanity to man from the black point of view. Langston Hughes is a pivotal figure in the transition of black poetry into the written literature of the twentieth century. As poet he used the mask of amused observer or ironic commentator, the image of a man who often must laugh to keep from crying. When he more directly revealed the anger of Black Americans against racism and exploitation, he used poetry as a weapon for achieving human justice, an expressive technique which the Haitian Jacques Roumain was to define later as a legitimate position of the poetic bard. Therefore Hughes, moved by his anger against injustice and the deteriorating conditions of black life, wrote a long poem satirizing the Waldorf Astoria through the voice of a poor man observing the luxury of the privileged few, or he wrote "Christ in Alabama," or "Park Bench," below, in which he speaks directly out of the suffering of black people with the familiar flick of irony that here masks a threat at the end:

> I live on a park bench,
> You, Park Avenue.
> Hell of a distance
> Between us two.
>
> I beg a dime for dinner—
> You got a butler and maid.
> But I'm wakin' up!
> Say, ain't you afraid
> That I might, just maybe
> In a year or two,
> Move on over
> To Park Avenue?

Predictably, the poems he wrote during this period drew the attention of the congressional Un-American Activities Committee, whose members summoned him for questioning about his presumed ties with communism and the Communist Party. Although cleared, his writing was largely ignored by the usual channels available to him for publication. The few editors and critics inclined to recognize a writer of Hughes's stature either left him alone or did not admit his poetry of dissent into their anthologies. Folk themes, song and dance, and Africanity were safer. Yet Langston Hughes continued to make statements against injustice, to call for change. In a poem written for *New Masses,* September 1932, Hughes opens, "Listen Revolution,/ We're buddies, see . . ." and calls clearly for change that would give power to people. "Together" the poem continues,

> We can take everything:
>
> . . . . . . . . . .
> (Great day in the morning!)
> Everything—
> And turn 'em over to the people who work.
> Rule and run 'em for us people who work.

During the same period, Hughes's poetry spoke out against the meaning of war, its ugly implications for the community of men. In response to the Spanish Civil War he wrote "Hero—International Brigade," in which he expresses his sense of unity with all mankind, in suffering and in hope:

> I've given what I wished
> and what I had to give
> That others live.
> And when the bullets
> Cut my heart away,
> And the blood
> Gushed to my throat
> I wondered if it were blood
> Gushing there.
> Or a red flame?
> Or just my death
> Turned into life?
> They're all the same
> Our dream!

Hughes was a direct observer of what he wrote. In the company of Nicolás Guillén, whom he joined in Paris, Hughes traveled to Spain as a correspondent for the Baltimore Afro-American newspaper. The opening lines of "Madrid—1937" again present Hughes's reaction to the meaning of the civil war in Spain:

> Put out the lights and stop the clocks.
> Let time stand still.
> Again man mocks himself
> And all his human will to build and grow.
> Madrid!
> The fact and symbol of man's woe.
> Madrid!

The closing lines are the poet's response to Fascism:

> In the darkness of her broken clocks
> Madrid cries NO!
> In the timeless midnight of the Fascist guns,
> Madrid cries NO!
> To all the killers of man's dreams.
> Madrid cries NO!
>   To break that NO apart
>   Will be to break the human heart.

In the decade of the thirties, Hughes's concern with world issues did not curtail his writing poetry that dealt specifically with racism in the United States. Poems such as "Black Seed" and "Sunset in Dixie," as well as the poetry of *Scottsboro Limited,* voice his commitment to racial justice, which would continue to the end of his career. Thus in 1941 a poem denouncing the treatment of blacks in the South, "Sunset in Dixie," anticipates the civil rights movement of the 1960s, and in a strongly worded poem written in 1957, "Memo to Non-White Peoples," he warns of new instruments for enslaving black people:

> They will let you have dope
> Because they are quite willing
> To drug you or kill you. . . .
>
> They will gleefully let you
> Kill your damn self any way you choose
> With liquor, drugs, or whatever . . .
>
> It's the same from Cairo to Chicago,
> Cape Town to the Caribbean, . . .
> Exactly the same.

It should not be difficult to gauge the depths of Hughes's disillusionment as he observed the world around him. As a poet, he wanted to free men spiritually from institutions and systems that denied them dignity as human beings, but he was also politically aware that freedom of the spirit is seldom achieved on an empty stomach. Thus as with Roumain and Guillén, political activism and poetic vision merged in a poetry that rebelled, demanded, and then actively searched for alternative systems under which people might live and develop.

SUSAN L. BLAKE

# Old John in Harlem: The Urban Folktales of Langston Hughes

"If you want to know about life," says Simple in the story that introduces him to readers of *Simple Speaks His Mind* and *The Best of Simple*, "don't look at my face, don't look at my hands. Look at my feet and see if you can tell how long I been standing on them." In the well-known catalogue of things Simple's feet have done—the miles they've walked; the lines they've stood in; the shoes, summer sandals, loafers, tennis shoes, and socks they've worn out; and the corns and bunions they've grown—Langston Hughes characterizes Jesse B. Semple, Harlem roomer, as the personification of the accumulated black experience. But what is especially significant about Simple is that he not only acknowledges his past, but uses it to shape his present. When his bar-buddy Boyd challenges him to name one thing his feet have done that makes them different from any other feet in the world, Simple points to the window in the white man's store across the street and replies that his right foot broke out that window in the Harlem riots and his left foot carried him off running, because his personal experience with his history had taught him, as he says, "to look at that window and say, 'It ain't mine! Bam-mmm-mm-m' and kick it out."

In creating the Simple stories, Hughes has done the same thing with the black folk tradition that his character does with black history—made it live and work in the present. It is easily recognized that Hughes has a relationship to the folk tradition. He wrote poetry in vernacular language and blues form. He edited *The Book of Negro Humor* and, with Arna Bontemps, *The Book of Negro Folklore,* which includes several of his own

From *Black American Literature Forum* 14, no. 3 (Fall 1980). © 1980 by Indiana State University.

poems and Simple stories as literature "in the folk manner." Simple himself has been called a "folk character" on the basis of half a dozen different definitions of the term: sociological average, composite of Southern folk types, epic hero, ordinary man, wise fool, blues artist. But Simple is more than vaguely "folk," and Hughes's relationship to the folk tradition is direct and dynamic. Simple is the migrant descendant of John, the militant slave of black folklore, and the fictional editorials that Hughes wrote for the *Chicago Defender* from 1943 to 1966 function as real folktales in the political story-telling tradition of the John-and-Old-Marster cycle. Not only do they follow the pattern of the John tales in characterization and conflict, not only do they include traditional motifs, they also recreate on the editorial page of a newspaper the dramatic relationship between storyteller and audience that characterizes an oral storytelling situation.

The principal difference between folk and self-conscious literature is in the relationship between the work and the audience. Generally speaking, self-conscious literature, usually written, isolates the experience of individuals; is addressed to individuals, who may or may not share either personal or social experience with either the author or the characters; and is experienced by the individual as an individual. Folk literature, usually oral, isolates the experience of a socially defined group; is addressed to all members of the group; and is experienced by a group, even if it consists of only two members, as a group. The self-conscious artist tells a story to suit himself, and the audience takes it or leaves it. The folk storyteller chooses and adapts a traditional text according to the occasion and the audience. The folk audience, therefore, participates in the storytelling and, in a sense, is also part of the story told. The story is told by, to, and for the people it is about; it is part of their lives as they are part of it. The Simple stories close the gap between story and audience created by the medium of print in several ways. They, too, adapt traditional materials from black folk-lore, the Bible, U.S. history, and popular culture. They, too, are occasional, as they deal with current events and social conditions. Their consistent subject, race, is the one experience that unites and defines the folk group to which they are addressed. Their principal character is an avid reader of the very publication in which the audience encounters him. Their story-within-a-story structure creates a dialogue between characters and audience. And their purpose is to function in the social conflict in which both characters and audience are engaged.

The typical Simple story is narrated by Boyd, who reports an encounter with Simple in which Simple has narrated an experience of his own. Each story contains two conflicts—one expressed in Simple's confrontation with an outside antagonist, the other in the conversation with Boyd in which he narrates it. Both conflicts are based on the consequences of race, which Simple defines in this exchange:

> "The social scientists say there is *no* difference between colored and white," I said. "You are advancing a very unscientific theory."
>
> "Do I look like Van Johnson?" asked Simple.
>
> "No, but otherwise—"
>
> "It's the *otherwise* that gets it," said Simple. "There is no difference between me and Van Johnson, except *otherwise*. I am black and he is white, I am in Harlem and he is in Beverly Hills, I am broke and he is rich, I am known from here around the corner, and he is known from Hollywood around the world. There is as much difference between Van Johnson and me as there is between day and night. And don't tell me day and night is the same. If you do, I will think you have lost your mind."

The *otherwise* that Simple is talking about—the social, political, and economic disparity between blacks and whites—generates other disparities: between Christianity and racism, legislation and application, "race leaders" and black folks, "say-ola" and "do-ola," *ought* and *is*, the American Dream and the American Dilemma. These in turn produce the psychological disparity, the twoness that Du Bois classically defined, between being black and being American. In general, the story Simple narrates addresses the social disparity; his dialogue with Boyd addresses the psychological. The dual structure of the stories makes Simple both actor and storyteller; it makes Boyd actor, teller, and audience. It enables Hughes to explore all the implications of American race discrimination and to bring them home to the audience that experiences them.

In the inside story, Simple follows the model of John, the insubordinate slave in the cycle of folktales about the perpetual contest between John and Old Marster. John is Old Marster's favorite slave, his foreman, his valet, his confidant, his fortune-teller, his alter ego. When Old Marster throws a party, John plays the fiddle; when he gambles with his neighbors, he bets on John; when he goes on a trip, he leaves John in charge. John is as close to Old Marster as a slave can be, but he is still a slave. He spends his life trying to close the gap between himself and Old Marster, between slavery and manhood. In the words of Julius Lester, John does "as much living and as little slaving" as he can.

He does so by effectually swapping places with Old Marster. At every opportunity, he puts himself in Old Marster's shoes: throws a party in the big house when Old Marster takes a trip, appropriates Old Marster's hams and chickens, "borrows" his clothes and his best horse, copies his manners, kisses his wife, and generally assumes the prerogatives of manhood that Old Marster takes for granted. He also shows Old Marster what it is like to go barefoot. When Old Marster and Old Miss sneak back from their trip in ragged disguise to spy on his party, John sends them to the kitchen like white trash. When Old Marster sends John out at night to guard his cornfield from a bear, John ends up holding the gun while Old Marster plays ring-around-the-rosy with the bear.

John is neither big nor strong, and he is more than clever. He is a political analyst. When he wins a round with Old Marster, his victory is the result of an objective understanding of the political and psychological principles of slavery that enables him to turn those principles back upon the institution. In one version of a popular tale called "The Fight," for example, John bluffs his opponent into forfeiting a fight on which Old Marster has staked his entire plantation by slapping Old Miss across the face. Since John has saved the plantation, Old Marster is reduced to diffidence when he inquires why John has violated the rock-bottom rules of slavery. When John explains, "Jim knowed if I slapped a white woman I'd a killed him, so he run," there is nothing further Old Marster can say. Even when John himself loses, the tale contains the analysis of slavery that represents the teller's and audience's intellectual control over their situation. Whether he wins or loses, John is the personification of this control.

Simple, the character in his own stories, like John, has the circumstances of a slave and the psychology of a free man. Although he works for a wage instead of for life, it's a subsistence wage, as evidenced by his chronic inability to save the One Hundred and Thirty-Three Dollars and Thirty-Four Cents to pay for his share of his divorce from Isabel so he can marry Joyce. Although he doesn't need a pass to leave Harlem, as John needs a pass to leave the plantation, Simple knows that there are barber shops, beaches, and bars outside Harlem where he would be unwelcome or in danger. Although his antagonists are as various as newspaper reporters, hotel clerks, Emily Post, and Governor Faubus, they all represent institutions of a society that excludes him, just as Old Marster represents slavery. But just as John refuses to behave like a slave, Simple refuses to be restricted by race: "What makes you think I'm colored?" he demands when told a factory is not taking on any "colored boys." "They done took such words off of jobs in New York State by law."

As a storyteller, Simple points out the same kinds of disparities that concerned the tellers of John tales. First, there are the practical disparities between life uptown and life downtown. The folk storyteller points out that John sees chicken on Old Marster's table and fat bacon on his own. Simple observes that Joyce buys her groceries downtown because "everything is two-three-four cents a pound higher in Harlem"; that he could get a hotel room if he asked for it in Spanish, but not if he asked for it in English; that white folks Jim Crow and lynch him "anytime they want to," but "suppose I was to lynch and Jim Crow white folks, where would I be?" Second, there is the disparity between stated and practiced values. Two of the themes that Simple returns to most frequently are also common themes in folk literature: the difference between Christian doctrine and Christians' doing, and the reversed status of people and animals when the people are black. In "Cracker Prayer," a variant of a traditional type of satiric prayer of which there is an example in Hurston's folklore collection *Mules and Men,* Simple impersonates a pious bigot who prays to the "Great Lord God, Jehovah, Father ... to straighten out this world and put Nigras back in their places." In "Golden Gate," he dreams a dream based on the traditional tale of The Colored Man Barred From Heaven, in which he arrives at the gate of Heaven and finds "Old Governor of Mississippi, Alabama, or Georgia, or wherever he is from," telling him to go around the back. Black folklore compares the lot of the black man, often disadvantageously, to that of the mule. Simple does the same thing with dogs. "Even a black dog gets along better than me," says Simple. "White folks socialize with dogs—yet they don't socialize with me." The army "Jim Crows me, but it don't Jim Crow dogs." In slavery days, Simple recalls, "a good bloodhound was worth more than a good Negro, because a bloodhound were trained to keep the Negroes in line." And dogs are still, he observes, more carefully counted than Negroes, better fed, sometimes even better clothed.

As an actor, Simple, like John, endeavors to resolve the disparities he has pointed out. His most common method is the folktale expedient of swapping places. He dreams that he is the one "setting on the wide veranda of my big old mansion with its white pillars, the living room just full of chandeliers, and a whole slew of white servants to wait on me, master of all I surveys, and black as I can be!" He turns himself into a general in charge of white troops from Mississippi: "They had white officers from Mississippi in charge of Negroes—so why shouldn't I be in charge of whites?" He sets himself up in the Supreme Court, where he uses the principle of swapping places to enforce the laws he promulgates: "For instant, 'Love thy neighbor as thyself.' The first man I caught who did not love his neighbor as hisself, I would make him change places with his neighbor—the rich with the poor, the white with the black and Governor Faubus with me."

Just as John not only seats himself at the head of Old Marster's table, but uses the opportunity to treat Old Marster as Old Marster has treated him, Simple insists not simply on integration, but on "reintegration": "Meaning by that, what?" asks his white boss. "That you be integrated with *me*," replies Simple, "not me with you." If a white reporter from one of the downtown newspapers were to interview him about life in Harlem, for example, Simple would suggest that they swap apartments for thirty days: " 'By that time, you will have found out how much the difference is in the price of a pound of potatoes uptown and a pound of potatoes down-town, how much the difference is for what you pay for rent downtown and what I pay for rent uptown, how different cops look downtown from how cops look uptown, how much more often streets is cleaned downtown than they is uptown. All kinds of things you will see in Harlem, and not have to be told. After we swap pads, you would not need to interview me,' I would say, 'so let's change first and interview later.' "

The circumstance that makes Simple act as John acts is the same one that makes Simple experience what John experiences. Slavery and Jim Crow are both manifestations of the idea that race determines place. The society dictates the theme of swapping places by creating places:

> "You talk just like a Negro nationalist," I said.
> "What's that?"
> "Someone who wants Negroes to be on top."
> "When everybody else keeps me on the *bottom*, I don't see why I shouldn't be on top. I will, too, someday."

What Simple really wants is not for top and bottom to be inverted but for there to be no top or bottom, no "place," to swap:

> "Anyhow," said Simple, "if we lived back in fairy tale days and a good fairy was to come walking up to me and offer me three wishes, the very first thing I would wish would be:
> THAT ALL WHITE FOLKS WAS BLACK
> then nobody would have to bother with white blood and black blood any more."

But Simple does not live back in fairy-tale days, so he tries to combat racism by showing how unfair it would look if the tables were turned. The principle of swapping places is literally the principle of revolution. But the elimination of places is equally revolutionary. Hughes's purpose in Simple's stories is to make revolution look simple.

To the extent that inside and outside plots can be separated, the inside plot of a Simple story is addressed to the problem of Jim Crow and the outside plot to the people who suffer from it. The narrator of the Simple stories, identified in the later stories as Boyd (though "Boyd" in the earlier stories is the name of another roomer in Simple's house), is both the immediate audience of Simple's narrative—and, thus, a stand-in for the newspaper audience—and one of Simple's antagonists. For although Simple and Boyd are both black, and in full agreement on what *should* be, they disagree about what *is*. Because Boyd views reality in terms of American ideals and Simple views it in terms of black experience, their friendly disagreements focus on the psychological disparity between being black and being American.

Boyd talks American. He is a romantic, an idealist, one of the two hundred ninety-nine out of a thousand people, as George Bernard Shaw figured it, who recognize the conventional organization of society as a failure but, being in a minority, conform to it nevertheless and try to convince themselves that it is just and right. Simple talks black. He is Shaw's realist, the one man in a thousand "strong enough to face the truth the idealists are shirking." The truth he faces and Boyd shirks is the importance of race. Though Boyd is black, rooms in Harlem, listens to Simple nightly, sees the evidence of race discrimination all around him, he keeps trying to believe that what ought to be is. The police are there to "keep you from being robbed and mugged"; "violence never solved anything"; "bomb shelters will be for everybody"; "Negroes today are . . . advancing, advancing!" "I have not advanced one step," counters Simple, getting down to cases, "still the same old job, same old salary, same old kitchenette, same old Harlem and the same old color." "You bring race into everything" complains Boyd. "It is in everything," replies Simple.

Boyd considers Simple's race-consciousness provincial, chauvinistic, and un-American. He repeatedly encourages Simple to "take the long view," "extend a friendly hand," get to know more white people, try some foreign foods. But Simple insists on his Americanness as much as his blackness. In his imaginary encounters with representatives of all the institutions that exclude him because he is black, he replies, "I am American." The difference between Simple's and Boyd's assumptions about what it means to be American is dramatized by their response to a folk joke Simple tells about an old lady who enters a recently integrated restaurant, orders various soul-food specialties, is politely but repeatedly told "we don't have that," and finally sighs, "I knowed you-all wasn't ready for integration":

> "Most ethnic groups have their own special dishes," I said. "If you want French food, you go to a French restaurant. For Hungarian, you go to Hungarian places."
> "But this was an American place," said Simple, "and they did not have soul food."

To Boyd, as to the hotel clerks and employers Simple encounters, "Negro" and "American " are mutually exclusive; "American" identity is an achievement upon which "Negro" identity may be put aside. To Simple, they are mutually necessary. America is not American *unless* it has room for him, "black as I can be," "without one plea." From Simple's point of view, Boyd's is not American at all, but white. Though Boyd voices the ideals of freedom, he represents the influence of racist conventions in his interpretation of them. The repartee between Simple and Boyd puts a contemporary conflict of attitudes into the context of the historical conflict between John and Old Marster. Through Boyd, Hughes shows that to deny the reality of racial oppression is actually to support it.

Since Boyd, as Simple's audience, also represents the reading audience, Simple's argument with him becomes an argument with his audience as well. The framework conversation with Boyd applies the meaning of Simple's narrative to the audience and anticipates their objections. Through it Simple the folk narrator confronts the legacy of Old Marster in the audience as Simple the folk hero confronts Jim Crow. Folktales could not free the slaves who told them, but they could keep the slaves from being tricked into believing they were meant to be slaves; the tales could keep the distinction between living and slaving clear. The Simple stories do the same for the distinction between American ideals and black reality. The principle of the Simple stories is that the way to overcome race discrimination is to confront it, and they keep their audience confronted not only with the principle of confrontation but also with the evidence of discrimination. In the words of Ellison's definition of the blues, they keep alive the painful details and episodes of black experience and transcend them—keep them alive in order to transcend them—just as Simple remembers his past in order to free his future.

The similarity between Simple's conflict and John's makes the Simple stories resemble folktales, but the active engagement in the audience's social and psychological experience makes them be to an urban newspaper-reading folk what the John tales must have been to a rural storytelling folk: a communal affirmation of the group's own sense of reality. Like the folk storyteller, Hughes speaks of and to the group. He speaks of their immediate experience, by commenting on current events, and puts it into the context of their historical experience and the fundamental fact of their group identity, race. He uses the medium, the newspaper, that draws the largest audience, and a narrative form that not only simulates narrator-audience exchange in the dialogue between Simple and Boyd, but stimulates it by making Simple and Boyd personify conflicting attitudes he knows his audience—individually as well as collectively—holds. The Simple stories seek to show that, though the forms of life in mid-twentieth-century Harlem are different from those on the ante-bellum plantation, the fundamentals are the same. The stories themselves are written and published on this same principle; and the adaptation of their form to the realities of an urban, literate, mass society is what in fact allows them to function as folktales.

Implicitly in the Simple stories, Hughes has redefined the notion of black folk tradition. Most of the writers who consciously used black folk materials in the first half of the twentieth century located "the folk tradition" in the South, in the past, in a pastoral landscape. They either employed it— as did Toomer, Hurston, O'Neill in *The Emperor Jones,* Heyward in *Porgy*—or rejected it, as did Wright, as a retreat from the social complexities of modern life into either pastoral simplicity or the individual psyche. But Hughes's definition of black folk tradition is dynamic. Limited by no time, place, or landscape, it is simply the continuity of black experience—an experience that is "folk" in that it is collective and a "tradition" in that it defines the past, dominates the present, and makes demands on the future.

Hughes asks his audience to recognize their place in this tradition and use it as Simple uses the history stored up in his feet. The force and purpose of his writing is to project his understanding of the folk tradition out among the folk, to bind black people together in a real community, united by their recognition of common experience into a force to control it. Modestly, like a relay runner, Langston Hughes picks up the folk tradition and carries it on toward the goal of social change in the real world.

RICHARD K. BARKSDALE

# Hughes: His Times and His Humanistic Techniques

In one of his critical essays, "Tradition and the Individual Talent," T. S. Eliot suggested that there is a necessary creative tension between a given tradition and most writers who choose to write in that tradition. The tradition defines an approach and a set of guidelines that tend to restrict the creativity of the individual writer, and the writer in reaction seeks to assert his independence and modify the tradition. So tradition speaks to writer and writer speaks to tradition. At times, a writer affects a given tradition little or not at all. For instance, a nineteenth-century romantic poet like Philip Freneau did not change the tradition of romantic poetry at all. On the other hand, Algernon Swinburne, because of his literary and physical encounter with sadism and various kinds of eroticism, revolted against the tradition of Victorian neoromanticism, and the tradition was never quite the same after Swinburne.

The case of Langston Hughes is not exactly comparable, but there is substantial evidence that by 1926, with the publication of his *Weary Blues,* he had broken with one or two rather well-established traditions in Afro-American literature. By no means was he alone in this act of literary insurrection; Claude McKay, Jean Toomer, and other poets of the 1920s stood with him. First, Hughes chose to modify the poetic tradition that decreed that whatever literature the black man produced must not only protest racial conditions but promote racial integration. There was little or no place in such a literary tradition for the celebration of the black lifestyle for its own sake. With obviously innocuous intent, Dunbar had attempted

From *Black American Literature and Humanism,* edited by R. Baxter Miller. © 1981 by the University Press of Kentucky.

some celebration of the black lifestyle in the post-Reconstruction rural South, but his pictures of happy pickaninnies and banjo-plucking, well-fed cabin blacks did not square with the poverty and racial violence that seared that period. In any event, by 1920 a poetry of strong social protest which attempted to plead cultural equality with white America had become a fixed tradition in Afro-American literature. It was thought that black America's writers could knock on the door of racial segregation and successfully plead for admission into a presumably racially integrated society. Of course, admission would not be gained unless these writers, painters, and sculptors had all been properly schooled in Western techniques and practices and thus fully qualified for acceptance. It might be pointed out in this context that to effect this end, even the so-called spirituals or sorrow-songs of the slaves were Europeanized—songs whose weird and sadly provocative melodies had had such a marked effect on northern Whites when first heard on the Carolina Sea Islands in 1862. In 1916, Harry T. Burleigh, the black organist at New York's ultra-fashionable St. George's Episcopal Church, published his *Jubilee Songs of the United States* with every spiritual arranged so that a concert singer could sing it, "in the manner of an art song." Thus, the black man's art in song and story was to be used primarily to promote racial acceptance and ultimately achieve racial integration. And it was clear that it had to be a Europeanized art.

Necessarily excluded from consideration in any such arrangement was the vast amount of secular folk material which had been created throughout the years of the black man's persecution and enslavement in America. For during slavery black people had used song and story to achieve many social and political goals. They had covertly ridiculed "massa" and "missus" in song and story and had overtly expressed their disdain and hatred for the "niggah driber." And since slavery, they had sung the blues on waterfront levees and in juke joints; they had built railroads and sung about John Henry and other laboring giants; they had been on chain gangs and as prisoners had been leased out to cruel masters to cut the tall cane on the Brazos to the tune of the slashing whip and under a blazing sun which they called "Ole Hannah." They had sung as they chopped cotton on tenant farms and scrubbed and ironed clothes in the White folks' kitchens. All of this orature, as some critics have called it, was, in the opinion of certain twentieth-century monitors of Afro-American culture, to be totally excluded from common view. Innocuous tidbits might be acceptable, like James Weldon Johnson's "Since You Went Away," which was one of the "croon songs" published in his 1916 volume *Fifty Years and Other Poems*. But generally, the richly complex burden of secular folk material—the songs and stories that came out of the sweat, sorrow, and occasional joy of black people of the lower classes—might impede integration and hence was to be expunged from the racial literary record.

The crystallization of a tradition which outlawed black folk literature and song inevitably fostered some attitudes which adversely affected the jazz and blues which were just beginning to be established in the early 1920s when Hughes first settled in New York City. For the indictment of folk material resulted in the cultural censure of the blues singing of Bessie and Clara Smith; the jazz playing of Duke Ellington, Louis Armstrong, and Fletcher Henderson; and the song-and-dance and vaudeville showmanship of Bill Robinson, Bert Williams, Eubie Blake, and Noble Sissell. Ironically, one of the cultural monitors of the period, James Weldon Johnson, had written that the cakewalk and ragtime were two of black America's principal contributions to American culture. Johnson had been a music man himself at one time in his career. But other strong-minded monitors of black culture ignored Johnson and deemed that the dancing, singing, laughing, blues-singing, jazz-playing black was too uncomfortably close to a despised folk tradition to project a proper integrationist image. In retrospect, one is forced to observe that in view of how deeply black jazz and music have influenced both twentieth-century American and European lifestyles, this attempt to demean the image of the black entertainer and music man of the early 1920s is indeed one of the great ironies in Afro-American cultural history.

So Langston Hughes and other young poets of the early years of the Harlem Renaissance had to confront a point of view which had quickly crystallized into a binding and restricting tradition. Hughes also developed a dislike for the tradition of racial exoticism which, largely promoted by white patrons, began to be an absorbing concern of black writers by the mid-1920s. Although his resistance to racial exoticism eventually ruptured his relationship with his patron, Mrs. R. Osgood Mason, his fight against a tradition barring orature and the rich folk material of the lower classes of blacks became his major struggle. The discussion to follow focuses not on how he waged a successful fight to change that tradition, but on the humanistic techniques which he used in his poetry to reflect and communicate the rich folk culture of black people.

Before making any specific attempt to describe Hughes's use of humanistic techniques in his folk poetry, one may make at least three generalizations about his folk poetry. First, most of his folk poems have the distinctive marks of orature. They contain many instances of naming and enumerating, considerable hyperbole and understatement, and a strong infusion of street talk rhyming. Also, there is a deceptive veil of artlessness in most of the poems. Actually, there is much more art and deliberate design than one immediately perceives. I should point out in this context that Hughes prided himself on being an impromptu and impressionistic writer of poetry. His, he insisted, was not an artfully constructed poetry. But an analysis of some of his better monologues and his poems on economic and social class issues will reveal that much of his poetry was carefully and artfully crafted. The third generalization is that Hughes's folk poetry shares certain features found in other types of folk literature. There are many instances of dramatic ellipsis and narrative compression. Also, we find considerable rhythmic repetition and monosyllabic emphasis. And, of course, flooding all of his poetry is that peculiar mixture of Hughesian irony and humor—a very distinctive mark of his folk poetry.

The foregoing generalizations have a particular relevancy when one studies some of Hughes's dramatic monologues. In most instances, these are artfully done; the idioms of black folk speech and street talk abound; and very often the final lines drip with irony and calculated understatement. An example is "Lover's Return":

> My old time daddy
> Came back home last night.
> His face was pale and
> His eyes didn't look just right.
>
> . . . . . . . . . . . .
> He says to me, "Mary, I'm
> Comin' home to you—
> So sick and lonesome
> I don't know what to do."

First, there are two levels of monologue in this poem; the persona describes to the reader her elderly lover's return, and then, in lines which the poet italicizes, there is an interior monologue in which the persona talks to herself. These italicized lines clearly reveal the heightened anxiety and emotional tensions that haunt her:

> *Oh, men treats women*
> *Just like a pair o' shoes.*
> *You men treats women*
> *Like a pair o' shoes—*
> *You kicks 'em round and*
> *Does 'em like you choose.*

This interior monologue contains a repressed truth, and one can imagine the tremendous psychological pressure such a repressed truth has on the psyche of the persona. Moreover, these words in the interior monologue have a double-edged relevancy; they define the persona's particular dilemma and they also effectively generalize about a larger and more universal dilemma in the arena of sexual conflict. The full psychological impact of this monologue, however, is felt in the last stanza of the poem, where the conflict between outward compassion and inner condemnation is clearly delineated:

> I looked at my daddy—
> Lawd! and I wanted to cry.
> He looked so thin—
> Lawd! that I wanted to cry.
> But de devil told me:
> > Damn a lover
> > Come home to die!

Inevitably, as the result of the carefully controlled narrative compression commonly found in the well-crafted dramatic monologue, many facts remain explicitly unstated. But Hughes calls upon the perceptive and imaginative reader to fill out the details of this miniature but poignant drama. The persona, deserted by her lover many years ago, is now forced by an obviously unfair kind of social obligation to receive him once again. Her code of faithfulness and her sense of social propriety pull her in one direction. Her sense of fair play and justice pulls her in another direction. In the end, the harassed woman is torn between a deeply instinctual desire to avoid pain and distress and a strong sense of obligation to honor an elderly lover "come home to die." Characteristically, Hughes defines the dilemma and then leaves the resolution carefully unstated. By so doing, he suggests that the vulnerable, dilemma-ridden, anti-heroic persona truly counts in the larger human equation.

Further examples of Hughes's humanistic techniques can be found in certain of his blues poems and his dialogue and debate poems. In his gutsy reaction against the tradition which censured the blues as offensive and devoid of cultural import, Hughes wrote a lot of blues poems. In fact, *Fine Clothes to the Jew* (1927), *Shakespeare in Harlem* (1942), and *One-Way Ticket* (1949) have more than their fair share of such poems. Many are uncomplicated blues statements like:

> When hard luck overtakes you
> Nothin' for you to do.
> When hard luck overtakes you
> Nothin' for you to do.
> Gather up your fine clothes
> An' sell 'em to de Jew.

or:

> I beats ma wife an'
> I beats ma side gal too.
> Beats ma wife an'
> Beats ma side gal too.
> Don't know why I do it but
> It keeps me from feelin' blue.

In these poems there is a Hughesian blend of irony and humor but no psychological complexity. One contains some advice about how to handle hard luck with minimum psychological damage; the second poem describes the casual self-acceptance of a chronic woman-beater who apparently is unaware of the extent of his problem. But in "In a Troubled Key" there is a difference. The blues form is here, but the persona is emotionally insecure:

> Still I can't help lovin' you,
> Even though you do me wrong.
> Says I can't help lovin' you
> Though you do me wrong—
> But my love might turn into a knife
> Instead of to a song.

The harassed persona is helplessly entwined in love, but there is the possibility that instead of a song of love, there will be knife-work in the night. Similarly, the blues poem "Widow Woman" has an unexpectedly ironic ending. After promising to be ever-faithful to a recently deceased "mighty lover" who had "ruled" her for "many years," in the last two lines the persona suddenly becomes aware of the full import of the freedom that is about to become hers. So the poem ends with the kind of ironic juxtaposition Hughes loved. The outwardly distraught widow stands sobbing by the open grave as she watches the grave-diggers throw dirt in her husband's face. But, inwardly, her heart soars joyfully at the prospect of freedom: ". . . you never can tell when a/Woman like me is free?"

In addition to the humanizing techniques used by Hughes in some of his dramatic monologues, the poet also sometimes presented two personae in a dramatic dialogue form of poetry. In one or two instances, the dialogue broadens into a debate which the poet humanizes by carefully illuminating the two opposing points of view. For instance, in "Sister," one of the poems in *Montage of a Dream Deferred,* a dialogue occurs between a mother and her son about his sister's involvement with a married man. The brother is embarrassed by his sister's behavior and asks: "Why don't she get a boyfriend/I can understand—some decent man?" The mother somewhat sur-prisingly defends her daughter; actually her Marie is the victim of the grim economic lot of the ghetto dweller. She "runs around with trash" in order to get "some cash." Thus a grim and dehumanizing economic determinism is in control of the lives of all three—the mother, the son, and the daughter. The son, however, still does not understand; he asks, "Don't decent folks have dough?" The mother, out of the wisdom of a bitter cynicism, imme-diately replies, "Unfortunately usually no!" And she continues: "Did it ever occur to you, boy,/that a woman does the best she can?" To this the son makes no reply, but a voice, probably the poet's, adds: "So does a man." Hughes is saying that, like the distressed, fragmented, and fallible personae of most folk poetry, human beings do the best that they can, and their failures and defeats are actually the mark of their humanity.

Another poetic dialogue, entitled "Mama and Daughter," has a slightly different thrust and meaning. There is no polarizing conflict between the two personae, but obviously each reacts quite differently to the same sit-uation. The mother helps her daughter prepare to go "down the street" to see her "sugar sweet." As they talk, the mother becomes increasingly agi-tated because she remembers when she, too, went "down the street" to see her "sugar sweet." But now the romantic tinsel is gone forever from her life; her "sugar sweet" married her, got her with child, and then, like so many ghetto fathers, abandoned her to a life of unprotected loneliness. So a dramatic contrast develops between the naively hopeful daughter who is eager to join the young man she can't get off her mind, and the disillusioned mother who for different reasons can't get her errant husband off her mind. When the mother expresses the hope that her husband—"that wild young son-of-a-gun rots in hell today," her daughter replies: "*Mama, Dad couldn't be still young.*" The anger of the mother's final comment is the anger of all the abandoned women of all of America's urban ghettos. And what she leaves unsaid is more important than what she actually says:

> He *was* young yesterday.
> He *was* young when he—
> Turn around!
> So I can brush your back, I say!

Love and sex have tricked the mother and left her lonely and full of bitter memories, but the "down-the-street" ritual must be repeated for the daugh-ter. Disappointment and disillusionment very probably await her later; but to Hughes disappointment and disillusionment await all lovers because these are, once again, the necessary and essential marks of the human condition.

There are three other poems by Hughes which provide interesting examples of his use of humanistic techniques. The first, "Blue Bayou," is a tersely wrought dramatic monologue in which the persona describes the circumstances leading to his death by lynching. In essence, it is an age-old southern tale of an interracial love triangle that inevitably turns out badly for the black man. What is striking about the monologue is the poet's use of the folk symbol of the "setting sun." In some of the old blues standards, this image is a recurring motif with various overtones of meaning:

> In the evenin', in the evenin'
> When the settin' sun go down
> Ain't it lonesome, ain't it lonesome
> When your baby done left town.

or:

> Hurry sundown, hurry sundown
> See what tomorrow bring
> May bring rain
> May bring any old thing.

And at the beginning of "Blue Bayou," the "setting sun" could be a symbol of "any old thing." The persona says: "I went walkin'/By de Blue Bayou/ And I saw de sun go down." Using the narrative compression and dramatic ellipsis usually found in the folk ballad, the persona then tells his story:

> I thought about old Greeley
> And I thought about Lou
> And I saw de sun go down.
> > White man
> > Makes me work all day
> > And I works too hard
> > For too little pay—
> > Then a White man
> > Takes my woman away.
> I'll kill old Greeley.

At this point, the persona's straight narration ends. In the next stanza, sundown as a reddening symbol of violent death is introduced, and the italicized choral chant of the lynchers is heard:

> De Blue Bayou
> Turns red as fire.

> *Put the Black man*
> *On a rope*
> *And pull him higher!*

Then the persona returns to state with a rising crescendo of emotional stress: "I saw de sun go down."

By the time the final stanza begins, "De Blue Bayou's/A pool of fire" and the persona utters his last words:

> And I saw de sun go down,
> Down,
>     Down!
> Lawd, I saw de sun go down.

The emphasis in this last stanza is on the word "down," used four times in the four lines, and in lines two and three "down, down!" are the only words used. And Hughes arranges the monosyllabic words so that the second literally is placed "down" from the first. Thus concludes this grim little tragedy of a triangular love affair that ended in a murder and a lynching.

Several additional critical observations may be made about this poem. First, it is interesting to note how Hughes manipulates the meaning of the setting sun. It is done with great verbal economy and tremendous dramatic finesse. At the beginning, when the persona views the setting sun, it is part of a beautiful Blue Bayou setting. But the persona's mood is blue just like the anonymous blues singer who shouts:

> In the evenin', in the evenin'
> When the settin' sun go down
> Ain't it lonesome, ain't it lonesome
> When your baby done left town.

Hughes's persona quickly and succinctly relates what has happened to his baby, Lou. We do not know whether she left voluntarily with old Greeley or had no choice. In any event, as the sun is setting, the persona decides to assert his manhood and kill old Greeley. A short time after the deed is done, the lynchers catch him by the Blue Bayou. Again the sun is setting, but now all nature begins to reflect and mirror the victim's agony. The bayou turns red with his blood; and then it becomes a pool of fire mirroring the flames that begin to burn his hanging, twisting body. Finally, the victim symbolically sees his own death as he repeats, "Lawd, I saw de sun go down." It is through his poetic technique that Hughes, the "artless" poet, conveys to the reader the brutal and agonizing slowness of the persona's death. Just as the setting sun in the American southland provides a scene of slow and lingering beauty as it sinks down, down, down over the rim of the earth, so the death of the victim is a slow and lingering agony as he sinks down, down, down into the pit of death.

It should also be stressed that, although this poem has a recurring blues motif in its use of the setting-sun image, it has a finality hardly ever found in the standard blues. In fact, all good blues reflect survival and recovery. In "Stormy Monday Blues," for instance, it takes Lou Rawls six days to get rid of his blues; then, after the "ghost walks on Friday," on Saturday he "goes out to play" and on Sunday he goes "to church to pray." In the real blues the persona is always waiting hopefully to see "what tomorrow brings." But in Hughes's "The Blue Bayou," the persona has no tomorrow. Had the poem described a tomorrow, the reader would have seen a bayou flooded with the bright colors of a beautiful sunrise; and, mirrored in the bayou's sun-flecked waters, one would see the persona's body slowly twisting in the early morning breeze. The stench of burning flesh would be everywhere and no birds would sing to greet the multi-colored dawn.

A discussion of Hughes's humanistic techniques in poetry should include two additional poems: "Jitney," an experimental poem celebrating a highly particularized mode of the black lifestyle, and "Trumpet Player: 52nd Street," which reflects the poet's consummate artistry in one mode of genre description. Essentially, both are folk poems. "Jitney" is an exuberant salute to the jitney cabs that used to wind up and down South Parkway in Chicago and Jefferson Street in Nashville, Tennessee. They have long been supplanted by better modes of transportation, but in the 1930s and 1940s the jitneys were very much part of black Chicago and black Nashville.

In his poem, Hughes attempts to capture the uniqueness of the experience of riding a jitney cab on two round trips between Chicago's 31st and 63rd streets. Like the cab, the poem snakes along; each stop—31st, 35th, 47th—is a single line, thus providing the reader with the sense of movement in space. Not only does the form reflect the content in this poem; the form is the content.

The great merit of the poem is not its experimental form, however. "Jitney" is a microcosm of a moving, surging, dynamic black Chicago. Thus the poem celebrates not so much a mode of transportation unique to Chicago's black Southside; rather it celebrates the Southside folk who ride jitneys and hustle up and down South Parkway to go to church, to go to the market, to go to night school, to go to nightclubs and stage shows and movies. Or sometimes the time spent riding in a jitney becomes a peaceful

interlude in the hectic struggle to survive in a swiftly paced urban society—
an interlude to gossip or signify:

> Girl, ain't you heard?
> *No, Martha, I ain't heard.*
> I got a Chinese boy-friend
> Down on 43rd.
> 47th,
> 51st,
> 55th,
> 63rd,
> Martha's got a Japanese!
> Child, ain't you heard?

As people come and go, facts and circumstances obviously change; but
apparently the mood in a jitney cab is one of warm, folksy friendliness—
the kind Chicago's black residents remembered from their "down-home"
days. Indeed, the poem suggests that in a large metropolis like black Chicago, one refuge from the cold anonymity of urban life is the jitney cab:

> 43rd,
> I quit Alexander!
> Honey, ain't you heard?
> 47th,
> 50th Place,
> 63rd,
> Alexander's quit Lucy!
> Baby, ain't you heard?
> . . . . . . . . .
> If you want a good chicken
> You have to get there early
> And push and shove and grab!
> I'm going shopping now, child.

The pervasive mood of "Jitney," then, is one of racial exuberance and
vitality. As the cab moves up and down South Parkway, the Southside folks
who jump in and out and are busy about their business have no time to
talk about deferred dreams. Obviously, Chicago's black citizens had as
many as Harlem's black citizens; but the jitney provided neither the time
nor the place for in-depth discussions of racial dilemmas. It is significant
that by the time black urban America exploded into riot and racial con-

frontation, the jitneys of Chicago's South Parkway and Nashville's Jefferson Street had long since disappeared from the urban scene.

Finally, "Trumpet Player: 52nd Street" reveals a fine blending of the best of Hughes's humanistic techniques. In the portrait of the musician we see both a particular person and a folk symbol. For Hughes, who had started writing about "long-headed jazzers" and weary blues-playing pianists back in the 1920s, regarded the black musician as a folk symbol with deep roots in the racial past. Thus in the poem's first stanza we greet the symbol, not the man. What the persona remembers, all black musicians have remembered throughout all of slavery's troubled centuries:

> The Negro
> With the trumpet at his lips
> Has dark moons of weariness
> Beneath his eyes
> Where the smoldering memory
> Of slave ships
> Blazed to the crack of whips
> About his thighs.

The instrument he is playing has no significance; it could be a banjo, a drum, or just some bones manipulated by agile black fingers; the memory is the same. And the memory makes the music different. Etched in pain, the sound is better, the beat more impassioned, the melody more evocative. And the music flows forth with greater ease, as Dunbar's Malindy proved in "When Malindy Sings." Actually these musicians have found the "spontaneous overflow of powerful emotions" that the youthful Wordsworth was in search of and actually never found, for too often in Western artistic expression, traditional structures intervene and negate spontaneous creativity.

The poem also has its fair share of Hughesian irony. Where in ancient times man through his music sought the moon and the beautiful, ever-surging sea, now matters have changed:

> Desire
> That is longing for the moon
> Where the moonlight's but a spotlight
> In his eyes,
> Desire
> That is longing for the sea
> Where the sea's a bar-glass
> Sucker size.

So no fanciful escape from the hard facts of nightclub life is permitted. We can and must remember the past but we cannot escape the present, and through Hughes's gentle reminder one stumbles on one of history's great and o'erweening truths. If art does provide an escape from the present, it is but a temporary escape. But the memory of past pain and the awareness of the present's difficulties and deferred dreams are themes that make the *comédie humaine* so truly comic.

Finally, as the poem draws to a close, the poet presents the trumpeter himself:

> The Negro
> With the trumpet at his lips
> Whose jacket
> Has a fine one-button roll,
> Does not know
> Upon what riff the music slips
> Its hypodermic needle
> To his soul.

The figure of the hypodermic needle penetrating the soul of the music man suggests that the music provides only temporary relief from the difficulties of the present: jazz is a useful narcotic to allay the world's woes. But the poetic image of the hypodermic needle also suggests that jazz lovers can develop addictive personalities and become dependent on a little music that excludes the terror and woe of human existence. It is not only good for the soul but absolutely necessary for the psyche.

The final stanza of this extraordinarily well-made poem repeats what was said at the beginning of the poem about the historical role of the black maker of music.

> But softly
> As the tunes come from his throat
> Trouble
> Mellows to a golden note.

The music anesthetizes both performer and listener against remembered pain. In fact, the 52nd Street trumpeter with his "patent-leathered" hair and his jacket with "a *fine* one-button roll" disappears from view and a folk music man of ancient origin reappears. His role has long been to convert "trouble" into beautiful music. But Hughes humanizes the function of art and music. In "Trumpet Player: 52nd Street" the poet suggests that the black man's music nullifies the pain of the past and seals off the woe of the present. Admittedly, the poem, with its sophisticated imagery, is probably not orature of the kind found in other poems discussed above, but the black music man described herein has long been a focal figure in producing the songs and stories that black people have orated and sung down through the centuries.

There are many more instances of Hughes's use of humanistic techniques throughout the full range of his poetry. But this discussion has been limited to his folk poetry—to his orature. It is now clear that Hughes's devotion to this kind of poetry had two major consequences: he broke the back of a tradition which sought to exclude secular folk material from the canon of black literature. And, in his use of the language of the black lower classes, Hughes prepared the way for the use and acceptance of the revolutionary black street poetry of the late 1960s.

CHIDI IKONNE

# Affirmation of Black Self

When Countee Cullen wondered whether some of Langston Hughes's poems were poems at all, he was not alone. Eugene F. Gordon and Thomas Millard Henry's description of *The Weary Blues* as a "doggerel" and "product of the inferiority complex" has already been noted. Hughes's second volume of poetry, *Fine Clothes to the Jew* (1927), was unequivocally condemned by a section of the black press. The *Pittsburgh Courier* called "LANGSTON HUGHES' BOOK OF POEMS TRASH." The *New York Amsterdam News* called Hughes himself "THE SEWER DWELLER," while the *Chicago Whip* named him "The poet lowrate of Harlem." Even his friend, Wallace Thurman, almost agreed with his critics that Hughes wrote "trash" when he suggested that Langston Hughes "needs to learn the use of the blue pencil and the waste-paper basket."

Thurman, nevertheless, offers one of the reasons why most of the Negro literati could not have approved of some of Langston Hughes's subject matter: the apparently anti-assimilationist hue of his treatment. Thurman writes: "He went for inspiration and rhythms to those people who had been the least absorbed by the quagmire of American Kultur, and from them he undertook to select and preserve such autonomous racial values as were being rapidly eradicated in order to speed the Negro's assimilation."

Langston Hughes's early poetry contained such pieces as "Young Prostitute," which is about a growing but already overworked harlot—the kind [that] come cheap in Harlem/So they say"; "To a Black Dancer in 'The Little Savoy,' " which focuses on a girl whose "breasts [are]/Like the pillows

From *DuBois to Van Vechten: The Early New Negro Literature 1903–1926.* © 1981 by Chidi Ikonne. Greenwood Press, 1981.

of all sweet dreams"; "The Cat and the Saxophone," that jerky sputtering of a tipsy love-thirsty couple that knocked Countee Cullen "over completely on the side of bewilderment, and incredulity"; and the poem about a prostitute in a British colony—possibly in Africa—Natcha. She offers love "for ten shillings." All these are raw slices of life cut from Harlem and Africa with no palliative or the Freudian "incitement premium" offered. The pretty and sexy "wine-maiden" drunk with "the grapes of joy" in "To a Black Dancer in 'The Little Savoy'" is, possibly, only a reflection (a literary transplant) of a young black woman whom the poet must have met, one night, in the cabaret—The Little Savoy.

Thus the source of Hughes's trouble with some black critics was not that he was not being Negro but that his work was too Negro self-expressing. He threw wide, to use Countee Cullen's words, "every door of the racial entourage, to the wholesale gaze of the world at large" in defiance of the black middle-class assimilationist "code" of decency.

The last paragraph of his reply to George S. Schuyler's article "The Negro-Art Hokum" is an adequate definition of what he and many of his close associates—especially his co-founders of *Fire*—were trying to do:

> We young Negro artists who create now intend to express our individual dark-skinned selves without fear or shame. If white people are pleased we are glad. If they are not, it doesn't matter. We know we are beautiful. And ugly too. The tom-tom cries and the tom-tom laughs. If colored people are pleased we are glad. If they are not, their displeasure doesn't matter either. We build our temple for tomorrow, strong as we know how, and we stand on the top of the mountain, free within ourselves.

George S. Schuyler, who believed that "the Aframerican is merely a lampblacked Anglo-Saxon," had contended that there could be nothing "expressive of the Negro soul" in the work of the black American whose way of life was hardly different from that of other Americans. He is, Schuyler argued, "subject to the same economic and social forces that mold the actions and thoughts of the white Americans. He is not living in a different world as some whites and a few Negroes would have us believe. When the jangling of his Connecticut alarm clock gets him out of his Grand Rapids bed to a breakfast similar to that eaten by his white brother across the street . . . it is sheer nonsense to talk about 'racial differences' as between the American black man and the American white man." Therefore any attempt on the part of the black American to aim at the production of any art distinctively Negro borders on self-deception, for "Negro art" belongs somewhere else. It "has been, is, and will be among the numerous black nations of Africa; but to suggest the possibility of any such development among the ten million colored people in this republic is self-evident foolishness."

Langston Hughes's response was direct in spite of the young poet's initial faux pas when he strained logic by equating a desire "to be a poet—not a Negro poet" with a wish "to be white." Without repudiating the Americanness of the Afro-American, he defined how a work of art by a black American can be Negro, the artist's Americanness notwithstanding. The basis is his choice of object and of manner of imitation. The black artist stands a good chance of capturing the Negro soul if he looks for his material not among the "self-styled 'high-class' Negro[es]," but among "the low-down folks, the so-called common elements." These, Hughes claimed, unlike the type of Negroes who have "Nordic manners, Nordic faces, Nordic hair, Nordic art (if any), and an Episcopal heaven," "furnish a wealth of colorful, distinctive material for any artist because they still hold their own individuality in the face of American standardizations." They could easily be found "on Seventh Street in Washington or State Street in Chicago and they do not particularly care whether they are like white folks or anybody else."

To construct works of art distinctively Negro with these elements, Hughes argued, all the Afro-American artist has to do is to bring to bear on them "his racial individuality, his heritage of rhythm and warmth, and his incongruous humor that so often, as in the Blues, becomes ironic laughter mixed with tears." It is this marriage between Negro material and the artist's "racial individuality," as a basis for the creative process, that makes Jean Toomer's *Cane* and Paul Robeson's singing "truly racial" or expressive of the Negro self. He concluded: the development of this type of black self-expressive art was his and his close associates' prideful aim.

The New Negroness of Langston Hughes resides, therefore, in one attitude of the mind: race-pride. It supports and is often indistinguishable from his African motif; it is at the base of his application of the Negro folk treatment to Negro folk material.

Langston Hughes and his associates were not the first Afro-Americans to apply folk treatment to Negro folk material. James Edwin Campbell, Paul Laurence Dunbar, Daniel Webster Davis, J. Mord Allen, the early James Weldon Johnson, and many others had written about the "common [black] elements" in Negro dialect. Not all their works, however, anticipated the self-pride and self-expression of the Harlem Renaissance literature. Many of them belonged to the minstrel tradition. In many cases, although their subject looked black and their language of creation supposedly was Negro, their end product lacked the Negro soul. Created purposely for the delectation of the white folk whose self-aggrandizement they also sought to sustain, these earlier works comprised mainly those Negro elements which experience had proved to be pleasurable to the white ego. They were, essentially, attempts to recreate the white man's concept of the black man. In other words, the Negro artists often borrowed their black material from the white man's imagination. With regard to their form, the dialect (folk) poems most often differed from their literary counterparts only in orthography. In some cases their folk treatment did not go beyond a distortion of English syntax.

Consequently, when Langston Hughes arrived on the scene the process he was to adopt was almost nonexistent, even though some critics confused it with the old minstrel tradition and feared that it might cater to the old self-aggrandizement of the white folk. Drawing his subjects straight from real (as distinct from imagined) Negro folks, he experimented with the blues and jazz forms and employed the real dialect of real Negroes, mainly of Washington, D.C., Harlem, and the South Side, Chicago. Among the results of his first experiments are "The Weary Blues," "Jazzonia," and "Negro Dancers"—poems which are important not only because they are three of his best, but also because they were the very ones that he showed to Vachel Lindsay at the Wardman Park Hotel, Washington, D.C., in December 1925. They set the tone for much of Langston Hughes's later poetry; as such they deserve a closer look.

Thomas Millard Henry was not completely wrong when he applied the phrase "a little story of action and life" to "The Weary Blues," which earned Hughes the forty-dollar first prize in the poetry section of *Opportunity's* 1925 contest. An attempt to paint a folk creator of the blues in the very action of creation, the poem is essentially a process analysis, a rhetorical pattern which is very close to narrative. Its title notwithstanding, it is hardly a true imitation of the folk blues—a genre which James Weldon Johnson rightly described as a "repository of folk-poetry." At least its form does not agree with the description of the blues pattern as given by Langston Hughes himself in 1927:

> The Blues, unlike the *Spirituals,* have a strict poetic pattern: one long line repeated and a third line to rhyme with the first two. Sometimes the second line in repetition is slightly changed and sometimes, but very seldom, it is omitted. The mood of the *Blues* is almost always despondency, but when they are sung people laugh.

Yet "The Weary Blues" is a successful poem. The monotonous, and therefore boring, sentence patterns with very little or no attention to syntax combine with the folk artist's "droning," "rocking," and swaying as well as the implication of the "old gas light," the "poor piano," and the "rickety stool" to underscore the dreariness of the player's life. We feel his blues-infected soul not only in the "sad raggy tune" squeezed out of the "poor" moaning piano, or in the "drowsy syncopated tune" and "mellow croon," but also in his helplessness vis-à-vis the song which rises in him and overflows, almost unaided, his tired voice in the semi-darkness of "an old gas light." The mood is that of "despondency." It is the mood of blues, an art form which Hughes thought was more dolorous than the spirituals because its sorrow is untempered by tears but intensified by an existentialistic laughter.

With regard to its coming too close to being an ordinary narrative, "a little story of action and life," it is even doubtful that it could have done otherwise, since the blues as a poetic expression is an exposé of an active experience physically lived through, or being contemplated mentally or internally ongoing. Witness the movement of the famous "St. Louis Blues" or the sequential approach of "Hard Times Blues." Unexpected interjections of moods and sentiments may disturb the logical sequence of the action being rehearsed or being lived mentally; they hardly disrupt the basic layout of the experience. "What's stirrin', babe?" which, incidentally, is a good example of the blues in one of its earlier stages of development, will make this point clearer:

> Went up town 'bout four o'clock;
> > What's stirrin', babe; stirrin', babe?
> When I go dere, door was locked:
> > What's stirrin', babe, what's stirrin', babe?
>
> Went to de window an' den peeped in:
> > What's stirrin', babe; stirrin', babe?
> Somebody in my fallin' den—
> > What's stirrin', babe; stirrin', babe?

The question "What's stirrin', babe?" is interjected in the first stanza to reactualize the past experience and underscore the speaker/singer's emotion: a combination of surprise and jealousy. Yet the basic structure of the action is not destroyed, as can be seen if we relocate the interjecting question where it really belongs—after the first line of the second stanza: that is, when the speaker/singer really sees something "stirrin' " in his "fallin' den [his bed]."

It is because the blues is an account of an experience lived, or an experience being lived, or an experience that will be lived, that "it was assumed," as LeRoi Jones correctly points out, "that *anybody* could sing the blues. If someone had lived in this world into manhood, it was taken for granted that he had been given the content of his verses." Langston Hughes sees the relationship between the blues and the experience of its author in his account of the singing habit of one George, a joy-seeking wretch who shipped out to Africa with him. According to Hughes "he used to make up his own Blues—verses as absurd as Krazy Kat and as funny. But sometimes when he had to do more work than he thought necessary for a happy living, or, when broke, he couldn't make the damsels of the West Coast believe love worth more than money, he used to sing about the gypsy who couldn't find words strong enough to tell about the troubles in his hard-luck soul." Janheinz Jahn is also aware of this storifying nature of the blues when he says that "the texts of the blues follow the African *narrative style almost entirely*." This feature itself is not surprising since the blues is only a distant descendant of West African folk songs through the Afro-American work songs, saddened by the black man's experience in the New World.

Whatever the case, "The Weary Blues" has something which can pass as the blues in its own right: one aspect is shown by the speaker's imitation (in the line "He did a lazy sway. . . ./He did a lazy sway. . . .") of the rhythm which the folksinger is trying to create; a second blues quality appears in the last stanza of the lyric that the pianist is in the process of composing. This stanza approximates the blues form to the extent that it could be extracted and sung as an independent folk song:

> "I got the Weary Blues
> And I can't be satisfied.
> Got the Weary Blues
> And can't be satisfied—
> I ain't happy no mo'
> And I wish that I had died."

As a matter of fact, Langston Hughes confesses in his autobiography that it is a real "blues verse"—the first he "ever heard way back in Lawrence, Kansas, when [he] was a kid."

It conforms with the three-point movement of a typical blues stanza: affirmation, reaffirmation, determination. Above all, it obeys the rule of repeated lines as well as the *a b a b c b* rhyme scheme which some of Hughes's later and more confident attempts follow, as evidenced by this stanza from "Bad Man":

I'm a bad, bad man
Cause everybody tells me so.
I'm a bad, bad man
Everybody tells me so.
I take mah meanness and ma licker
Everywhere I go.

Or by the third stanza of "Po' Boy Blues":

I fell in love with
A gal I thought was kind.
Fell in love with
A gal I thought was kind.
She made me lose ma money
An' almost lose ma mind.

Or by the last stanza of "Hard Daddy":

I wish I had wings to
Fly like de eagle flies.
Wish I had wings to
Fly like de eagle flies.
I'd fly on ma man an'
I'd scratch out both his eyes.

And by this stanza from "Bound No'th Blues":

Goin' down de road, Lawd,
Goin' down de road.
Down de road, Lawd.
Way, way down de road.
Got to find somebody
To help me carry dis load.

Just as "Aunt Sue's Stories" is a celebration of the oral tradition—that bastion of black civilization and cultural experience—and a product of the oral tradition, "The Weary Blues" is both a folk poem and a dramatization of the creation of a folk poem.

This is also true of the systematic, though disorganized, rhythm of "Jazzonia," which is modeled on jazz music whose flexible structure, like African musical habits from which it takes at least part of its roots, makes for improvisations capable of provoking a sigh or a smile or both. The speaker manipulates the rhythm and the imagery to create the gay, urgent,

and often grotesque atmosphere inherent in jazz music. The refrain with
its exotic dazzling tree (of life in the Garden of Eden) and river (Nile)
heightens the gaiety and seeks to stabilize the tempo as well as the theme.
Yet like a real piece of jazz music whose rhythm and duration are unpre-
dictable, it comes to an abrupt end at a moment when we want more of
it—not only because we want to know more about "Eve's eyes" and Cleopatra's "gown of gold" (the focus of the fourth stanza and the frame of
reference of the refrain) but also because the very two lines that crash-stop
the piece have started with a promise of at least two other lines to follow
(since they are modeled on the first two lines of the second stanza, which
has four lines):

> In a whirling cabaret
> Six long-headed jazzers play

The total effect is that of joy and sorrowful disappointment, two opposing moods which adequately reflect those of the dancing girl—an embodiment of Eve and Cleopatra, their initial joyous allurements and eventual
sorrows combined. Like real American Negro jazz, "Jazzonia" has an undercurrent of sorrow.

Indeed this could be said of most of Langston Hughes's jazz poems
before and after 1926. Witness the mournful pessimism beneath the otherwise Dionysian gaiety of "Harlem Night Club" and the frustration that
boils under the hilarious "Brass Spittoons." Jazz is like "that tune" in "Jazz
Band in a Parisian Cabaret," "that tune/That laughs and cries at the same
time." Langston Hughes had earlier indicated this happy-sorrowful nature
of jazz, which he tried to capture in most of his jazz poems:

> They say a jazz-band's gay.
> Yet as the vulgar dancers whirled
> And the wan night wore away,
> One said she heard the jazz-band sob
> When the little dawn was grey.

"Negro Dancers," the last of the poems which Hughes showed to
Vachel Lindsay, is also a folk material effectively treated in a folk manner
in spite of the jarring threat implicit in the two-line third stanza:

> White folks, laugh!
> White folks, pray!

The rhythm this time is that of the Charleston. With a combination of short
lines made up mainly of monosyllabic words and gasping punctuation, the

speaker captures the sprightful rhythm of the folk dance as well as the urgency of the folk dancer's announcement. The second and third stanzas, with their less-hurried tempo and the double entendre of a pessimistic speaker, highlight the gaiety of the rhythm of the folk dance and cast a shadow (of doubt) on the exuberance of the folk dancer. The total effect, once again, is joy with an undercurrent of sorrow—a combined reflection of the folk dancer's apparent happiness and the pessimism of the speaker who, beneath the joy of the folk dancer's publication of "two mo' ways to do de buck," seeks to uncover what looks like "I'm laughin' to keep from cryin'." Yet "Negro Dancers" is a successful imitation of the Charleston— that folk dance whose roots several students have followed beyond the Afro-American community in Charleston, S.C., into Africa.

When Langston Hughes wrote his poems or when he used the jazz and the blues forms, he thought of his manner of imitation as Afro-American, as distinct from African. Nevertheless, it could safely be assumed that he would not be shocked by the idea that his poetry reveals faint rhythms of African tom-toms and African musical habits, such as the call-and-response technique. For one thing, his "POEM For the portrait of an African boy after the manner of Gauguin" sees the rhythm of the tom-tom as a component of the African blood:

> All the tom-toms of the jungles beat in my blood,
> And all the wild hot moons of the jungles shine in my soul.
> I am afraid of this civilization—
> > So hard,
> > > So strong,
> > > > So cold.

The Afro-American, we learn from another poem, "Afraid," also is lonely and afraid "among the skyscrapers"—symbols of the non-African Western civilization—"as our ancestors" were lonely and afraid "among the palms in Africa." As another blood component, Hughes often hears a jungle timbre and feels a jungle rhythm in jazz music and jazz dance, as in "Nude Young Dancer." The young dancer, like the "night-veiled girl" of "Danse Africaine," obviously owes part of the effectiveness of her performance to her connection with the jungle.

Unlike many other Afro-Americans who used African motifs in their works, Hughes did not have to rely solely on secondhand exotic pictures of Africa in books and on celluloids. He had been physically in contact with the black continent before publishing—if not writing—most of his poems that use Africa either as a motif or as a reinforcing image in his black-is-beautiful theme. Even if he had written them before visiting Africa, it is a mark of his satisfaction with the accuracy of his conception of the ancestral continent that the poems were published after he had had the opportunity of knowing, to use his own words, "the real thing, to be touched and seen, not merely read about in a book." The attitudes of his speakers towards Africa could, therefore, be credited with a measure of sincerity instead of being simply discarded as another faddish moonshine of the Jazz Age.

Admittedly, Hughes could not always resist the temptation of trying to soothe the thirst in the 1920s for the exotic and the primitive. Some of his autobiographical short stories reveal a sacrifice of realities on the altar of masturbatory exoticism. "Luani of the Jungles," a story which appeared in the November 1928 issue of *Harlem* magazine, is a good example.

In this piece, Hughes's first-person narrator describes the physical milieu where the action takes place as accurately as his white interlocutor depicts the reception given to Luani when she returns from Europe:

> There a hundred or more members of the tribe were waiting to receive her,—beautiful brown-black people whose perfect bodies glistened in the sunlight, bodies that shamed me and the weakness under my European clothing. That night there was a great festival given in honor of Luani's coming,—much beating of drums and wild fantastic dancing beneath the moon,—a festival in which I could take no part for I knew none of their ceremonies, none of their dances. Nor did I understand a word of their language. I could only stand aside and look, or sit in the door of our hut and sip the palm wine they served me.

The story, however, moves irrecoverably towards the exotic as the white man describes Luani's behavior in her home village in Nigeria, and portrays her as going "hunting and fishing, wandering about for days in the jungles."

Firstly, it is doubtful that women among any tribe in Nigeria "went hunting and fishing . . . with members of the tribe" in the 1920s—at least not a chief's daughter who had lived in England and France. Secondly, it is doubtful that a Nigerian girl like Luani would leave her husband's bed of a night to walk about naked, making love with another man under palm trees—even if her husband were impotent. Perhaps a woman can, in 1981 Nigeria, tell her husband whom she has cheated sexually that "a woman can have two lovers and love them both." A society which had not greatly evolved from what it was in the days of Chinua Achebe's Okonkwo would have fallen completely apart before being required to listen to such an outrageous claim.

Indeed it strains credulity to accept the idea of a white man's going to live with an African wife in her African "jungle" village. A more realistic picture is that which emerges from Langston Hughes's own account of the experience of the mulatto Edward and his black African mother. The mother was only a house servant of a white man who lived at a special place reserved for whites. When the white man returned to England, "the whites inside the compound naturally would have nothing to do with them [Edward and his mother], nor would they give him [Edward] a job, and the Negroes did not like his mother, because she had lived for years with a white man, so Edward had no friends in the village, and almost nobody to talk to."

Nevertheless, the attitudes of Langston Hughes's speakers towards Africa should be credited with a measure of sincerity. Unlike the narrators of his "African" short stories (and they are too few to be significant) who tend to subscribe to the exotic image of Africa, most of them who speak of or allude to Africa were created by Hughes before 1926. It was during the post-1926 period that the genuine Afro-American's attempt to express himself and his ancestral heritage was falling into decadence as some New Negro writers consciously sought to please their audience instead of seeking to express their dark selves. Thus, if Langston Hughes had chosen after 1926 to repudiate the articles of his "manifesto" completely (and he did not do so) his action could not have affected most of his poems that deal with Africa either directly or indirectly. Besides, the inaccuracies of his speakers notwithstanding, the picture of Africa that emerges from those poems is more authentic than the images that emerge from the writings of many other New Negro authors. For instance, unlike Countee Cullen's romantic Africa where, as in *Heritage,* "cinnamon tree" grows, Langston Hughes's Africa grows "palm trees," as in "Afraid."

It is this considerably high degree of accuracy in the conception of the face of Africa that separates Hughes's "African" poems from those of his fellow New Negroes (who used the same motifs) without, however, depriving them of the basic New Negro awareness of the Dark Continent's presence in the Afro-American's life.

Hughes's black Americans, whose attitudes his first-person speakers voice, have no illusions either of the remoteness of Africa both in time and space or of their unquestionable right to full American citizenship. They all "sing America"; they are all Americans, the darkness of their skins notwithstanding. Even in the poem "Dream Variation"—where the speaker longs "to fling [his] arms wide/In some place of the sun,/To whirl and to dance/Till the white day is done./Then rest at cool evening/Beneath a tall tree/While night comes on gently"—it is America that is being sung. The dream is a wish fulfillment. Unable to belong effectively to his live society, the speaker wishes for a place where he could relax. The motivation of this "dream" is the motivation of the numerous back-to-Africa movements. The dream would not occur if the live situation were not painful. This can also be said of "Our Land," which the poet tellingly subtitled "Poem for a Decorative Panel"—fine art, another channel of wish fulfillment. As a re-action to "this land where life is cold," the speaker wishes for a dreamland which exists nowhere on this planet.

Nonetheless, Langston Hughes's Afro-Americans recognize and affirm their relations with Africa, whose heritage and experience they cherish and revere as sources of pride-inspiring characteristics. In "The Negro Speaks of Rivers" the characteristic is stability which, ironically, has developed from the instability of the speaker's experience. The impermanence of his situation (as an enslaved African), from life on the Euphrates of ancient history to the Mississippi of relatively modern times, has toughened his mind and skin, making him as stable as the rivers whose rise and fall in importance have not destroyed them: "My soul has grown deep like the rivers." He could as well say as a mother says to a son in a later poem:

> I'se still goin', honey,
> I'se still climbin',
> And life for me ain't been no crystal stair.
>
> ("Mother to Son")

Stability through the instability of Africa and her sons is also the point of "Proem," which, in a way, resembles "The Negro Speaks of Rivers." The blackness of the speaker's skin relates him directly to the blackness of night and of the depths of Africa. Just as the blackness of night and of the depths of Africa is an unchangeable fact, so also is the speaker's blackness with all its fortitude already tested and confirmed. He IS. His blackness, derived from Africa, has exposed him to a toughening experience. He IS now as real as his experience WAS.

In many other poems by Hughes the inherent characteristic of the Afro-American African ancestry is beauty. We see this in "When Sue Wears Red," a poem which Hughes wrote at the age of seventeen about a seventeen-year-old "brownish girl" who had recently arrived from the South, and sometimes "wore a red dress that was very becoming to her." Susanna Jones, beautiful in her "red dress," is portrayed as a reincarnation of a dead African queen, possibly Cleopatra in view of her obvious coquetry or tantalizing charm which "burns . . . a love-fire sharp like pain" in the speaker's heart. The piece "Poem," which was first published in the June 1922 number of *The Crisis,* is a direct assertion of the beauty of the black race:

> The night is beautiful
> So the faces of my people.
>
> The stars are beautiful,
> So the eyes of my people.
>
> Beautiful, also, is the sun.
> Beautiful, also, are the souls of my people.

In most of Hughes's poems *night* is interchangeable with *blackness*; the two words as well as *sun* often relate the subject in focus to Africa as the foundation or the starting point of black life and experience in America.

Langston Hughes's speakers are hardly loud in their acknowledgment of their relationship with Africa. When they try to be, as in "Afro-American Fragment" (which, though published in 1930, is a good summary of the speakers' attitudes towards Africa), their voices tremble with an anti-African note. The repetition of the first three lines ("So long,/So far away/Is Africa") at the end of the first stanza (and, indeed, at the end of the next and only other stanza) underscores the speaker's wish that his disassociation of himself from Africa be taken seriously. Nevertheless, beneath the disassociation is a strong undercurrent of affirmation of the speaker's kinship with "Africa's Dark Face." It is one thing to stop the "drums"; to muffle the sound already produced is another. While the production of drum sounds requires a conscious and, under normal conditions, a voluntary effort, resurgence of the sound after the process that produced it has been discontinued can take place in spite of the feeling and preoccupation of the person in whose mind it has been registered.

Langston Hughes in the 1920s wrote poems like "Winter Moon," "March Moon," "Sea Calm," "Cross," "The Jester," and "The Minstrel Man." These are either nonracial, or extemely racial. When nonracial, they contain nothing that could be described as distinctively Negro. Splendid as it is, for instance, the three-line "Suicide's Note" could have been written by Alfred, Lord Tennyson:

> The calm,
> Cool face of the river
> Asked me for a kiss

When extremely racial, they assume various aspects of the writings of the Old Negro authors—from the Niagara fume of "The South," which could

have come from W. E. B. Du Bois's pen to the Old Negro Christlike virtue
of "The White Ones."

Based on the experience of the black man in the New World though
these poems are, they did very little or nothing to affirm with pride the
Negro self. This assignment was left for the poems where Hughes considerably exploited the Negro folk material and folk medium of creation or
acknowledged, even if ambivalently, his ancestral heritage as it related to
Africa.

These were the basis of his New Negroness. He expressed the dark self
of the Afro-American without for the most part trying to please or displease
the black man or his white brother. "With quiet ecstatic sense of kinship
with even the most common and lowly folk," as Alain Locke puts it, he
"discovers in them, in spite of their individual sordidness and backwardness,
the epic quality of collective strength and beauty." These were also the basis
of his originality, which, ironically, laid him open to attacks, especially from
black scholars and critics who, with Benjamin Brawley, saw his themes as
"unnecessarily sordid and vulgar" and his manner of treating them as a
good example of "imperfect mastery of technique."

This, however, was mainly a cover for the belief that Hughes was only
catering to the pleasure of white faddists who had allegedly influenced him
in a bad way. Even Wallace Thurman, his fellow traveler on the bandwagon
of "Fire," thought as much when he charged that "urged on by a faddistic
interest in the unusual, Mr. Hughes has been excessively prolific, and has
exercised little restraint.

The strongest and most direct charges, however, came from Benjamin
Brawley in his article "The Negro Literary Renaissance," published in the
*Southern Workman,* and from Allison Davis, who claimed that "the severest
charge one can make against Mr. Van Vechten is that he misdirected a
genuine poet, who gave promise of a power and technique exceptional in
any poetry,—Mr. Hughes." Both of them drew immediate responses, one
from Carl Van Vechten and the other from Langston Hughes.

Benjamin Brawley had implied that Van Vechten had influenced Langston Hughes's first volume of poetry, *The Weary Blues,* which contains a
preface written by Carl Van Vechten. In his reply, therefore, Van Vechten
tried to show that that could not have been possible:

> *The Weary Blues* had won a prize before I had read a poem by
> Mr. Hughes or knew him personally. The volume, of which this
> was the title poem, was brought to me complete before Mr.
> Hughes and I ever exchanged two sentences. I am unaware even

to this day, although we are the warmest friends and see each other frequently, that I have had the slightest influence on Mr. Hughes in any direction. The influence, if one exists, flows from the other side, as any one might see who read my first paper on the *Blues,* published in *Vanity Fair* for August, 1925, a full year before *Nigger Heaven* appeared, before, indeed, a line of it had been written. In this paper I quoted freely Mr. Hughes' opinion on the subject of Negro folk song, opinions which to my knowledge have not changed in the slightest.

Unfortunately for his argument, however, the opening part of his statement does not agree with established facts from other reliable sources— including his own introduction to the book in question: *The Weary Blues.* He met Langston Hughes and Countee Cullen for the first time on November 10, 1924, the very day Langston Hughes returned from sea, and was introduced to him by Walter White at a party given by the NAACP. He met and spoke with Langston Hughes again a year later at the 1925 Awards dinner of *Opportunity,* where the poem "The Weary Blues" was awarded the first prize for poetry. Obviously, "the volume, of which this was the title poem," was not given to him for onward transmission to Alfred Knopf until later. Furthermore, the claim that he had not written "a line" of his *Nigger Heaven* by August 1925 is misleading, for in a letter dated March 26, 1925, Langston Hughes hoped " 'Nigger Heaven' 's successfully finished. It is, isn't it?"

Langston Hughes's rejoinder was stronger. Allison Davis, writing after Van Vechten's denial of Benjamin Brawley's charge, had argued that if the author of *Nigger Heaven* did not influence *The Weary Blues,* he "undoubtedly *did* influence" *Fine Clothes to the Jew,* Hughes's second volume of poems, which was dedicated to Carl Van Vechten. In his letter to the editor of *The Crisis* Langston Hughes offered "a correction" based on verifiable facts. He had written many of the poems in both *The Weary Blues* and *Fine Clothes to the Jew* before November 10, 1924, when he met Van Vechten for the first time:

> I would like herewith to state and declare that many of the poems in said book were written before I made the acquaintance of Mr. Van Vechten, as the files of THE CRISIS will prove; before the appearance of *The Weary Blues* containing his preface; and before ever he had commented in any way on my work. (See THE CRISIS for June, 1922, August, 1923, several issues in 1925; also *Buccaneer* for May, 1925.) Those poems which were written

after my acquaintance with Mr. Van Vechten were certainly not about him, not requested by him, not misdirected by him, some of them not liked by him nor so far as I know, do they in any way bear his poetic influence.

He returned to the matter in 1940 and explained that most of the poems that supposedly revealed Carl Van Vechten's influence on *Fine Clothes to the Jew* were not included in the earlier volume "because scarcely any dialect or folk-poems were included in the *Weary Blues.*" While what Hughes means by "folk-poems" is not clear, the emphasis in his statement is on the modifier "scarcely," because *The Weary Blues* does contain folk poems.

In any event, Langston Hughes could not have owed his interest in the blues and jazz to Carl Van Vechten. His pre-August 1925 correspondence with Van Vechten confirms the latter's claim with regard to the possibility of Hughes's having influenced his concept of the blues although they had different tastes. Hughes's interest in the blues could be traced to the time when, at the age of nine, he heard the blues on Independence Avenue and on Twelfth Street In Kansas City. With regard to jazz, he wrote one of his best jazz poems, "When Sue Wears Red," at the age of seventeen. He met Carl Van Vechten at the age of twenty-two.

A careful study of his development as a writer shows that the credit for influence has often been misdirected. The three persons who most deserve it are frequently forgotten: (1) Paul Laurence Dunbar, whose dialect poems he liked and tried to imitate as a child; (2) Ethel Weimer, his English teacher at Central High School in Cleveland, who introduced him to the writings of Carl Sandburg, Amy Lowell, Vachel Lindsay, and Edgar Lee Masters; (3) Carl Sandburg, whose influence on his budding poetic temperament is evident in the form and content of some of his juvenilia and who, obviously, helped to start him on the road which eventually led him to the stark realism—both in subject and style—that shocked some of his critics. Hughes described Sandburg as his "guiding star" in 1940; he had as a boy written a poem about him.

Vachel Lindsay only helped to enlarge his audience since Hughes had already been published by *The Crisis* before he met and showed Lindsay his "Jazzonia," "Negro Dancers," and "The Weary Blues" at the Wardman Park Hotel in December 1925. As a matter of fact, the three poems had already been published in magazines before Lindsay saw them: "Jazzonia" in *The Crisis,* August 1923; "Negro Dancers" in *The Crisis,* March 1925; "The Weary Blues" in *Opportunity,* May 1925, after winning a prize. In any case, Hughes's work does not reveal as much influence of Vachel Lindsay as Countee Cullen's use of the African motif does, for instance.

Still more conspicuous is the absence of the influence of Hughes's famous patron on his work. Incidentally, Langston Hughes was introduced to her only in 1928. At that time he had already published his first two volumes of poetry. He started work on his first novel, *Not without Laughter,* in the summer of that year. Although the grant he received from her enabled him to complete and revise the novel, any influence she must have had on its form or content is not apparent. The relationship came to an end in December 1930 because Hughes could not satisfy her wish that he "be primitive and know and feel the intuitions of the primitive."

Carl Van Vechten's interest in his writing must have been pleasing and encouraging to the young author. Given, however, Langston Hughes's strong sense of independence of opinion and of action, both as a child and as an adult, it is fairly reasonable to assume that his choice of subject and of manner of treatment could have been exactly as he had worked them out (before his acquaintance with Van Vechten) with or without the interest and encouragement of the author of *Nigger Heaven* or anyone else.

He was predisposed to identification with the common man—the black masses or, to use a more recent phrase, "the soul people." He was one of them. He looked through their eyes and felt through their senses. His art, therefore, was black self-expression.

DAVID MICHAEL NIFONG

# Narrative Technique
# *in* The Ways of White Folk

*After all, I suppose, how anything is seen depends on whose eyes*
*look at it.*
                                        —*I Wonder as I Wander*

The young Langston Hughes, intent on making a living through his writing, ventured in 1933 into what was for him a relatively new genre, "and
once started," Hughes recalls, "I wrote almost nothing but short stories."
The resulting collection, *The Ways of White Folks,* serves two important
purposes for the critic of Black American literature. First, it offers stories
which deal truthfully, ironically, and (oftentimes) humorously with "some
nuance of the race relation." Second, the collection offers a unique opportunity for the study of numerous different narrative points of view in a
single volume. While the first purpose has intrigued readers for years, the
second has been ignored. A close reading of the collection reveals the effectiveness of Hughes's conscious or subconscious experimentation with
narrative perspective, and a review of formalistic critical theory further
illuminates these techniques. Hughes's strategies include three first-person
narratives: a well-crafted oral monologue ("A Good Job Gone"), a disap-
pointing epistle ("Passing"), and a beautifully constructed stream-of-con-
sciousness/internal monologue ("Red-Headed Baby"). An omniscient
narrator convincingly probes the minds of three main characters in the only
story to use this difficult perspective ("Father and Son"). The more numerous third-person narratives range from a straightforward character

From *Black American Literature Forum* 15, no. 3 (Fall 1981). © 1981 by Indiana
State University.

169

sketch ("Berry") to a psychological central intelligence study ("Little Dog"). The final strategy, one rarely attempted by authors, is a dramatic monologue with an effaced narrator ("Mother and Child"). Here Hughes moves away from the egocentric and nosy narrators to one who seemingly does not exist. This incredible variety of perspectives makes the study of *The Ways of White Folks* both enjoyable and enlightening.

One can easily see the inseparability of form and content in the study of poetry where form controls and shapes the content just as the content determines the form. While there are some ideas which simply cannot be expressed in sonnet form, there are others which can be expressed in no other way. The close interrelationship between form and content of poetry has been widely discussed by the formalist critics, and it is only natural that the critical concepts which they developed should be carried into the study of fiction. As the formalistic critical theories have been applied to works of fiction, there has been born a renewed awareness of technique and of the importance which narrative point of view plays in shaping a work of fiction.

Mark Schorer is one of the most influential spokesmen of the formalist movement, and his essay "Technique as Discovery" is one of the central essays in modern criticism of the novel because

> it states most explicitly and emphatically the formalist attitude toward fiction, in which the unit is the word, the embodiment the technique, and the result an aesthetic whole that is valid on its own terms.
>
> (R. M. Davis, *The Novel: Modern Essays in Criticism*)

The far-reaching effects of Schorer's essay, written in 1948, can be seen in the writings of Robert Scholes, Robert Kellogg, Norman Friedman, John E. Tilford, and Wayne C. Booth. These men acknowledge the importance of Schorer's concepts and base their theories on his premise that technique and subject matter are inseparable and that technique is something more crucial than mere embellishment.

According to Schorer, modern criticism has clearly demonstrated that "in art beauty and truth are indivisible and one." Revising this statement, Schorer substitutes "form" for "beauty" and "content" for "truth" and further narrows the distinction by saying that "in art technique and subject matter are indivisible and one." Content divorced from form is simply experience, while "achieved content" is a work of art. Therefore, "the difference between content, or experience, and achieved content, or art, is technique." Schorer's widely quoted definition states that

> Technique is the means by which the writer's experience, which is his subject matter, compels him to attend to it; technique is the only means he has of discovering, exploring, developing his subject, of conveying its meaning, and finally, of evaluating it.

Furthermore, when applying the term "technique" to fiction, Schorer uses the term to signify two fundamentals of writing. First, technique refers to the manner in which language is used to express the experience which the author wishes to relate; second, technique refers to the use of point of view "not only as a mode of dramatic delineation, but more particularly of thematic definition."

Wayne Booth, in *The Rhetoric of Fiction*, echoes Schorer's emphasis:

> We all agree that point of view is in some sense a technical matter, a means to larger ends; whether we say that technique is the artist's way of discovering his artistic meaning or that it is his way of working his will upon his audience, we can still judge it only in the light of the larger meaning or effects which it is designed to serve.

The best way to judge the effectiveness of point of view as technique is to study the different narrative postures in several works of art and decide whether the artist succeeds in reaching his desired audience response. The critic who has read widely will have no trouble in comparing various approaches of authors to narrative point of view. It is exciting, however, to discover a collection of short stories which makes the study of point of view relatively simple. In *The Ways of White Folks* one discovers that Langston Hughes experiments with seven points of view and meets with varying degrees of success.

The first-person narrator appears in three stories in *The Ways of White Folks*, yet each is slightly different. "A Good Job Gone," a story about a wealthy white man who goes crazy after his black mistress leaves him, is related as an historic monologue from the point of view of the black houseboy who finds himself without a job after Mr. Lloyd's breakdown. Scholes and Kellogg point out that there is a quite useful distinction between the first person speaker in empirical narrative and the first person speakers of fictional narrative. By the "telling" of this story, Hughes limits the reader to information which the protagonist shares. Everything appears through this unnamed protagonist's eyes, and the only picture of the protagonist available to the reader is a mirror's reflection. One must also realize that the entire story is written in the historic past. By reporting what has already happened, the narrator further selects and limits what the reader perceives. This retrospective point of view also gives the story a folk tale quality, especially when one realizes by the last sentences ("Say boy, gimme a smoke will you? I hate to talk about it.") that the story has been presented orally and "overheard" by the reader. As John Tilford explains, by telling the story from the "inside"—that is, having one of the characters tell it—there is a certain tone, focus, conviction, meaning, and flavor of style which could not be retained if the story were told in the third person.

The short sketch entitled "Passing" is also written in the first person but is in the form of a letter. Jack, the son of a black mother and a white father, writes to thank his mother for pretending she did not know him when he and his white fiancée passed her on the street. The narrative focus is so limited in the epistolary form that it is questionable as to whether "Passing" can be called a short story. The characterization, setting, and plot are so tied up in the implied author's choice of words that, as a traditional short story, it simply does not suffice. Jack finds it necessary to tell his mother details of which she would not need to be reminded unless she were senile and blind. For instance, he writes that his brother Charlie is "darker than you, even, Ma," and recalls the generosity of his white father who "did buy you a house and send all us kids through school." In case she has forgotten where he went to college, Jack adds, "I'm glad I finished college in Pittsburgh before he died." The structural irony of the piece is its sole redeeming quality. Jack has already passed but has not yet severed his last tie to the black community—his relationship with his mother. The only thing which still holds them together is their correspondence through letters. In what Scholes and Kellogg term "empirical narration" through an autobiographical confessor, Jack lets his mother know that it was not the presence of his white girl friend that kept him from speaking to her, but that it was the whole concept of "crossing the color line." Early in the letter he states, "If I hadn't had the girl with me, Ma, we might have talked," and later he writes, "But I don't mind being 'white,' Ma." The pitiful closing of the letter pleads: "Even if we can't meet often, we can write, can't we, Ma?" Jack, who has definitely constructed his whole world and has determined his own future, knows that he and his mother can no longer write, that when he betrayed his heritage by passing his mother on the street he had completed the passing process and could now refer to himself as white—without the quotation marks.

Hughes creates a most effective story by combining the first-person point of view with a poetic internal monologue in "Red-Headed Baby." This powerfully written piece, about a white sailor who returns to the house of his black lover and finds himself face to face with his three-year-old, red-headed, deaf and dumb son, would easily fit between the covers of Jean Toomer's *Cane*. Poetry and fiction are successfully fused as Hughes allows his creativity full reign. One observes the futile life of Clarence, a poor white sailor whose existence is nothing but "Mosquitoes, sand, niggers." The stagnation of Clarence's life is made quite obvious through the restlessness of the narrative style. Short choppy sentences show a man wanting to run but with no place to go except back to Betsy. Once reunited with her, Clarence hopes to calm his mind, but Hughes presents the following passage which has a distinct Joycean aura:

> Soft heavy hips. Hot and browner than the moon—good licker. Drinking it down in little nigger house Florida coast palm fronds scratching roof hum mosquitoes night bugs flies ain't loud enough to keep a man named Clarence girl named Betsy old woman named Auntie from talking and drinking in a little nigger house on Florida coast dead warm night with the licker browner and more firey than the moon. Yeah man! . . . and everybody drinking . . when . . the door . . slowly . . . opens.

This stream-of-consciousness technique is reminiscent of "Penelope" in *Ulysses,* a book with which Hughes probably became familiar in Paris even before it was allowed into the United States. Clarence's complete rejection of his son, and his need to prostitute the evening by paying for his drinks, brings this excellent story to a conclusion of complete pathos.

Perhaps the most difficult point of view to incorporate in one's writing is that of the omniscient narrator. Scholes and Kellogg deny the availability of omniscience as a method for the modern writer. Since omniscience includes the god-like attribute of omnipresence,

> a narrator in fiction is imbedded in a time-bound artifact. He does not "know" simultaneously but consecutively. He is not everywhere at once but now here, now there, now looking into this mind or that, now moving to other vantage points.
>
> (Robert Scholes and Robert Kellogg, *The Nature of Narrative*)

The range of the story is wide open since the narrator is often compelled to tell the reader everything about every character in every situation. The closest which Hughes comes to this approach in *The Ways of White Folks* is in the lengthy story entitled "Father and Son." The plot of this tale revolves around the homecoming of Bert, the twenty-year-old son of Cora, a black housekeeper, and Colonel Norwood, a white plantation owner. The conflict arises when Bert refuses to be a "white folks' nigger" and expects to be treated like the well-educated man he is. Bert's pride and his father's obstinacy lead to patricide, Cora's mental breakdown, Bert's suicide, and the lynching of both Bert's dead body and the live body of his brother Willie—the perfect "white folks' nigger."

The narrator does not exploit his omniscient capabilities but allows the reader to see behind the different characters at certain times. Therefore, one is able to see that Colonel Norwood is eagerly awaiting his son's return even though his actions around the other characters would never indicate this. The narrator, in the third paragraph, states: "Colonel Norwood never would have admitted, *even to himself,* that he was standing in his doorway waiting for his half-Negro son to come home. But in truth that is what he was doing" (my italics). One quickly sees that the narrator is separated from Norwood and is capable of observing the Colonel's mental state and motives when the Colonel cannot even do this himself. The narrator obviously has power. In section 5 he begins to set the tone of Bert's rebellion:

> There are people (you've probably noted it also) who have the unconscious faculty of making the world spin around themselves, throb and expand, contract and go dizzy. Then, when they are gone away, you feel sick and lonesome and meaningless.

Here the narrator foreshadows the forthcoming trouble caused by Bert's refusal to be a "white folks' nigger." Through the use of the parenthetical expression, the narrator steps out of the boundaries of the story and directly addresses the reader. Hughes enjoys making these parenthetical "asides," and there are seventy-three in the book. The ultimate result of the omniscient narrator in this story is the full characterization of Bert, Cora, and Colonel Norwood. Since the point of view is not limited to any one of these main characters, each is able to be developed to an extent not possible with any other narrative perspective.

The simple third-person point of view is used in the majority of the selections in *The Ways of White Folks.* Hughes adds variety to this common narrative approach by giving the implied author or narrator a definite skin color. The reader readily understands that he is viewing the characters and situations through racial eyes, and this understanding adds an extra depth to the stories. "Berry" is a rather short sketch about the mistreatment of a young black man who works at a summer camp where crippled children receive care which is far inferior to what their middle-class white parents have paid for. Milberry, or Berry as the children call him, is uneducated but possesses "plenty of mother wit and lots of intuition about people and places." His insightfulness allows him to see through the scam of the children's home, but since jobs are scarce, Berry puts up with the inept white staff until he is mercilessly dismissed. The first sentence of the story ironically reveals the race of the narrator: "When the boy arrived on the four o'clock train, lo and behold, he turned out to be colored!" From this point, the narration proceeds in a matter-of-fact fashion, commenting on the characters and their relationships with this one black employee. The narrator realizes that Milberry is being overworked, but "Still he did everything and didn't look mad—jobs were hard to get, and he had been hungry too long in town." The naive young man then speaks the passage from which the title of the book is taken:

> "Besides," Milberry said to himself, "the ways of white folks, I mean some white folks, is too much for me. I reckon they must be a few good ones, but most of 'em ain't good—leastwise they don't treat me good. And Lawd knows, I ain't never done nothin' to 'em, nothin' a-tall."

The reader is forced to respond with anger when he sees the injustice performed against Milberry. As Booth points out, the implied author can be more or less distant from other characters and can be inferred as approving of actions almost completely while the reader, as chief "reflector," definitely disapproves of the social injustices. Thus, the one good character of the story—a young man who shows love to the crippled children—is sent away without pay. Thereby, the world of the indifferent white narrator triumphs over the helpless black man.

In "Little Dog," Hughes follows the Jamesean technique of further developing the third-person narrator into a central intelligence. In what [Norman] Friedman terms "selective omniscience," the reader is limited to the mind of only one of the characters. "Instead, therefore, of being allowed a composite of viewing angles, he is at the fixed center." Here, the narrator focuses on the thoughts and actions of Miss Clara Briggs, a forty-five-year-old white spinster who fantasizes about the black janitor who brings meat and bones to her little white dog. The reader is not limited to the shadowing of Miss Briggs's actions by an outsider, but is able to get inside her mind. One sees a lonely, introverted lady who tries to share her life with her little white dog but who runs when she is faced with the possibility of sharing her life with her big black janitor. The strangely sexual imagery of this black man nightly bringing his meat to the lady is fully exploited by the narrator and is reflected in Miss Briggs's mind:

> When the Negro really knocked on the door with the meat, she
> was trembling so that she could not go to the kitchen to get it.
> "Oh, Flips," she said, "I'm so hungry." She meant to say "*You're*
> so hungry." So she repeated it. "You're so hungry! Heh, Flipsy,
> dog?"
>
> And from the way the little dog barked, he must have been
> hungry. He loved meat.

Through the use of the central intelligence, one is fully acquainted with the strange thoughts and actions of Miss Clara Briggs. "The result is unity of focus, intensity, strong identification of the reader with one character, and a certain esthetic distance not possible in first person narration."

One final point of view is found in "Mother and Child," a story about the birth of a black baby to a white family and the resulting turmoil in the small Ohio town. The baby's father, Douglass Carter, a twenty-six-year-old black farmer, refuses to run as the black community advises; the resolute Carter stays in Boyd's Center waiting for his lover's husband to turn out both baby and mother. In this story Hughes employs the effaced narrator in a dramatic dialogue. Having eliminated the author and the narrator, Hughes is now ready to dispose of mental states altogether. A story with an effaced narrator, as Friedman suggests, is

> in effect a stage play cast into the typographical mold of fiction.
> But there is some difference: fiction is meant to be read, drama
> to be seen and heard, and there will be a corresponding difference
> in scope, range, fluidity, and subtlety.

This technique (also used by Hemingway in "The Killers") would seemingly be difficult to incorporate since all of the story's vital information must be presented in the conversation of the characters without the aid of Shavian stage directions. However, the technique works exceptionally well in this particular story since the characters involved in the dialogue are a bunch of old ladies who doubtlessly like nothing better than spreading the latest gossip. An outside narrator probably couldn't get a word in edgewise! When the ladies are finally called to order by Madam President, the irony of the story is made apparent:

> "The March meeting of the Salvation Rock Ladies Missionary
> Society for the Rescue o' the African Heathen is hereby called
> to order. . . . Sister Burns, raise a hymn. . . . Will you-all ladies
> *please* be quiet? What are you talking 'bout back there anyhow?"

Amidst the singing, the Sisters realize that there are heathens in need of rescue much closer than Africa. Once again, the narrative technique works for Langston Hughes in this interesting dramatic sketch.

Thus, as one studies narrative technique and applies the theories to a given work of art, he discovers the vast, controlling importance of point of view.

> Once made, the author's choice of point of view and the mode of language appropriate to it will influence his presentation of a character, incident, and every other thing represented. For the reader, however, point of view is not an esthetic matter but a mode of perception. The point of view in a given work controls the reader's impression of everything else.
>
> (Scholes and Kellogg)

As one reads *The Ways of White Folks*, it is easy to enjoy the well-developed plots and the masterful character studies, but when the reader takes a closer look to analyze just what it is that makes this collection of short stories good, he discovers Hughes's excellent use of point of view. Whether he is creating the self-centered narrator of "A Good Job Gone" or the all-seeing narrator of "Father and Son," Hughes carefully molds the narrator to fulfill the function of shaping experience into art. The result is an exceptional assortment of narrative perspectives which do not appear as superfluous embellishment but prove to be integral parts of the aesthetic whole.

ARNOLD RAMPERSAD

# The Origins of Poetry in Langston Hughes

In his study *The Life of the Poet: Beginning and Ending Poetic Careers* (1981) Lawrence Lipking asks three main questions, one of which concerns me here in the case of Langston Hughes: "How does an aspiring author of verses become a poet?" In the case of John Keats, for example, how did the poet arrive at "On First Looking into Chapman's Homer," that great leap in creative ability in which Keats, sweeping from the legend of "the realms of gold" toward modern history, "catches sight not of someone else's dream but of his own reality? He stares at his future, and surmises that he may be a poet. The sense of possibility is thrilling, the moment truly awesome. Keats has discovered Keats." Or in the well-known words of Keats himself: "The Genius of Poetry must work out its own salvation in a man: It cannot be matured by law & precept, but by sensation & watchfulness in itself—That which is creative must create itself."

Can one ask a similar question about the origins of poetry in Langston Hughes, who in June 1921, at the age of nineteen, began a celebrated career when he published his own landmark poem "The Negro Speaks of Rivers" in W. E. B. Du Bois's *Crisis* magazine? Like Keats before "Chapman's Homer," Hughes had written poems before "The Negro Speaks of Rivers." Much of the poetry before "Rivers" is available for examination, since Hughes published steadily in the monthly magazine of his high school in Cleveland, Ohio. Certain aspects of this verse are noteworthy. It has nothing to do with race; it is dominated by images of the poet not as a teenager but as a little child; and, in Hughes's junior year, he published his first

From *The Southern Review* 21, no. 3 (July 1985). © 1985 by Louisiana State University.

poem in free verse, one that showed the clear influence of Walt Whitman for the first (but not the last) time. Revealing an increase in skill, Hughes's early poetry nevertheless gives no sign of a major poetic talent in the making. At some point in his development, however, something happened to Hughes that was as mysterious and as wonderful, in its own way, as the miracle that overtook John Keats after the watchful night spent with his friend Charles Cowden Clarke and a copy of Chapman's translation. With "The Negro Speaks of Rivers" the creativity in Langston Hughes, hitherto essentially unexpressed, suddenly created itself.

In writing thus about Hughes, are we taking him too seriously? With a few exceptions, literary critics have resisted offering even a modestly complicated theory concerning his creativity. His relentless affability and charm, his deep, open love of the black masses, his devotion to their folk forms, and his insistence on writing poetry that they could understand, all have contributed to the notion that Langston Hughes was intellectually and emotionally shallow. One wonders, then, at the source of the creative energy that drove him from 1921 to 1967 to write so many poems, novels, short stories, plays, operas, popular histories, children's books, and assorted other work. As a poet, Hughes virtually reinvented Afro-American poetry with his pioneering use of the blues and other folk forms; as Howard Mumford Jones marveled in a 1927 review, Hughes added the verse form of the blues to poetry in English (a form that continues to attract the best black poets, including Michael Harper, Sherley Anne Williams, and Raymond Patterson). One wonders, too, in his aspect as a poet, why this apparently happy, apparently shallow man defined his creativity in terms of unhappiness. "I felt bad for the next three or four years," he would write in *The Big Sea* about the period beginning more or less with the publication of "The Negro Speaks of Rivers," "and those were the years when I wrote most of my poetry. (For my best poems were all written when I felt the worst. When I was happy, I didn't write anything.)"

Hughes actively promoted the image of geniality to which I have alluded. Wanting and needing to be loved, he scrubbed and polished his personality until there was no abrasive side, no jagged edge that might wound another human being. Publicly and privately, his manner belied the commonly held belief that creativity and madness are allied, that neuroses and a degree of malevolence are the fair price of art. His autobiographies, *The Big Sea* (1940) and *I Wonder as I Wander* (1956), made no enemies; to many readers, Hughes's mastery of that form consists in his ability to cross its chill deep by paddling nonchalantly on its surface. And yet in two places, no doubt deliberately, Hughes allows the reader a glimpse of inner turmoil. Both appear in the earlier book, *The Big Sea*. Both involve personal and emotional conflicts so intense that they led to physical illness. Because of their extreme rarity, as well as their strategic location in the context of his creativity, these passages deserve close scrutiny if we hope to glimpse the roots of Hughes's originality as a poet.

The first of these two illnesses took place in the summer of 1919, when Hughes (at seventeen) saw his father for the first time in a dozen years. In 1903, James Hughes had gone to Mexico, where he would become a prosperous property owner. In a lonely, impoverished, passed-around childhood in the Midwest, his son had fantasized about the man "as a kind of strong, bronze cowboy, in a big Mexican hat, going back and forth from his business in the city to his ranch in the mountains, free—in a land where there were no white folks to draw the color line, and no tenements with rent always due—just mountains and cacti: Mexico!" Elated to be invited suddenly to Mexico in 1919 at the end of his junior year in high school, Langston left the United States with high hopes for his visit.

The summer was a disaster. James Hughes proved to be an unfeeling, domineering, and materialistic man, scornful of Indians and blacks (he was himself black) and the poor in general, and contemptuous of his son's gentler pace and artistic temperament. One day, Langston could take no more: "Suddenly my stomach began to turn over and over. And I could not swallow another mouthful. Waves of heat engulfed me. My eyes burned. My body shook. I wanted more than anything on earth to hit my father, but instead I got up from the table and went back to bed. The bed went round and round and the room turned dark. Anger clotted in every vein, and my tongue tasted like dry blood." But the boy, ill for a long time, never confessed the true cause of his affliction. Having been moved to Mexico City, he declined to help his doctors: "I never told them . . . that I was sick because I hated my father." He recovered only when it was time to return to the United States.

Hughes's second major illness came eleven years later. By this time he had finished high school, returned to Mexico to live with his father for a year, attended Columbia University for one year (supported grudgingly by James Hughes), dropped out of school, and served as a messman on voyages to Africa and to Europe, where he spent several months in 1924 as a dishwasher. All the while, however, Hughes was publishing poetry in a variety of places, especially in important black journals. This activity culminated in books of verse published in 1926 (*The Weary Blues*) and 1927 (*Fine Clothes to the Jew*) that established him, with Countee Cullen, as one of two major black poets of the decade. In 1929, he graduated after three and a half years at black Lincoln University, Pennsylvania. In 1930, Hughes published his first novel, *Not without Laughter*.

This book had been virtually dragged out of him by his patron of the preceding three years, "Godmother" (as she wished to be called), an old, white, very generous but eccentric woman who ruled Hughes with a benevolent despotism inspired by her volatile beliefs in African spirituality, folk culture, mental telepathy, and the potential of his genius. But the result of her largesse was a paradox: the more comfortable he grew, the less Hughes was inclined to create. Estranged by his apparent languor, his patron finally seized on an episode of conflict to banish him once and for all. Hughes was devastated. Surviving drafts of his letters to "Godmother" reveal him deep in self-abasement before a woman with whom he was clearly in love. Ten years later, he confessed in *The Big Sea:* "I cannot write here about that last half-hour in the big bright drawing-room high above Park Avenue . . . because when I think about it, even now, something happens in the pit of my stomach that makes me ill. That beautiful room . . . suddenly became like a trap closing in, faster and faster, the room darker and darker, until the light went out with a sudden crash in the dark, and everything became like . . . that morning in Mexico when I suddenly hated my father.

"I was violently and physically ill, with my stomach turning over and over. . . . And there was no rationalizing anything. I couldn't." For several months, according to my research (Hughes erroneously presents a far briefer time frame in *The Big Sea*), he waited in excruciating hope for a reconciliation. As in Mexico, he wasted time and money on doctors without revealing to them the source of his chronic illness (which one very ingenious Harlem physician diagnosed as a Japanese tapeworm). Rather than break his silence, Hughes even agreed to have his tonsils removed. Gradually it became clear that reconciliation was impossible. Winning a prize of four hundred dollars for his novel, Hughes fled to seclusion in hot, remote Haiti. When his money ran out some months later, he returned home, healed at last but badly scarred.

Although they occurred more than a decade apart, the two illnesses were similar. Both showed a normally placid Hughes driven into deep rage by an opponent, a rage which he was unable to ventilate because the easy expression of personal anger and indignation was anathema to him. In both cases, he developed physical symptoms of hyperventilation and, eventually, anemia. More importantly, both were triggered in a period of relatively low poetic creativity (as when he was still a juvenile poet) or outright poetic inactivity (as with his patron). In each instance, Hughes had become satisfied with this low creativity or inactivity. At both times, a certain powerful figure, first his father, then "Godmother," had opposed his right to be content. His father had opposed any poetic activity at all; "Godmother" had opposed his right to enjoy the poetical state without true poetical action, or writing. In other words, a powerful will presented itself in forceful opposition to what was, in one sense, a vacuum of expressive will on Hughes's part. (Needless to say, the *apparent* absence of will in an individual can easily be a token of the presence of a very powerful will.) The result on both occasions, which was extraordinary, was first Hughes's endurance of, then his violent rebellion against, a force of will that challenged his deepest vision of the poetic life.

I use the term "will" knowing that to many people it is an obsolete concept, in spite of the revival of interest in Otto Rank, or continuing critiques of Freud's use of the term as, for example, Harold Bloom's excellent essay "Freud's Concepts of Defense and the Poetic Will." But I am referring here mainly, though not exclusively, to the will as a function of consciousness, as in the case of "Godmother's" will, or that of Hughes's father, or— far less demonstrably—Hughes's own volition. And what do I mean by Hughes's "vision of the poetic life"? I refer to what one might call unshaped or amorphous poetic consciousness, poetry not concretized or written down, but the crucial element (when combined with poetic "material") out of which written or oral poetry is made. In an old-fashioned but still significant way, the poet Richard Eberhart has written of "Will and Psyche in Poetry" (in Don Cameron Allen's *The Moment of Poetry*, 1962). Poems of the will value the body, activity, struggle, and the things of this world; poems of the psyche endorse spirit, "an uncontaminated grace," and the "elusive, passive, imaginative quality" of the world beyond this world. A poem of will, such as Marvell's "To His Coy Mistress," might involve a man calling a woman to bed; for an exemplary poem of psyche, Eberhart chose Poe's "To Helen," where desire leads directly away from sexuality toward spirit.

The notorious placidity of surface in Hughes, as I see it, bespeaks the extent to which he was a poet who preferred his poems unwritten—a poet, like his great mentor Walt Whitman, who saw his life itself as a poem greater than any poem he could possibly write. Hughes's greatest poetical instinct was to preserve his unformed or dormant poetic consciousness as the highest form of poetry. Such an instinct may suggest infantilism; one remembers Freud's unfortunate words about the link between creative writing and daydreaming. Infantilism would be wrong as an explanation. But, in Hughes's case, I suspect, the instinct had something to do with the youthfulness of the self he clearly regarded as his authentic, or most cherished self. Placidity of surface, anxiety to please and to be loved, apparent asexuality (the most consistent conclusion—rather than that of homosexuality, for which there is no evidence—about his libido among people who knew him well), and the compulsion against concretized or written poetry reflect a sense of self as prepubescent, or apubescent; in other words, a sense of self as an eternal child. At some level, Hughes saw himself ideally as a child—a dreamy genius child, a perfect child, a princely child, a loving child, even a mothering and maternal child—but first and foremost as a child (almost never is he the destructively rebellious child, in spite of his radical poetry).

It must be stressed that such a sense of self, although it modulates art (as does every other factor of comparable importance), is by no means an inherent handicap to a creative person. In any event, Hughes teetered between a sense of confidence (a sense of being loved by a particular person to whom he was emotionally mortgaged) and a rival, harrowing sense, born in his own childhood, of abandonment and despair. The latter was closer to the origins of his poetry. Release Hughes as an artist from the stabilizing social context and he flies almost immediately toward themes of nihilism and death. For example, take his poem "Border Line":

> I used to wonder
> About living and dying—
> I think the difference lies
> Between tears and crying.
>
> I used to wonder
> About here and there—
> I think the distance
> Is nowhere.

Or "Genius Child":

> . . . *Nobody loves a genius child.*
>
> Can you love an eagle,
> Tame or wild?
>
> Wild or tame,
> Can you love a monster
> Of frightening name?
>
> *Nobody loves a genius child.*
>
> *Kill him*—and let his soul run wild!

Or "End":

> There are
> No clocks on the wall,
> And no time,
> No shadows that move
> From dawn to dusk
> Across the floor.
>
> There is neither light
> Nor dark
> Outside the door.
>
> *There is no door!*

In Hughes's writing, there is precious little middle ground between such verse and that for which he is far better known (and deservedly so), the poems steeped in race and other social concerns. Nature as flora and fauna bored the man who preferred Harlem in hot summer to the cool New England woods, as he once joked, because "I prefer wild people to wild animals." Hughes understood wherein his salvation rested.

This bleakness, almost always ignored in critical treatments of Hughes, evolved out of the saturation of his dormant poetical consciousness by the powerful will toward death stimulated in him by his loneliness as a child. But Hughes did not surrender passively to the force of his father and "Godmother" when they turned against him. These attacks, in fact, elicited in him a massive retaliatory display of willfulness, at first (while he was ill) as uncontrolled and uncontrollable as the right to the passive poetic consciousness it defended. The invocation of will in such massive degree could easily have remained as toxic as it was while he was sick with his silent rage. Only the modification of will, a compromise between passive poetic consciousness and the purposefulness needed to defend that consciousness, could prevent the consummation of poetry (amorphous or concrete) by rage. And only an appeal to a third force that was neither Hughes nor his enemy could allow him to fashion a balance between will and his unformed poetical consciousness.

Both in the experience with his father in Mexico and in the struggle with "Godmother," the third force was represented by the black race. Hughes's attitude to the black masses is too complicated to detail here. But my argument depends on the crucial understanding that Hughes was virtually unique among major black writers not so much because of the considerable depth of his love of black people, but because of *the depth of his psychological dependence on them.* Hughes became dependent because of a relatively complicated set of circumstances in his youth, when he was reared by his poor but very proud grandmother, the aged, wrinkled, and laconic Mary Langston, whose first husband had died at Harpers Ferry with John Brown. But Mary Langston's zeal to defend the rights of her race was offset for her grandson by her personal remoteness both from him and the race, and by the severity of her pride—a pride compounded by her very light skin, her Indian rather than predominantly African features, her Oberlin education, and her high-toned religion, which all kept her distant from the black masses. She did not attend black churches, did not sing black spirituals (much less the blues); she spoke in a clipped manner, rather than a folksy drawl, and she detested popular culture—as Hughes spelled out partially in *The Big Sea,* but more completely in an unpublished portrait prepared in 1943.

What Mary Langston offered in the abstract, however, was made wonderfully concrete to young Hughes by two persons with whom he lived from time to time (when his grandmother was forced to rent out her house, and after she died) and whom he described in an Arcadian paragraph in *The Big Sea*—"Uncle" and "Auntie" Reed. "Uncle" James Reed, who dug ditches for the city, smoked his pipe and stayed home on Sundays. "Auntie" Reed (later Mrs. Mary J. Reed Campbell) took Langston to St. Luke's A.M.E. church (a church apparently not good enough for his grandmother) and taught the Sunday School there in which the boy was the brightest star. Through the childless Reeds, who clearly adored the boy, he learned how to love the race, its church ways and folk ways, and its dreams and aspirations, of which the handsome, scrubbed, light brown boy, the grandson of "Colonel" Charles Langston (whose brother John Mercer Langston had served in the U.S. Congress and as an ambassador of the United States) was the shining embodiment. And it was a lie he told to the Reeds (that Jesus had come to Hughes at a revival meeting, after "Auntie" Reed had prayed that this would happen) that led to the major trauma of his childhood, as related in *The Big Sea*—a long weeping into the night (the second to last time he cried, Hughes wrote) because he had waited for Jesus, who had never come, then had lied to the people who loved him most. In *The Big Sea* Hughes would admit to hating his father; he would partly ridicule his mother; he would admit that he did not cry when his grandmother died. The Reeds, however, were different: "For me, there have never been any better people in the world. I loved them very much."

In his bitter struggles with his father and "Godmother," Hughes turned to the black race for direction. But one needs to remember that this appeal in itself hardly gave Hughes distinction as a poet; what made Hughes distinct was the highly original manner in which he internalized the Afro-American racial dilemma and expressed it in poems such as "When Sue Wears Red," "The Negro Speaks of Rivers," "Mother to Son," "Dream Variations," and "The Weary Blues," poems of Hughes's young manhood on which his career would rest. Of these, the most important was "The Negro Speaks of Rivers."

I've known rivers.
I've known rivers ancient as the world and older
    than the flow of human blood in human veins.

My soul has grown deep like the rivers.

I bathed in the Euphrates when dawns were young.
I built my hut near the Congo and it lulled me to sleep.
I looked upon the Nile and raised the pyramids above it.
I heard the singing of the Mississippi when Abe Lincoln
    went down to New Orleans, and I've seen its muddy
    bosom turn all golden in the sunset.

I've known rivers:
Ancient, dusky rivers.

My soul has grown deep like the rivers.

Here, the persona moves steadily from dimly starred personal memory ("I've known rivers") toward a rendezvous with modern history (Lincoln going down the Mississippi and seeing the horror of slavery that, according to legend, would make him one day free the slaves). The death wish, benign but suffusing, of its images of rivers older than human blood, of souls grown as deep as these rivers, gives way steadily to an altering, ennobling vision whose final effect gleams in the evocation of the Mississippi's "muddy bosom" turning at last "all golden in the sunset." Personal anguish has been alchemized by the poet into a gracious meditation on his race, whose despised ("muddy") culture and history, irradiated by the poet's vision, changes within the poem from mud into gold. This is a classic example of the essential process of creativity in Hughes.

    The poem came to him, according to Hughes (accurately, it seems clear) about ten months after his Mexican illness, when he was riding a train from Cleveland to Mexico to rejoin his father. The time was sundown, the place the Mississippi outside St. Louis. "All day on the train I had been thinking of my father," he would write in The Big Sea. "Now it was just sunset and we crossed the Mississippi, slowly, over a long bridge. I looked out of the window of the Pullman at the great muddy river flowing down toward the heart of the South, and I began to think what that river, the old Mississippi, had meant to Negroes in the past—how to be sold down the river was the worst fate that could overtake a slave in bondage. Then I remembered reading how Abraham Lincoln had made a trip down the Mississippi on a raft, and how he had seen slavery at its worst, and had decided within himself that it should be removed from American life. Then I began to think of other rivers in our past—the Congo, and the Niger, and the Nile in Africa—and the thought came to me: 'I've known rivers,' and I put it down on the back of an envelope I had in my pocket, and within the space of ten or fifteen minutes, as the train gathered speed in the dusk, I had written this poem."

Here, starting with anguish over his father, Hughes discovered the compressed ritual of passivity, challenge, turmoil, and transcendence he would probably have to re-create, doubtless in variant forms, during the great poetic trysts of his life. Even after he became a successful, published poet, the basic process remained the same, because his psychology remained largely the same even though he had become technically expert. In his second major illness, caused by his patron "Godmother," Hughes wrote poetry as he struggled for a transcendence that would be long in coming. The nature of that interim poetry is telling. When he sent some poems to a friend for a little book to be printed privately, she noticed at once that many spoke of death—"Dear lovely Death/That taketh all things under wing—/Never to kill. . . ." She called the booklet *Dear Lovely Death*. In "Afro-American Fragment," unlike in "The Negro Speaks of Rivers," Africa is seen plaintively:

> . . . Subdued and time-lost
> Are the drums—and yet
> Through some vast mist of race
> There comes this song
> I do not understand,
> This song of atavistic land,
> Of bitter yearnings lost
> Without a place—
> So long,
> So far away
> Is Africa's
> Dark face.

But when Hughes returned home, scarred but healed, after months in seclusion in Haiti, he no longer thought of loss and death. Instead, he plunged directly into the life of the black masses with a seven-month tour of the South in which he read his poetry in their churches and schools. Then he set out for the Soviet Union, where he would spend more than a year. Hughes then reached the zenith of his revolutionary ardor with poems (or verse) such as "Good Morning Revolution," "Goodbye Christ," and "Put One More 'S' in the USA."

"Good Morning Revolution," for example, and "The Negro Speaks of Rivers" are very different poems. The former is the polar opposite of the poetry of nihilism; the latter blends aspects of existential gloom with the life-affirming spirit of the black race. Together, the poems illustrate the wide range of possibility in the mixture of will and passivity which characterizes Hughes's art (although one can argue that "Good Morning Revolution"—by far the lesser poem—marks an overreaction of will, and thus is not truly representative of Hughes's poetic temperament in that it contains no element of passivity). But the creative process has remained the same. The right to amorphous poetic consciousness is challenged. The will is aroused in defense of that consciousness. Illness (an extreme version of Wallace Stevens's "blessed rage for order"?) marks the struggle of will against opposing will. The long-endured illness, in silence, gradually allows the mutual fertilization of will and poetic consciousness that is needed for concrete art. Illness ends when that ratio is achieved or perceived, and writing begins. Creativity, in Keats's term, has created itself. A poet, or a poem, is born.

To some extent, this process is nothing more than Wordsworth's definition of poetry as the final recollection "in tranquility" (a phrase often underplayed or even ignored in quoting Wordsworth's definition) of emotion that had once spontaneously overflowed. What is different, of course, is that Wordsworth (and Keats and Stevens) did not have to contend with race as a factor in his creativity. For many writers, perhaps even most, race is a distracting, demoralizing force. Hughes's genius, or his good fortune, consisted in his ability to accommodate race harmoniously within the scheme of creativity common to all major poets, and to turn it from an anomaly into an intimate advantage.

# Chronology

| | |
|---|---|
| 1902 | Born February 1 in Joplin, Missouri, to James Nathaniel Hughes and Carrie Mercer Langston. |
| 1902–21 | Spends an unsettling childhood with mother in several cities, with grandmother in Kansas, with father in Mexico, and on his own. |
| 1921–1922 | Attends Columbia University for one year. |
| 1922–26 | Drifts to New York, to Paris, and to sea. Occasional readings and minor publications of his poetry. |
| 1926–29 | *The Weary Blues* published. Receives a bachelor's degree at Lincoln University, Pennsylvania. Spends his summers reading his poetry and collecting folklore with Zora Neale Hurston. Writes the novel *Not without Laughter* (1930). |
| 1931 | Wins the Hammond Gold Award for *Not without Laughter*. Tours the South reading his poetry and then sails to Cuba. |
| 1937 | Covers the Spanish Civil War for *The Baltimore Afro-American*. |
| 1938 | Founds the Harlem Suitcase Theater—one of many subsequent experimental troupes—to perform his play *Don't You Want to Be Free? New Song*, a volume of poems celebrating the international workers' movement, published. |
| 1940 | *The Big Sea: An Autobiography* published. |
| 1943 | The *Simple* columns begin appearing weekly in *The Chicago Defender*. |

1947    *Fields of Wonder* published. Buys a Harlem brownstone. With Mercer Cook translates Jacques Roumain's *Masters of the Dew*.

1948    Translates Nicholás Guillén's *Cuba Libre* with Ben Frederic Carruthers.

1949    Edits his *The Poetry of the Negro, 1746–1949* with Arna Bontemps. *One-Way Ticket* appears. His musical *Troubled Island* opens in New York.

1950    *Simple Speaks His Mind,* first of several column collections, published.

1951    Translates Federico Garcia Lorca's *Romancero Gitano. Montage of a Dream* published.

1952    *The First Book of Negroes* and *Laughing to Keep from Crying* published.

1953    Questioned by Senator Joseph McCarthy's HUAC committee.

1954–55   *Famous American Negroes, The First Book of Rhythms, The First Book of Jazz,* and *Famous Negro Music Makers* published. Many similar primers follow.

1956    *I Wonder as I Wander,* second autobiography, appears.

1959    The novel *Tambourines to Glory* and *Selected Poems* published.

1960    Awarded NAACP's Spingarn Medal.

1961    Elected to National Institute of Arts and Letters.

1963    *Something in Common and Other Stories* and *Five Plays by Langston Hughes* published. Play based on *Tambourines to Glory* opens on Broadway. Receives Doctor of Letters degree from Howard University.

1965    Lectures in Europe for the U.S. Information Agency.

1967    Edits *The Best Short Stories by Negro Writers. The Panther and the Lash,* his final book of poetry, appears. Dies in New York, May 22.

# Contributors

HAROLD BLOOM, Sterling Professor of the Humanities at Yale University, is the author of *The Anxiety of Influence, Poetry and Repression,* and many other volumes of literary criticism. His forthcoming study, *Freud: Transference and Authority,* attempts a full-scale reading of all of Freud's major writings. A MacArthur Prize Fellow, he is general editor of five series of literary criticism published by Chelsea House. During 1987–88, he served as Charles Eliot Norton Professor of Poetry at Harvard University.

DARWIN T. TURNER is Professor of English at the University of Iowa and the author of *In a Minor Chord.*

GEORGE E. KENT taught Afro-American literature at the University of Chicago. He is the author of *Blackness and the Adventure of Western Civilization.*

ROGER ROSENBLATT, formerly literary editor of *The New Republic,* is the author of *Black Fiction.*

RAYMOND SMITH writes on American culture.

ONWUCHEKWA JEMIE is the author of *Langston Hughes: An Introduction to the Poetry.*

R. BAXTER MILLER is Professor of English and Director of the Black Literature Program at the University of Tennessee, Knoxville. He is the author of *Langston Hughes and Gwendolyn Brooks: A Reference Guide* and the forthcoming *For a Moment I Wondered: The Literary Imagination of Langston Hughes.*

MARTHA COBB teaches Spanish at Howard University. She is the author of *Harlem, Haiti, and Havana: A Study of Langston Hughes, Jacques Roumain, and Nicolas Guillen.* She has published widely on the black writers of the Caribbean.

SUSAN L. BLAKE is Associate Professor of English at Lafayette College and writes widely on black literature.

RICHARD K. BARKSDALE is a member of the Department of English at the University of Illinois, Urbana, where he serves as associate graduate dean. He is the editor of *Langston Hughes: The Poet and His Critics* and, with Kenneth Kinamon, of *Black Writers of America: A Comprehensive Anthology*.

CHIDI IKONNE has been Assistant Professor and Acting Chairman of Afro-American Studies at Harvard University. He is the author of *From Du Bois to Van Vechten: The Early New Negro Literature, 1903–1906*.

DAVID MICHAEL NIFONG has taught English at the University of Tennessee.

ARNOLD RAMPERSAD, Hughes's definitive biographer, is Professor of English at Rutgers University. In addition to his ongoing work on Hughes, he is the author of *The Art and Imagination of W. E. B. Du Bois*.

# Bibliography

Ako, Edward O. "Langston Hughes and the Négritude Movement: A Study in Literary Influence." *CLA Journal* 28 (1983–84): 46–56.

Barksdale, Richard K. *Langston Hughes: The Poet and His Critics*. Chicago: American Library Association, 1977.

Berry, Faith. *Langston Hughes: Before and beyond Harlem*. Westport, Conn.: Lawrence Hill, 1983.

Blake, Susan L. "The American Dream and the Legacy of Revolution in the Poetry of Langston Hughes." *Black American Literature Forum* 14 (1980): 100–104.

Brown, Lloyd W. "The Portrait of the Artist as a Black American in the Poetry of Langston Hughes." *Studies in Black Literature* 5, no. 1 (1974): 24–27.

Bruck, Peter. "Langston Hughes: 'The Blues I'm Playing' (1934)." In *The Black American Short Story in the 20th Century: A Collection of Critical Essays*, edited by Peter Bruck, 71–83. Amsterdam: B. R. Gruner, 1977.

Carey, Julian C. "Jesse B. Semple Revisited and Revised." *Phylon* 32 (1971): 158–63.

Clark, VeVe. "Restaging Langston Hughes' *Scottsboro Limited:* An Interview with Amiri Baraka." *Black Scholar* 10 (1979): 62–69.

Clarke, John Herrik. "The Neglected Dimensions of the Harlem Renaissance." *Black World* 20 (November 1970): 118–29.

Cobb, Martha K. "Concepts of Blackness in the Poetry of Nicholás Guillén, Jacques Romain and Langston Hughes." *CLA Journal* 18 (1974–75): 262–72.

Cullen, Countee. "Poet on Poet." *Opportunity* 4 (March 1926): 73.

Davis, Arthur P. "The Harlem of Langston Hughes' Poetry." *Phylon* 13 (Winter 1952): 276–83.

———. "Langston Hughes." In *From the Dark Tower*, 61–72. Washington, D.C.: Howard University Press, 1974.

———. "The Tragic Mulatto Theme in Six Works of Langston Hughes." *Phylon* 16, no. 2 (Spring 1955): 195–204.

Dickinson, Donald C. *A Bio-Bibliography of Langston Hughes, 1902–1967*. Hamden, Conn.: Archon, 1967.

———. "Langston Hughes and the Brownie's Book." *Negro History Bulletin* 31 (December 1968): 8–10.

Dixon, Melvin. "Rivers Remembering Their Source: Comparative Studies in Black Literary History—Langston Hughes, Jacques Romain, and Negritude." In *Afro-*

*American Literature: The Reconstruction of Instruction,* edited by Dexter Fisher and Robert B. Stepto, 25–43. New York: Modern Language Association, 1979.

Emanuel, James A. *Langston Hughes.* New York: Twayne, 1967.

Fauset, Jesse. Review of *The Weary Blues. Crisis* 34 (March 1926): 239.

Garber, Earlene D. "Form as a Complement to Content in Three of Langston Hughes' Poems." *Negro American Literature Forum* 5 (1971): 137–39.

Gomes, E. "The Crackerbox Tradition and the Race Problem in Lowell's *The Bigelow Papers* and Hughes' Sketches of Simple." *CLA Journal* 27 (1983–84): 254–69.

Hansell, William H. "Black Music in the Poetry of Langston Hughes: Roots, Race, Release." *Obsidian* 4 (Winter 1978): 16–38.

Hudson, Theodore R. "Technical Aspects of the Poetry of Langston Hughes." *Black World* 22 (September 1973): 24–25.

Jackson, Blyden. "Claude McKay and Langston Hughes: The Harlem Renaissance and More." *Pembroke Magazine* 6 (1975): 43–48.

———. "From One 'New Negro' to Another." In *Black Poetry in America: Two Essays on Historical Interpretation,* 51–58. Baton Rouge: Louisiana State University Press, 1974.

———. "Renaissance in the Twenties." In *The Twenties: Fiction, Poetry, Drama,* edited by Warren French, 303-16. Deland, Fla.: Everett/Edwards, 1975.

———. "A Word about Simple." *CLA Journal* 11 (1967–68): 310–18.

Jemie, Onwuchekwa. *Langston Hughes: An Introduction to the Poetry.* New York: Columbia University Press, 1976.

Johnson, Patricia A., and Walter C. Farrell. "How Langston Hughes Used the Blues." *Melus* 6 (Spring 1979): 55–63.

Kent, George E. "Langston Hughes and Afro-American Folk and Cultural Tradition." *Blackness and the Adventure of Western Culture.* Chicago: Third World Press, 1972.

Klotman, Phyllis R. "Langston Hughes's Jesse B. Semple and the Blues." *Phylon* 36 (1975): 68–72.

———. "Jesse B. Semple and the Narrative Art of Langston Hughes." *Journal of Narrative Technique* 3 (1973): 66–75.

Larkin, Margaret. "A Poet of the People—A Review." *Opportunity* 5 (March 1927): 84–85.

Locke, Alain. "The Weary Blues." *Palms* 4 (1926–27): 27–28.

Martin, Dellita. "Langston Hughes' Use of the Blues." *CLA Journal* 22 (1978–79): 151–59.

Miller, R. Baxter. " 'Even after I Was Dead': *The Big Sea*—Paradox, Preservation, and Holistic Time." *Black American Literature Forum* 11 (1977): 39–45.

Mullen, Edward J. *Langston Hughes in the Hispanic World and Haiti.* Hamden, Conn.: Archon, 1977.

Nichols, Charles H., ed. *Arna Bontemps and Langston Hughes: Letters 1925–1967.* New York: Dodd, Mead, 1980.

Nifong, David Michael. "Narrative Technique and Theory in *The Ways of White Folks.*" *Black American Literature Forum* 15 (1981): 93–96.

O'Daniel, Therman B. "Lincoln's Man of Letters." *Lincoln University Bulletin,* July 1964, 9–12.

————, ed. *Langston Hughes, Black Genius: A Critical Evaluation.* New York: William Morrow, 1971.

Presley, James. "The Birth of Jesse B. Semple." *The Southern Review* 38 (1973): 219–25.

————. "Langston Hughes: A Personal Farewell." *Southwest Review* 54 (1969): 79–84.

Prowle, Allen D. "Langston Hughes." In *The Black American Writer.* Vol. 2, *Poetry and Drama.* Edited by C. W. E. Bigsby, 77–87. Deland, Fla.: Everett/Edwards, 1969.

Quinot, Raymond. *Langston Hughes, ou L'Etoile Noire.* Bruxelles: Editions C.L.F., 1964.

Randall, Dudley. "The Black Aesthetic in the Thirties, Forties, and Fifties." In *The Black Aesthetic,* edited by Addison Gayle, Jr., 212–21. Garden City, N.Y.: Doubleday (Anchor), 1972.

Redding, Saunders J. *To Make a Poet Black.* Chapel Hill: University of North Carolina Press, 1939.

Review of *The Weary Blues. Times Literary Supplement,* 29 July 1926, 515.

Smith, Raymond. "Langston Hughes: Evolution of the Poetic Persona." *Studies in the Literary Imagination* 7 (Spring 1974): 49–64.

Tolson, Melvin. "The Harlem Group of Negro Writers." M.A. thesis: Columbia University, 1940.

Tracy, Steven C. "Simple's Great Afro-American Joke." *CLA Journal* 27 (1983–84): 239–53.

Turner, Darwin T. "Langston Hughes as Playwright." *CLA Journal* 11 (1967–68): 297–309.

Wagner, Jean. "Langston Hughes." In *Black Poets of the United States from Paul Laurence Dunbar to Langston Hughes.* Urbana: University of Illinois Press, 1973.

Waldron, Edward E. "The Blues Poetry of Langston Hughes." *Negro American Literature Forum* 5 (1971): 140–49.

Winz, Cary D. "Langston Hughes: A Kansas Poet in the Harlem Renaissance." *Kansas Quarterly* 7 (Summer 1975): 58–71.

Yestadt, Sister Marie. "Two American Poets: Their Influence on the Contemporary Art-Song." *Xavier University Studies* 10 (Spring 1971): 33–43.

# Acknowledgments

"Hughes as Playwright" (originally entitled "Langston Hughes as Playwright") by Darwin T. Turner from *CLA Journal* 11, no. 4 (June 1968), © 1968 by the College Language Association. Reprinted with permission.

"Hughes and the Afro-American Folk and Cultural Tradition" (originally entitled "Langston Hughes and Afro-American Folk and Cultural Tradition") by George E. Kent from *Blackness and the Adventure of Western Civilization* by George E. Kent, © 1972 by George E. Kent. Reprinted with permission.

"*Not without Laughter*" by Roger Rosenblatt from *Black Fiction* by Roger Rosenblatt, © 1974 by the President and Fellows of Harvard College. Reprinted with permission of Harvard University Press.

"Hughes: Evolution of the Poetic Persona" by Raymond Smith from *Studies in the Literary Imagination* 7, no. 2 (Fall 1974), © 1974 by the Department of English, Georgia State University. Reprinted with permission.

"Jazz, Jive, and Jam" by Onwuchekwa Jemie from *Langston Hughes: An Introduction to the Poetry* by Onwuchekwa Jemie, © 1973, 1976 by Columbia University Press. Reprinted with permission.

" 'No Crystal Stair': Unity, Archetype and Symbol in Hughes's Poems on Women" (originally entitled " 'No Crystal Stair': Unity, Archetype and Symbol in Langston Hughes's Poems on Women") by R. Baxter Miller from *Negro American Literature Forum* 9, no. 4 (Winter 1975), © 1975 by Indiana State University. Reprinted with permission.

"Langston Hughes" by Martha Cobb from *Harlem, Haiti, and Havana* by Martha Cobb, © 1979 by Three Continents Press, Washington, D.C. Reprinted with permission.

"Old John in Harlem: The Urban Folktales of Langston Hughes" by Susan L. Blake from *Black American Literature Forum* 14, no. 3 (Fall 1980), © 1980 by Indiana State University. Reprinted by permission.

"Hughes: His Times and His Humanistic Techniques" (originally entitled "Langston Hughes: His Times and His Humanistic Techniques") by Richard K. Barksdale from *Black American Literature and Humanism*, edited by R. Baxter Miller,

© 1981 by the University Press of Kentucky. Reprinted with permission of the publishers.

"Affirmation of Black Self" by Chidi Ikonne from *Dubois to Van Vechten: The Early New Negro Literature 1903–1926* by Chidi Ikonne, © 1981 by Chidi Ikonne. Reprinted with permission of Greenwood Press. Excerpts from *Nigger Heaven* by Carl Van Vechten, © 1926 by Alfred A. Knopf, Inc., and renewed 1954 by Carl Van Vechten; *Selected Poems of Langston Hughes,* © 1959 by Alfred A. Knopf, Inc.; and *The Weary Blues* by Langston Hughes, © 1926, renewed by Langston Hughes, reprinted with permission of Alfred A. Knopf, Inc.

"Narrative Technique in *The Ways of White Folks*" (originally entitled "Narrative Technique and Theory in *The Ways of White Folks*") by David Michael Nifong from *Black American Literature Forum* 15, no. 3 (Fall 1981), © 1981 by Indiana State University. Reprinted with permission.

"The Origins of Poetry in Langston Hughes" by Arnold Rampersad from *The Southern Review* 21, no. 3 (July 1985), © 1985 by Louisiana State University. Reprinted with permission.

# Index